Making Crime Television

This book employs actor–network theory in order to examine how representations of crime are produced for contemporary prime-time television dramas. As a unique examination of the production of crime dramas, particularly their writing process, *Making Crime Television: Producing Entertaining Representations of Crime for Television Broadcast* examines not only the semiotic relations between ideas about crime, but the material conditions under which those meanings are formulated.

Using ethnographic and interview data, Anita Lam considers how textual representations of crime are assembled by various people (including writers, directors, technical consultants, and network executives), technologies (screen-writing software and whiteboards), and texts (newspaper articles and rival crime dramas). The emerging analysis does not project but instead concretely examines what and how television writers and producers know about crime, law and policing. An adequate understanding of the representation of crime, it is maintained, cannot be limited to a content analysis that treats the representation as a final product. Rather, a television representation of crime must be seen as the result of a particular assemblage of logics, people, creative ideas, commercial interests, legal requirements, and broadcasting networks. A fascinating investigation into the relationship between television production, crime and law, this book is an accessible and well-researched resource for students and scholars of Law, Media, and Criminology.

Anita Lam is an Assistant Professor of criminology in the Department of Social Science at York University, Canada.

Making Crime Television

Producing Entertaining Representations of Crime for Television Broadcast

Anita Lam

a GlassHouse Book

First published 2014
by Routledge
2 Park Square, Milton Park, Abingdon, Oxfordshire OX14 4RN

Simultaneously published in the USA and Canada
by Routledge
711 Third Avenue, New York, NY 10017

First issued in paperback 2014

A GlassHouse Book

Routledge is an imprint of the Taylor and Francis Group, an informa business

© 2014 Anita Lam

The right of Anita Lam to be identified as author of this work has been asserted by her in accordance with sections 77 and 78 of the Copyright, Designs and Patents Act 1988.

All rights reserved. No part of this book may be reprinted or reproduced or utilised in any form or by any electronic, mechanical, or other means, now known or hereafter invented, including photocopying and recording, or in any information storage or retrieval system, without permission in writing from the publishers.

Trademark notice: Product or corporate names may be trademarks or registered trademarks, and are used only for identification and explanation without intent to infringe.

British Library Cataloguing in Publication Data
A catalogue record for this book is available from the British Library

Library of Congress Cataloging-in-Publication Data
A catalog record has been requested for this book

ISBN 978-0-415-63288-1 (hbk)
ISBN 978-1-138-91513-8 (pbk)
ISBN 978-0-203-40544-4 (ebk)

Typeset in Baskerville by
Florence Production Ltd, Stoodleigh, Devon

Contents

Figures		vi
Acknowledgements		vii
	Introduction	1
1	Setting the stage: a literature review and analysis	11
2	On method: trail-sniffing ants and breadcrumbs of reflexivity	35
3	Breaking *The Bridge*: documenting the heterogeneous knowledge inputs into the laboratory of the writers' room	60
4	The case of the missing 'bad apples': transforming 'Injured Cop' into the 'Unguarded Moment'	97
5	Showcasing Hamilton: how place becomes relevant in the making of Canadian crime dramas	133
	Conclusion	169
	Bibliography	179
	Index	197

Figures

3.1 The writers' room of *The Bridge* — 63
4.1 Summary of story revisions — 126
5.1 The number of scripted pilots commissioned and aired by major North American broadcasters between fall 2009 and spring 2010 — 147
5.2 Gorky's Medical Rehabilitation Centre (formerly known as Porky's Strip Bar) — 155
5.3 Screenshot of Hamilton as illustrated in *Lawyers, Guns and Money*'s opening title sequence — 163

Acknowledgements

Once upon a time, this book was more than just words, pages and binding. These pages were alive, packed with the dramatic collision of people, texts, and things. For the book to exist as it does, I cannot thank enough the television producers, writers, directors, and other production personnel who had not only allowed me access to their television productions, but also expressed their ideas and experiences with such candour and humour.

I am indebted to Mariana Valverde for the profound ways in which she shaped not only my research, but also my sense of being a scholar. I am grateful to Shyon Baumann, Dru Jeffries, Ron Levi, and Desmond Manderson for their helpful comments on earlier versions of the manuscript. Many thanks are also due to the Routledge team – Colin Perrin, Rebekah Jenkins, Jack Webb, and Thomas Lodge – for their assistance in preparing this book.

Finally, I dedicate this book to my family. Here's to you for all of the important ways in which you have reassured, strengthened, encouraged, and inspired me.

This research was partially funded through a doctoral fellowship from the Social Science and Humanities Research Council. Permission has also been secured to include portions of material that have appeared in the following previously published material: 'Making "Bad Apples" on *The Bridge*: A Production Study of the Making of a Police Drama', in Peter Robson and Jessica Silbey (eds), *Law and Justice on the Small Screen* (2012). Oxford: Hart Publishing, pp. 63–86.

Introduction

The year that *CSI: Crime Scene Investigation* was born, the most popular[1] television drama in North America was a medical procedural named *ER*. Inside a season of its airing in 2000, *CSI* – a fictional crime drama that follows a team of Las Vegas forensic scientists and police detectives as they solve criminal cases and determine an individual's guilt through the use of presumably infallible forensic evidence – became the tenth most highly watched television program by (North) American viewers, although it was still over-shadowed by the novelty of a reality TV program that placed ordinary people on an island where they battled for survival. The year *CSI* turned two, it became the second most-watched television series in North America, eclipsed only by a situational comedy about a group of six coffee-loving friends living in New York City. In its third season, *CSI* was not only named the most highly watched television program in North America, but also able to spawn its first spin-off series *CSI: Miami*. In 2012 *CSI* received the International Television Audience Award in honour of being named the most-watched television drama series in 2011 across five continents. As crime dramas have come and gone in the last decade, *CSI* is notable for its staying power as an exemplar of popular television in the twenty-first century, especially since audience fragmentation has turned popularity into an increasingly ambiguous concept (Kompare 2010).

Despite being a surprise hit for American broadcaster CBS and a Canadian co-production in its first season,[2] *CSI*'s popularity has been explained by criminological scholars as though it were inevitable all along.[3] For example, Byers and Johnson (2009) explain that *CSI* was immediately popular because it managed to reproduce familiar socio-political discourses in dramatic form. Specifically, the show's initial success was a result of its synchronicity with the events of 9/11 and the social dominance of American neoliberal and neoconservative discourses on criminality and justice. Similarly, Rapping (2003: 27) describes *CSI* as an immediate hit because television producers were able to plug into successful programming trends and spin them in slightly new ways. Cavender and Deutsch (2007) explain *CSI*'s popularity through the popularity of the genre of crime dramas. Crime dramas attract a large audience because their plots are situated within dominant socio-political ideologies, and provide an understanding of crime and criminals that is consistent with criminological theories in vogue at the time (Rafter 2006). Academic criminologists are not the only ones to have noticed *CSI*'s popularity, as news outlets have been reporting on the so-called *CSI* effect since 2002. According to anecdotal evidence from legal professionals, laypeople who regularly watch *CSI* and other crime-related television dramas have inflated expectations about the significance of forensic evidence in criminal trials (Cole and Dioso-Villa 2009; Mopas 2007). Since the discovery of such an effect, criminologists and sociolegal scholars have attempted to empirically confirm or refute the effect's existence (e.g. Podias 2007). Sometimes, the *CSI* effect has even been used by some criminological scholars (e.g. Ferrell, Hayward and Young 2008: 119–20; Stevens 2011) as the example *par excellence* of how fictional television programs communicate misinformation to the public with devastating consequences, such as fuelling the public's increasingly punitive attitudes towards criminals.

Using the academic work done on *CSI* as a fairly typical example of criminological analyses of pop cultural products, we can note that criminologists have often presupposed that television writers and producers create certain messages about crime that are then disseminated to a mass audience. Academic criminologists have been concerned about these messages because they are not only presumed to be based on poor (i.e. non-academic, non-empirical and non-representative) sources of information, but also assumed to cause negative media effects. In contrast to much of the academic research on popular prime-time crime television dramas, this book does not examine media effects on mass audiences. Instead, it examines the *making of television fictions* – specifically, the production of prime-time North American crime dramas made in the shadow of *CSI* and its success. Contemporary crime dramas made for broadcast on major commercial networks tend to follow a pattern of storytelling set down by *CSI*, and this pattern is mimicked to the point that the term 'another *CSI*' has become a euphemism for the conservative, risk-averse storytelling approach taken by broadcast networks (Kompare 2010: 2). Even storytelling innovation on premium cable networks is defined against the norm set by *CSI*.

In this book, I explore how professional television writers and producers tell fictional, entertaining crime stories through the format of the television drama. While Latour and Woolgar (1979: 240) have remarked that '[t]he result of the construction of the fact is that it appears unconstructed by anyone,' the construction of television fiction has been rarely studied by criminological scholars despite a sense that such fiction is deliberately constructed. While criminologists have studied the production of crime news stories, they have not studied the making of fictional crime stories as particular social and cultural constructions. As these stories and representations are such constructions, I am interested in documenting the actual processes of their construction through the use of ethnography and interview data.

In focusing on issues of meaning, cultural representations and media, I situate this work in the intellectual space opened up by cultural criminology and popular criminology. Both cultural and popular criminologies acknowledge that mainstream academic criminology has often ignored pop cultural representations of crime, even though these representations form the largest public realm in which crime is imagined and understood. Cultural criminology assumes that the meaning of crime and crime control are themselves cultural constructions that are always under construction (Ferrell, Hayward and Young 2008: 123). Similarly, popular criminology focuses on images, representations and discourses about crime found in popular culture (Rafter 2007; Rafter and Brown 2011). Offering theories about crime and criminality, popular criminology is conceptualized as a way of knowing about crime, one that is complementary to the way academic criminology knows about and represents crime (Rafter 2007). Popular criminology, however, serves as a knowledge source about crime for a far larger audience than academic criminology. Following this conceptualization of popular criminology, I treat entertainment television production as a site of knowledge production. In doing so, however, I do not engage in a content analysis of crime dramas, whereby I examine popular criminology as a final product as most cultural criminologists have done. Neither do I project onto television writers and producers certain assumptions about what they know about crime.

Instead, I empirically document the making of popular criminology by addressing the following research questions: how do television writers and producers know about crime? How do they transform their knowledge into fictional representations of crime to fit within the format of the television drama?

Actor–network theory

To study the interrelated processes of knowing and representing, I make use of actor–network theory (ANT). As a theory about method, ANT considers successful final products to be *black boxes*. Black boxing refers to the effect of success, which entails erasing the various local, contingent processes and circumstances under which texts or objects were originally produced. Because cultural criminologists have tended to examine successful cultural products, such as long-running, popular television dramas, they have been primarily studying black boxes. As these black-boxed television programs gain credibility and popularity, they tend to lose reference to their originating local, contingent, semiotic and material conditions and instead appear as 'universal' stories about crime and policing. In using ANT, my research aims to open up the black box of entertainment television's fictional representations of crime, by studying them *in the making*.

By describing how particular representations are assembled through the concrete activities of media producers, an ANT account allows the actors to express themselves, by describing their own frames of reference, theories and contexts. ANT also holds that people, institutions, ideas, texts, technologies and logics are all actors, and more importantly, that they are all equally interesting analytically. Rather than reduce the production of a television drama to the vision of a singular human auteur or single intent, an ANT analysis documents instead how a television drama is *collaboratively* assembled by the coming together of heterogeneous actors in networks. Here, 'network' does not refer to an actual physical entity that appears in the shape of a network, but instead to a tool for describing a series of transformations and translations made between and among actors. To avoid confusion, I will use the term *actor* in the ANT sense throughout this book, and will refer to television actors as screen performers. While the term *network* will be used to refer to a broadcasting television network, *actor-network* will be used to denote the relations and transformations between heterogeneous people and things.

Throughout this book, I will be examining various translations made by actors within the television production process. As a key concept in ANT, translation involves practices that transform one thing into another thing, by making them equivalent in some way. The success or failure of a television drama, for instance, is dependent on its chains of translation. A television drama can only be successfully made if the multiple and heterogeneous (aesthetic, commercial and legal) translations of various actors in the production process align with one another. Because an ANT perspective is a myopic lens that focuses on particular details rather than on seeing the 'big picture,' the researcher lacks a privileged vantage point from which to perch, in order to see the construction and attribution of a representation's ultimate (or dominant) meaning. When conceptualizing the meaning of a representation, an ANT account traces how such meaning arises only as an outcome of the various strategies and struggles between various actors on the production team.

As a *material-semiotic* method of analysis (Law 2007), ANT is useful because it offers a way to bridge together the analytically distinct perspectives provided by social science and the humanities. When it comes to examining professional mass communications, the social science approach has been more attuned to how symbols are *materially* produced than to what they mean, focusing on the industrial and organizational context rather than the text itself (Ettema, Whitney and Wackman 1997: 33). In contrast, humanities-oriented analyses of mass cultural products have focused on the text's *semiotic* meanings, concentrating on the relation between symbols and ideas. Using ANT, I examine not only the semiotic relations between ideas about crime, but the material conditions under which those meanings are formulated in specific case studies. These case studies are concrete sites that allow us to observe the making of representations of crime by the actor-networks of popular criminology.

Case studies

> I'm not interested in telling Canadian stories because there is no such thing as a Canadian story. Ever since I got involved in [writing and producing this Canadian police drama, I have been asked], what makes it specifically Canadian? There's nothing that makes it specifically Canadian, and anybody who tells you differently is lying to you. Storytelling is storytelling, and it doesn't matter where it happens or who it happens to. Canadians would like to believe that there is a typical Canadian story, and I have never found it.
>
> (Canadian television writer DA 22 July 2012)

As ANT makes its arguments with reference to empirical case studies (Law 2007), the general theoretical points made in this book are drawn from interviews and observations of different sites of television production and practice. These specific research sites coincide with the following three case studies, all of which are English-language[4] Canadian crime television productions with some form of international distribution:

1. Internationally distributed by BBC Worldwide, *Cra$h & Burn*, formerly titled *Lawyers, Guns and Money*, is an original Canadian cable television drama that follows the adventures of insurance adjuster Jimmy Burn, as he navigates between the legitimate world of insurance and the illegitimate worlds of organized crime and insurance fraud in post-industrial Hamilton, Ontario. According to its executive producer, the series is patterned after the procedural storytelling format of *CSI* (e.g. each episode begins with an insurance incident that is then investigated by Jimmy). I worked as a paid researcher for the production company, Whizbang Productions, during the pre-production of the show's pilot (2008) and during the creation of its new media (Internet) website[5] (August to September 2009). As a result of my participation in the production process, I was able to observe much of the pre-production and shooting of the pilot during the summer and fall of 2008 over the course of four months.
2. *The Bridge* is a Canadian–American (CTV/CBS) co-produced one-hour police drama that follows Police Union President Frank Leo's quest to clean up corruption in the city's police departments. I interviewed the show's head writer and executive producer when *The Bridge* was beginning its pre-production in March 2009, and conducted a follow-up interview in July 2012. I observed the writing process for two episodes during the summer of 2009, where I followed the processes of story creation and revision from breaking story in the writers' room through to script changes across multiple story documents. *The Bridge* has since been distributed for airing in Australia and South Africa.
3. Airing not only in Canada but also the US, UK and some European countries, forensic crime docudramas, such as *F2: Forensic Factor*, *Cold Blood* (re-titled *True CSI* in the UK), and *Exhibit A*, make use of dramatic recreations in order to reconstruct for viewers the ways in which forensic science is used by police officers to solve past crimes in real life. Over the course of 2008 I conducted 11 in-depth interviews with producers, writers, directors, story coordinators and researchers for these shows, many of whom have worked on several crime-related docudramas. I paid special attention to the ways in which stories were selected, researched, and written. I also conducted a set visit to the shooting of a particular episode of *Forensic Factor*.

The bulk of this book draws from field observations that document the making of *The Bridge* and *Cra$h & Burn*. I do not, however, examine their entire production process, by detailing the making of an entire series. Instead, I examine each program at a particular phase of production: I describe the making of 1) a particular episode of *The Bridge*, 2) the pilot[6] of *Cra$h & Burn*, and 3) the research phase of forensic crime docudramas. Since ANT documents the assembly of ideas, people, logics, technologies, institutions and things, I have also organized the content of my chapters to highlight the process of such assembling. As a result, I do not devote any chapter to a single institution or to a significant member of the production unit. Instead, I document how these institutions and production staff members come together to make a particular representation of crime. Moreover, I also do not strictly separate my case studies into individual chapters. Since I focus on the practices of knowing and representing in television production, I juxtapose case studies in each of my chapters in order to emphasize the similarities and differences in how each television production knows and represents crime. Because each case study is a different research site, the conclusions in this book are drawn from the knowledge that we gain from moving from one site to another.

The juxtaposition of these case studies also allows me to describe the practices of North American television production. Despite the fact that these are Canadian case studies, the screenwriting and knowledge practices of Canadian television writers and producers are not distinctly different from those of their American counterparts for the following reasons. First, successful Canadian television writers, particularly showrunners (i.e. head writers) such as those of *The Bridge* and *Cra$h & Burn*, have often worked in the US as staff writers on television dramas for both major American broadcasters and premium cable channels. As a result, their screenwriting practices have been honed by their training in American writers' rooms.

Second, Canadian television writers are also consumers of American television dramas. While Canadian cultural nationalists tend to make an argument about the uniqueness and potential superiority of Canadian television dramas when compared to American television, Canadian audiences have routinely preferred non-Canadian programming (Beaty and Sullivan 2006: 10; Collins 1990: xv). As a result, Canadian audiences are not isolated from American television, and consequently understand the semiotics of a North American system of representation, often accusing Canadian police dramas of being 'too American' in their representation of crime and policing (DA 22 July 2012).

Lastly, the production practices of Canadian writers and producers are familiar to their American counterparts often because Canadian television producers seek American distribution as a first step in seeking international distribution for their television programs. While I do describe the particularities of the Canadian production context, Canadian television writers and producers are no longer solely writing for a Canadian audience, but for an increasingly large (geographically and culturally) undefined audience to whom 'universal' stories about crime and policing would appeal. In writing these 'universal' stories, Canadian writers themselves are de-emphasizing the Canadian content in their productions as a means of gaining some measure of international marketability. These universal storytelling attempts are linked to the financing structure of Canada's television industry, which has increasingly necessitated the making of co-productions (Fixmer 9 March 2009). Although the writers and producers described in this book work within the context of film and television production in Toronto, their commercial, aesthetic and legal considerations are being replicated in other countries that seek to export their television programs.

Chapter summaries

In exploring the translations made during the storytelling process of fictional television dramas, this book is organized along the metaphor of a travel guide. Analogous to the notion of translation, travel and transportation entail a point of departure, a terrain to be crossed, and a point of arrival. More importantly, a travel guide maps the paths we can take as we move from one point to the next across a territory. When documenting paths, the guide lets us know 'where it goes and what kind of traffic it has to carry' (Latour 1988: 179). The paths along which we travel determine not only what we see, but also how many of us see it.

As our point of departure, we begin on the intellectual superhighways or bypasses that have carried a heavy volume of research traffic. In Chapter 1, I review the criminological and sociolegal literature on mass-mediated, pop cultural representations. The bulk of this research has been methodologically structured by the use of content analyses and analyses of media effects. In treating representation as a final product, both of these methods have operated like superhighways in the sense that they have allowed researchers to speedily arrive at a pre-determined destination by relying on theoretical assumptions that may not be supported by empirical research. In particular, I argue that criminological and sociolegal scholars have tended to write as though there exists a singular culture industry (also known as *the* media) that is similarly responsible for all kinds of homogeneous cultural product, all of which are presumed to generate negative effects on mass audiences regardless of their medium specificity. In contrast to these theoretical and methodological assumptions, I suggest that we ought to undertake empirical research on the process of cultural production. When studying production, we ought to take into consideration the particular production processes of a specific medium (e.g. television), and not assume that *the* mass media exist as some singular, monolithic hegemonic entity. I end the chapter by laying the groundwork for using actor–network theory to study the process of television production.

By moving away from solely studying the text itself and its effects, we will be travelling away from the theoretical and methodological bypasses that have structured much criminological and sociolegal research. These bypasses have allowed researchers to circumvent the use of local roads with their slower traffic. To walk[7] along the local roads of television production, roads that have been less well paved because of their infrequent use by criminological and sociolegal scholars, I outline in Chapter 2 an ANT-inspired method for an empirical study of the culture industry. The chapter begins by explaining why ANT would be useful for an analysis of entertainment television production as a site of knowledge and textual production. I also explain how ANT diverges and converges from the production of culture perspective, which is a perspective used by scholars in political economy, sociology and cultural studies. The chapter ends with a description of how I gained access to television production sites in Toronto, Canada.

In following the local paths of television production, I document how television crime dramas start off as the work of a few individuals doing a specific series in a particular location – in this case, Toronto, Canada. Through unprecedented access, Chapter 3 takes the reader into the writers' room. Using the police drama *The Bridge* as a case study, I analyze the writers' room as a laboratory for the production of television fiction. I document the local and heterogeneous knowledge inputs into this laboratory during the process of breaking story (i.e. breaking an episodic story down to its component parts). Specifically, I discuss the role of the police technical consultant in providing writers with orally told, anecdotal story ideas about crime and policing. The extent to which television productions rely on police cooperation has an effect on how the shows ultimately represent the police. I also examine how broadcaster input, the showrunner's creative vision, and Errors and Omissions insurance shape those knowledge inputs into particular kinds of representations. In the case of *The Bridge*, representations are made episodic rather than serialized as a result of broadcaster demand. They are also universalized as a consequence of both legal/insurance requirements and the showrunner's Jungian-inspired storytelling preference.

While Chapter 3 follows knowledge inputs into an episode's formation, Chapter 4 follows the various story documents that are produced as outputs from the writers' room. Here, I am interested in documenting the textual transformations that an episodic story undergoes during the revision process. In doing so, I structure the chapter as a mystery: the case of the missing 'bad apples.' By examining how representations of 'bad apples' (i.e. corrupt police officers) disappear during the rewriting process of an episode of *The Bridge*, I describe how the meanings of representations are neither fixed nor stable during production. Instead, representations are bound up in alliances with particular spokespeople, such as writers, and are required to withstand multiple 'trials of strength' by various 'attackers,' such as network executives and producers. In addition, the study of textual transformations during the revision process can give us a sense of the different audiences that are mobilized in television production. While television writers and producers do create texts for an audience, this audience is not best understood as the (unknowable) consumer audience, but rather as the audience composed of network executives, insurers, Standards and Practices executives, and the show's own writers and producers. This production audience responds to and is activated by the multiple story documents, shaping story transformations before a singular television text is ultimately revealed to the consumer audience.

Chapter 5 leaves the writers' laboratory altogether in order to examine how place becomes relevant in the making of crime dramas, particularly at the stage of pilot development and production. The strategy of representing place (or setting) in a fictional crime drama is informed by the place of the commissioning broadcaster in the broadcasting landscape of the post-network television era. A broadcaster's place is located at the intersection of a quasi-legal broadcasting regulatory structure and a particular market orientation. Working in the tradition of 'quality,' North American premium cable networks cater to their niche market by providing crime dramas that are set in specific cities. In contrast, large broadcasting networks cater to their mass audience by generically setting their Canadian–American co-produced series in a large, urban city. Using case studies, I examine how recent Canadian–American co-produced police dramas – *The Bridge, Rookie Blue,* and *Flashpoint* – tend to translate Toronto into a 'world class city' analogous to any metropolitan (North American) city. In contrast, I examine how the showrunner of *Lawyers, Guns and Money* geographically relocated his series from New York City to Hamilton, Ontario, as the script moved from American premium cable network HBO to Canadian specialty channel Showcase. I end the chapter by examining how the specific representation of Hamilton is made relevant and feasible through translations undertaken by an actor-network consisting of governmental funding demands, Showcase's particular market orientation, the showrunner and director's narrative and aesthetic visions for the series, and knowledge about particular insurance scams.

Notes

1. Popularity is measured in this instance in terms of the total number of viewers per television program aired in a given year.
2. The first season of *CSI* was co-produced by Alliance Atlantis, a Canadian film and television production and distribution company.
3. There is evidence to suggest that *CSI* was sufficiently innovative to be considered a risky venture for major American broadcasters. Consequently, the series was not considered a guaranteed success by its broadcaster. The program was (in)famously the last series added to CBS' 2000–2001 programming schedule after all the major American broadcasters had passed on the script. It has been postulated that CBS was willing to pick up *CSI* and take such a programming risk because the broadcaster was coming out of the late 1990s at the back of the ratings pack (Kompare 2010). Together, these facts suggest that the producers and writers of *CSI* were not that successful at initially selling their show to American network executives, precisely because they were *not* talking about crime and criminality in ways that were sufficiently familiar to audiences.
4. This research does not document the making of French-language Canadian television productions, particularly series written and shot in Quebec. In contrast to English-language Canadian programming, Quebecois television enjoys a relatively larger audience, and is able to create and sustain a sense of coherent and unique (Francophone) identity (Beaty and Sullivan 2006).
5. The *Cra$h & Burn* website includes a section called 'Autotopsy,' which shows users the anatomy of a car accident complete with insurance ramifications. Autotopsy has since become an award-winning website. It won the Favourite Website Award (FWA) of the day on 3 March 2010. The FWA was created to recognize the latest and best cutting-

edge creativity, and is the most visited website award program in the history of the Internet.
6   The pilot is an episode that provides broadcasters with a sense of how the concept for a television series will be developed and executed.
7   Because an ANT account does not provide a general, structural overview of the world, it is often written as though the writer were taking her reader on a walking expedition during which they both explore a particular research site. Like a walking expedition, an ANT account covers a certain amount of space without giving an overview prior to exploring that space. This particular method of writing is inspired by Michel Serres' philosophy, especially his conceptualization of the *randonnée* – that is, a rambling kind of walking expedition. For Serres, the epistemology of journeys forges new relations between a human being and her world (Harari and Bell 1982). Thus, it is not surprising that Latour (2007) also provides an account of doing ANT through the metaphor of the hard-working ant who trudges about on a *randonnée* of its own. The point of the *randonnée* cannot be found in its destination, but in the processes of walking, rambling and trudging.

Chapter 1

Setting the stage: a literature review and analysis

In anticipation of the dawn of the twenty-first century, David Garland and Richard Sparks (2000) set out a programmatic research agenda that would re-conceptualize the discipline of criminology. They argue that academic criminology no longer monopolizes contemporary criminological discourse in society. Instead, this discourse can now be found circulating in public policy and popular culture often with little reference to or understanding of academic criminology. While academic criminology has historically focused on how public policy has constituted the issues of crime and crime control, it has generally ignored popular culture's criminological discourse. However, Garland and Sparks note that if academic criminology is to remain relevant today, it needs to understand the terms in which crime and crime control are being debated and discussed in popular culture. In seeking continued relevance, criminologists have embraced cultural studies in order to examine pop culture (Garland 2006). Pop culture is primarily conceptualized as the contextual domain of images, representations and meanings, many of which are mass-mediated. However, this enthusiastic embrace has generally occurred without much critical contemplation of exactly what it means to study culture (Garland 2006), particularly the production of mass-mediated, cultural representations. For the most part, this lack of critical reflection can be read as another instantiation of the observation that criminology has occurred largely in ignorance of recent conceptual debates in cultural studies (Carrabine 2008: 44) and in media studies (Sparks 1992). As a result, criminologists have tended to write as though there exists a singular culture industry (also known as *the* media) that is similarly responsible for all kinds of cultural product, all of which are presumed to generate negative effects on mass audiences regardless of medium.

To analyze this intellectual tendency, this chapter is organized into three parts. In Part 1, I will give a brief descriptive overview of the different banners under which research on media, culture and crime has proceeded. In Part 2, I will analyze the primary approaches that have been used by both criminologists and sociolegal scholars to study mass-mediated pop cultural representations. Implicitly, these scholars have proceeded under the assumption that culture *is* an industry that uses an assembly line to mechanically (re)produce homogeneous cultural products for mass consumption.[1] Lastly, in Part 3, I will argue that it is now time to break away from this particular conceptualization of the culture industry, and allow empirical research of the culture industries to anchor scholarly claims of what kinds of representation are produced by these industries and how.

Part 1: literature overview

Although criminology as a discipline can be traced back to the nineteenth century (Foucault 1977), the relationship between crime and culture has received little attention by criminologists until relatively recently (Young 2008). Criminologists interested in crime, media and culture have remarked upon the importance of mass-mediated, cultural representations of crime,[2] primarily because they constitute a mainstay of cultural consumption. After all, in North America, at least one crime television drama can be viewed in prime time almost any night of the week (Surette 2009). Crime stories are a staple of news media (see Jewkes 2004), and also feature in several movie genres, such as thrillers, police procedurals, and action movies among others. The popularity and prevalence of representations of crime in popular culture is said to be evidence of the public's growing fascination with crime and criminal justice (Mason 2003). This becomes problematic, especially to criminologists, because most ordinary people have limited direct experience or contact with criminal justice matters and rely on these media representations for their knowledge of such matters. Consequently, public consumption of media representations of crime is thought to affect public perceptions of criminals, victims and the criminal justice system (Mason 2003). As a result, the body of literature on crime, media and pop culture has been dominated by research on the effects of media representations on people's behaviour, fear of crime and ideological orientation (Carrabine 2008; Ericson 1991; Mason 2003; Reiner 2007). When studying media, criminologists have tended to focus on the (print) news media and the construction of crime news stories (e.g. Cohen and Young 1973; Ericson *et al.* 1987, 1991; Peelo 2006; Soothill and Walby 1991). However, since the beginning of the twenty-first century, criminologists have also increasingly attended to fictional representations of crime in films and on television (e.g. Rafter 2000, 2007; Valverde 2006).

Despite a shared interest in examining the intersection of crime, media and culture, criminologists have undertaken research on media representations of crime in popular culture under different banners: cultural criminology and popular criminology. In conceiving of popular criminology, criminologists have modelled this field of inquiry on popular legal studies and the interrelated study of law and film.

Cultural criminology

Studies of both news and fictional representations of crime have recently been subsumed under the banner of cultural criminology, which became a notable intellectual movement in criminology within the last decade. As Alison Young

(2008) notes, however, there are two strands of cultural criminology – namely, what she calls 1) subcultural criminology and 2) criminological aesthetics, each operating from different theoretical departure points.

Subcultural criminology

While subcultural criminology was more or less inaugurated by the publication of Jeff Ferrell and Clinton Sanders' *Cultural Criminology* (1995), it was not introduced to the wider community of criminologists until 2004 through the publication of a special issue of the journal *Theoretical Criminology* (see also Ferrell, Hayward, Morrison, and Presdee 2004). In presenting this new criminological perspective, Keith Hayward and Jock Young (2004: 259) described it in the following terms:

> [Cultural criminology] is the placing of crime and its control in the context of culture; that is, viewing both crime and the agencies of control as cultural products – as creative constructs. As such, they must be read in terms of the meanings they carry. Furthermore, cultural criminology seeks to highlight the interaction between these two elements ... Its focus is always upon the continuous generation of meaning around interaction; rules created, rules broken, a constant interplay of moral entrepreneurship, moral innovation and transgression.

In its manifesto form, subcultural criminology seeks to differentiate itself from what Hayward and Young (2004) call 'conventional' or 'administrative' criminology, which is a criminological perspective dominated by the instrumental and rational narratives of rational choice theory and positivism. In distinguishing itself, subcultural criminology's 'terms of engagement' are precisely binary opposites to those of 'conventional' criminology. 'Conventional' criminology privileges the use of quantitative methodologies; subcultural criminology uses qualitative methodologies, such as ethnography and qualitative content analyses. While 'conventional' criminology theorizes human subjects as rational beings, subcultural criminologists emphasize their 'irrationality' by focusing on their emotions. In particular, subcultural criminologists follow Jack Katz's (1988) insight that the act of (criminal) transgression is pleasurable, by focusing on the joys of transgression and the 'delight of deviance' (e.g. Presdee 2000). In contrast to 'conventional' criminology's focus on the community of victims and their fear of crime, subcultural criminologists tend to focus on subcultural participants (e.g. joy riders, gang members, young people at raves, graffiti artists, etc.). Their interest in media representations is related to the extent to which those representations make an impact on the style and aesthetic of subcultural participants, subjects who are theorized as consumers of mass mediated crime images.

In their understanding of media, subcultural criminologists primarily draw upon scholarly work done in the 1970s (Young 2008) – specifically, Stuart Hall *et al.*'s

(1978) *Policing the Crisis* and Stanley Cohen's (1972) early work on moral panics. Thus, subcultural criminologists endorse Hall *et al.*'s (1978) insight that the mass media play a highly significant role in both the labelling and communication of deviant subcultural identity, by fuelling moral panics. Hall *et al.* (1978) examined the moral panic surrounding mugging in Britain during the early 1970s. They connected the moral panic about mugging to the larger panic about the steadily rising rate of violent crime throughout the 1960s. Both of these panics, however, were about things other than crime *per se* (Hall *et al.* 1978: vii): as a condensation symbol for race, youth, and crime, mugging was a sign that the British way of life was falling apart, social order was disintegrating, and that society was in crisis. Mugging was used as an opportunity by the British state to construct an authoritarian consensus and to mobilize a law-and-order ideology. Similarly, in Cohen's (1972) analysis of the British mass media's construction of confrontations between the Mods and the Rockers in the 1960s, he demonstrated how the media demonized 'deviants' to reinforce society's boundaries of normality and order. While both are seminal works, it should be noted that both Hall *et al.*'s (1978) and Cohen's (1972) analyses are based on news representations rather than other kinds of fictional representation. The question remains to what extent insights derived from analyses of news representations can be applied without modification to understanding how fictional representations are produced, distributed and consumed.

Criminological aesthetics

Criminological aesthetics is a semiotic, textually oriented approach to analyzing the construction of crime as an image (Biber 2007; Hutchings 2001; Valier 2004), paying close attention to framing and editing devices as well as the linguistic tricks and turns through which crime becomes a topic (Young 1996: 16). This perspective begins with the observation that crime's images are structured according to a binary logic of representation: 'Oppositional terms (man/woman, white/black, rational/irrational, mind/body, and so on) are constructed in a system of value which makes one visible and the other invisible' (Young 1996: 1). The important point of analytic focus is not on the image's production, but on its interpretation by a spectator. According to Alison Young (2008: 24), criminological aesthetics pays attention to 'the matrix of intersections between spectator, the image and the context of reception.' For Young, these three terms are knit together through her definition of imagination: as the process by which people make images of crime, imagination evokes the drive of spectatorship, which turns on processes of identification *with*, *in* and *as* law and *against* crime and disorder. By and large, spectator identification is explored through the way a text constructs implied readers or viewers, and does not generally entail empirical research on the reception and identification of actual readers or viewers.

Popular criminology and popular legal studies

In the first comprehensive study of the genre of crime films done by a criminologist, Nicole Rafter (2000: 7) examines the content of such Hollywood films not for their accuracy, but for the ideological messages embedded in their narratives and imagery. More importantly, she begins to think through the implications of popular criminology. Crime films offer popular criminological explanations about who is a criminal, what is a crime, and what are the causes of criminal behaviour. They also tend to reflect the criminological theories in vogue at the moment they are produced (Rafter 2000: 48). For example, when criminological theories in the 1930s highlighted inner-city conditions and immigration as the causes of crime, films focused on ethnic mobsters' struggles for control in urban settings. When Freudian explanations of crime became popular in the late 1940s and 1950s, films began to present morally twisted characters in need of psychoanalytic diagnoses. However, crime films also continue to recycle discredited criminological theories. While academic criminologists move on to new theories of crime and criminal behaviour, crime films do not necessarily follow suit. Instead, they continue to represent the same kinds of popular criminological explanation irrespective of scientific credibility. While this tends to frustrate academic criminologists, it does not follow that they should ignore popular criminology.

Rafter (2007: 415) defines popular criminology as a category composed of discourses about crime found in film, on the Internet, on television, in newspapers, novels, rap music, and myth. Popular criminology, Rafter argues, covers much more territory than academic criminology in terms of raising ethical and philosophical issues. More importantly, it has greater social significance because it is more accessible and has a bigger audience than academic criminology. By presenting itself as scientific through the undramatic and dispassionate presentation of facts, theories and conclusions, academic criminology avoids the accessibility provided by popular criminology, effectively burying itself in 'the catacombs of conferences, journals and books' and the use of 'obfuscatory language and footnotes' (Rawlings 1998: 1–2). Despite the tension that exists between academic criminology and popular criminology, Rafter claims that they should be considered complementary discourses and ways of knowing about crime that exist under the larger umbrella category of criminology.

Because Rafter's conceptualization of popular criminology has been informed and inspired by popular legal studies, it would be worthwhile to consider the research questions that have stimulated the sociolegal study of popular culture. Popular legal studies (e.g. Chase 1986; Friedman 1988–9; Macaulay 1988–9) began in the form of discussions about how to study law and film. Film was taken as an example, and sometimes an exemplar, of a highly influential pop cultural product that sociolegal scholars should study because of their impact on ordinary people's perceptions of law. For example, as the first scholar to propose the study of law and film, Anthony Chase (1986) also proposed the creation of a systematic legal theory of American popular culture. He argued that pop cultural formats (e.g. fiction and non-fiction television, film, pop music and advertising) provide a fertile ground for a 'primitive accumulation' of mass culture's images of law and lawyers. An analysis of prime time, fictional television representations of law could be considered raw material for the popular social imagination, and offered a revealing look at American attitudes towards law and lawyers.

In general, there are three underlying assumptions that anchor the body of work done under the framework of popular legal studies. First, popular legal studies consider popular culture itself as a medium with a distinct format (Sherwin 2000). For example, William MacNeil (2007) examines various pop cultural texts without attention to their medium specificity. He considers fictional television series, novels, and film as exemplary instances of 'people's law' or *lex populi*, all of which serve to deliver jurisprudence from the rarified domain of legal professors to the public domain of the masses. The specific medium of various pop cultural products does not matter to these sociolegal researchers because they are more interested in the messages being transmitted by particular informational sources.

Second, from the beginning, popular legal studies was conceived as closely connected to considerations of ordinary people's perceptions of law. It sought to read pop cultural texts as evidence of people's attitudes towards law and justice. For example, Stephen Gillers (1988–9: 1622) argues that the popular television drama *LA Law* (1986–1994), broadcast to millions of viewers, 'may be seen as the single most important influence on the popular conception of lawyers' work and ethics. Accordingly, it may be criticized when it comes to distort what it pretends to describe.' Thus, Gillers provides a justification for corrective criticism: Because pop cultural texts are conceptualized as having such an immense effect on people's perceptions of law, sociolegal scholars need to highlight the gaps between (representations of) law *in* pop culture and (sociolegal representations of) law in action. The scholarly focus on the gap is in keeping with the tradition of sociolegal research, which has tended to focus on the gap between law on the books and the law in action (Sarat 1985; Sarat and Silbey 1988). Read within this tradition, popular legal studies merely highlight yet another gap to study. Like popular legal studies, popular criminology, as formulated by Rafter (2007: 415), also seeks to analyze the process through which popular criminology affects ordinary people's beliefs and perceptions about crime. In particular, academic criminologists should pay attention to how information about crime from popular criminological sources is organized in people's minds as frames and then as schemata.

Lastly, popular legal scholars are concerned with the effects of pop cultural texts on both ordinary people and on legal practitioners. The focus on ordinary people is often related to a concern that they will one day serve as jurors, and that their jury duty will be impacted by their consumption of pop cultural products. Certainly, this concern fuelled research on the *CSI* effect. There has been additional concern that the consumption of pop cultural products also shapes legal practices. In *Law Goes Pop* (2000: 17), Richard Sherwin asks what effect pop cultural forms, like advertising, Hollywood films, and television dramas, have on legal practice. He argues that as visual media, film and television have significantly altered the storytelling strategies used in the courtroom by trial lawyers, by highlighting the efficacy of visual persuasion. Because images are easily accessible (i.e. no training is required to understand them) and credible through the myth of 'seeing is believing,' they are especially persuasive to juries. Unlike MacNeil (2007), Sherwin (2000) sees the popularization of law in negative terms: when law goes pop, the ideals of law and justice are tarnished, by the mixing of fact with fiction and the introduction of visual logic to legal argument.

Law and film

As a complementary outgrowth of popular legal studies, the study of law and film is an interdisciplinary field animated by a basic research question that ultimately seeks to address how law films relate to law or the study of law (Freeman 2005). In pursuing this research question, the study of law and film comes together in a singular unit of analysis: the law film. Although law films were initially operationalized as courtroom dramas or films portraying lawyers (see the bibliography of early law and film articles in Machura and Robson 2001: 3–8), they have since been expanded to include any film that deals centrally with legal issues (Greenfield, Osborn, and Robson 2001). For example, scholars have also examined the Western *Unforgiven* (1992) as an exemplar of the revenge genre, in which vengeance is represented as a justified, equitable component to law (Miller 1998). One can read the expanding definition of law film as a sign of the growing importance of studying film in sociolegal studies.

The 'law and film' movement grew out of and parallels the structure of research done in the interdisciplinary field of 'law and literature,' which is a field that seeks to use literary insights to enhance the understanding of law while also using legal insights to enhance the understanding of literature (Posner 1988). In practice, scholars have examined law *in* literature, by examining how law is represented in literary classics (e.g. novels by Charles Dickens or Franz Kafka, the plays of William Shakespeare, etc.). They have also examined law *as* literature (see Levinson 1982), by using literary analyses to study legal texts. Lastly, 'law and literature' scholars have also compared the legal and literary modes of interpretation, concentrating on the ways in which rhetorical tools are similarly used in law and literature.

Similar to law *in* literature, the first sociolegal studies of law and film appearing in the late 1980s examined representations of law, particularly representations of lawyers in film. In one of the first edited anthologies on law and film, John Denvir (1996: xi) asserted that sociolegal scholars can learn a great deal about law from watching movies, and hence should study movies as legal texts. Since the late 1980s and 1990s, the bulk of the law and film literature still remains studies of law *in* film. Because the original mission of studying law and film was to provide a form of corrective criticism (Sarat *et al.* 2005) or forensic criticism (Black 1999), much of the literature on law *in* film is focused on policing film images that are inaccurate according to what sociolegal scholars knew about the law in action (e.g. Bergman and Asimow 2006). Other law and film scholars have progressed beyond examining a law film's accuracy, by analyzing representations of law and justice with the use of film theory, psychoanalysis, and semiotic theory.

Contemporary sociolegal scholars have also begun to examine film *as* law. In particular, they have begun to consider how film performs wide-scale legal indoctrination. For example, Orit Kamir (2005, 2006) follows Carol Clover (1998) by analyzing how law films position their viewers as active jurors through particular filmic techniques. In doing so, law films train viewers to enact judgment in ways that reflect and refract the dominant norms of a society, especially norms that presumably underlie both the production and reception of film and law in a society.

Other scholars have investigated how law and film are both powered by narrative, and the implications of their use of narrative regimes. For example, David Black (1999) considers how law and film are parallel narrative regimes. Both law and film have chosen narrative as their dominant organizing principle, even though the pleasure in film and the power in law escape narrativity. Black argues that the judicial system uses narrative to do what the cinema does: to draw attention away from its master purpose by advertising its ostensible function. While cinema advertises its entertainment function to obscure its master money-making purpose, the judicial system advertises its ability to administer justice in order to divert attention away from its master purpose of keeping the existing power structures in place. Rebecca Johnson and Ruth Buchanan (2001) are also interested in cinematic portrayals of law, not as representations of the truth of law, but as analogies for how law itself operates in constructing truth. Like cinema, law engages in a meaning-making process primarily through narrative, where it conflates narrative truth with historical truth in order to preserve the singularity of legal truth. A study of law would also be enhanced by a consideration of 'brute perception.' Because the audiovisual nature of cinema is a better analogy for the audiovisual real-life experience of the courtroom, analyses of 'brute perception' should consider cinematic elements of the courtroom experience.

Part 2: analysis of the main approaches used to study crime, media and culture

In contrast to the criminological literature on media and culture that has been dominated by an effects-centered study of non-fictional texts, the sociolegal literature has predominantly used text-centered approaches to examine fictional texts. However, both literatures make similar underlying assumptions about representations and popular culture.

For example, James Elkins (2006–7: 746) finds three basic propositions underlying sociolegal research on law and film, all of which are reiterated as 'crimes of the mass media' by Richard Ericson (1995) in his overview of criminological research on culture and communication. First, both Elkins and Ericson suggest that cultural products about crime and law are widely popular, especially in North America. Ericson associates this popularity thesis with the 'crime' of entertainment: mass mediated representations are popular precisely because they are fun.

Second, both Elkins and Ericson suggest that the mass media can have an educational effect on audiences because they have the capacity to teach people about the legal system or criminal justice. In Ericson's perspective, however, the mass media fail to effectively educate the audience because its representations are primarily formatted for entertainment. That is, a popular and entertaining format is assumed to have a narcotic and addictive effect on mass audiences, working to 'dull the mind, induce laziness, foster political alienation and produce cultural dopes' (Ericson 1995: xii). Lastly, both Elkins and Ericson suggest that media's educational capacity is compromised or certainly made questionable because its representations of crime and law are sometimes at variance with facts discovered by criminological and sociolegal scholars in the 'real world.' One of the negative effects of mass media, as Ericson explains, includes its 'criminal' inducement of fear and 'folly' in audiences. In undertaking research on such 'folly,' scholars assume that the mass media are organized in such a way that they inevitably produce distorted knowledge.

Following these three basic premises, both criminological and sociolegal research on pop cultural products have methodologically focused on the content and format of the products themselves, alternately treating them as art, texts to be corrected, or as symptomatic of a particular culture's ideological orientation. In addition, these scholars have examined the effects of cultural products on audiences, often assuming negative media effects on homogeneous mass audiences.

Studying the cultural product

The cultural product as art: semiotic approaches to studying representations of crime and law

In undertaking analyses of representations of crime and law, some criminological (e.g. O'Brien *et al.* 2005; Tzanelli *et al.* 2005; Valverde 2006) and sociolegal scholars (e.g. Kamir 2006; Sarat *et al.* 2005) use a semiotic approach to their content analysis. Most semiotic analyses are informed by a postmodern orientation as well as a subversive aim (Goodman 2006). The analysis is meant to reveal alternative meanings, and to provide a critical standpoint to interrogate and challenge the status quo. In theory, multiple meanings can be found within a single, polysemous text (Fiske 1989).

In using a semiotic approach, criminological and sociolegal scholars tend to elevate films and television programs to the status of art. Art is significant because it provides a sense of what might be possible in our world. For example, Sarat, Douglas, and Umphrey (2005: 2) justify the study of law and film precisely because law films chart 'might-have-beens' and 'might-bes.' Moreover, film's capacity to represent an alternative legal world is valuable: it allows legal scholars to imagine an alternative to the present legal world, and consequently to critique the present workings of the legal system (Sarat *et al.* 2005). For these researchers, films and television shows nourish the imagination of scholars.

In their consideration of cultural products as art, these scholars tend to proceed under the assumption that both culture and art ought to be considered separate from the economy. Implicitly following in the footsteps of scholars writing at the turn of the twentieth century (Steinert 2003), such as Max Horkheimer and Theodor Adorno (1972), contemporary criminologists and sociolegal scholars continue to presume that authentic, autonomous art can lift people into the sphere of culture, and should not be a product of the economy. Here, it is assumed that culture, a niche for all that is beautiful, good and true, should be governed only by its own rules. In contrast, cultural products that are subsumed under the logic of commodity production and exchange are thought to lose some of their critical potential (Thompson 1990). Governed by economic demands and commercial imperatives, the culture industry is assumed to churn out mass-produced products that reproduce formulaic stories and messages about crime rather than provide artistic creations that lead people into an alternate world of possibility.

We can see this assumed division between art/culture and the economy at work in two particular ways. First, some criminological and sociolegal scholars assume that the economy is a contaminating influence. Even MacNeil (2007), a scholar who celebrates massively appealing pop cultural products for their dissemination of popular jurisprudence, is suspicious about the contamination of these products by Capital. He notes that although pop cultural products should and could play an important part in democratizing the politics of law, they have an 'uneasy alliance with and co-optation by Capital' (MacNeil 2007: 157).

Second, culture and economy are kept separate in criminological and sociolegal analyses that tend to ignore the fact that cultural products are made possible by an economy. Instead, these scholars implicitly consider these products to be art, and as such choose to focus only on the aesthetics that govern representations of crime and law. Often, this consideration is related to the scholar's choice of cultural product for analysis, selecting one that is made by a director who is recognized as an auteur with a distinct authorial and stylistic signature. In general, these implicit auteurist arguments claim that the cultural product can transcend its industrial form of production and hence can be considered art (Stam 2000). Criminological and sociolegal scholars have also tended to select cultural products made outside of Hollywood, which can be considered the paradigmatic culture industry.[3] For example, *Rashomon* (1950) is a crime film that tends to attract sociolegal attention (e.g. Kamir 2005). Notably, it is a film made by a recognized auteur (Akira Kurasawa) as well as outside of the Hollywood studio system (i.e. it was made by a Japanese movie studio).

In addition to selecting cultural products made outside of Hollywood, criminological and sociolegal scholars tend to select relatively low-budget films with limited or questionable box office success. In other words, they tend to choose film exemplars that have remained relatively unscathed from the contaminating touch of Capital during both their production and reception. For example, in his Presidential Address to the 1999 Annual Law and Society Meeting, Austin Sarat (2000) chose the film *The Sweet Hereafter* (1997) for analysis. In doing so, he highlights the film's potential to illuminate alternative realities that would analytically contribute to sociolegal scholars' treatment of the law. However, it should be noted that *The Sweet Hereafter* is a Canadian film made on an estimated budget of $5 million. Since its release in theatres in 1997, the film has a total domestic box office gross[4] of roughly $3.3 million. As another example of the kinds of film chosen for analysis by sociolegal scholars, Alison Young (2008) chose Gus Van Sant's film *Elephant* (2003) as a case study to demonstrate the method of criminological aesthetics. Made with an estimated budget of $3 million, *Elephant* was produced by HBO Films,[5] a division of the cable television network HBO that is known for producing high-quality and ground-breaking productions mostly geared towards television distribution. The film opened in limited release across 100 American cinemas beginning in 2003 and accumulated a domestic gross total of $1.3 million over its 11-week run.

The selection of auteurist, low-budget cultural products with limited original success, as measured by box office receipts or television ratings, raises the question of whether these criminological and sociolegal scholars are tapping into pop cultural products that are indeed *popular*. If these are the products chosen for analysis in studies of popular criminology or popular legal studies, then it is not immediately clear how popular criminology or popular legal studies are themselves about 'the popular.' Obviously, not all films or television shows are popular with audiences. In fact, pop cultural theorist Henry Jenkins (4 September 2006) notes how there probably exists a 'canon' of television shows watched by many academics, but are still not highly rated by the rest of the world. For example, Jenkins believes that a PhD might be a pre-requisite for enjoying the ratings-challenged *Veronica Mars* (2004–2007), a television drama about a teenage private detective. Similarly, academic criminologists (e.g. Ferrell, Hayward, and Young 2008: 24), criminal law professors (e.g. Capers 2011), and sociologists[6] have been singing the praises of the HBO crime drama *The Wire* (2002–2008), a series that has received much critical success irrespective of its poor Nielsen ratings. As creator of *The Wire*, David Simon (Egner 5 April 2012), notes that the series' 'success' is part of a relatively recent and revisionist commentary, in which critics and fans now deem the show 'popular' when in fact it was not at the time of its airing.

These examples suggest that scholars tend to gravitate towards certain kinds of pop cultural product: specifically, those that are not massively popular, but rather critically well regarded. As such, there is an ambiguity in the term 'popular' as used by criminological and sociolegal scholars. It is not clear how 'popular' should be primarily understood: does 'popular' describe something that is intended to be massively popular or something that has proven to be massively appealing?[7] At what point can something be deemed massively appealing (e.g. are a group of TV critics somehow equivalent to millions of viewers?)? Or does 'popular' simply describe a mode of dissemination that allows for mass circulation? The distinction between these different definitions of popularity is partially related to whether one studies production or reception. When studying reception, popularity is often conceptualized as an effect of a 'successful' cultural product.

When studying production, however, a cultural product's popularity has yet to be established, but its format already takes into consideration how it will become accessible to potentially millions of viewers.

The facticity of cultural products: correcting representations of crime and law

Although some criminological and sociolegal scholars have undertaken semiotic analyses of representations of crime and law, most scholars use their analyses for the purpose of corrective criticism. For example, analyses of the popular American television show *CSI* have focused on its inaccurate representations of crime and policing (e.g. Cavender and Deutsch 2007; Stevens 2011; VanLaerhoven and Anderson 2009). Academics have focused on the show's 1) exaggerated portrayal of violent crimes, particularly murder; 2) representation of science as more unified and less contradictory than its actual practice; 3) representation of forensic science as always accurate and hence the Truth, making it necessary for the solving of crimes; and 4) the conflation of the work done by forensic scientists and primary police detectives. This is in keeping with other recent content analyses of entertaining media representations of crime and justice, which endeavour to report a sharp division between media representations and 'real-world' measures of crime and justice. In generalizing this divergence, Ray Surette (2009: 256) calls it 'the law of opposites': whatever the media show, it is the opposite of what is true. Similarly, Marilyn McShane and Frank Williams (1994: ix) claim the following in their foreword to an edited anthology about criminology and the mass media: 'Reality itself, clear and unadorned, is not to be found in the information provided by the media.'

In general, this kind of corrective analysis focuses on highlighting inaccurate images of crime and law and in doing so, reinforces the idea that there exists an objectively true reality to which these images should correspond. In contrast to that which is shown by popular media outlets, this factually accurate reality is often defined by official crime statistics and scholars' own knowledge of crime, law and science. For example, compared to police statistics, criminologists tout how the mass media over-represent murder and other forms of serious violent crime and under-represent property crime (Ericson 1991; Surette 2009). In making these corrective claims, however, these scholars implicitly conceive of the popular, mass-mediated realm and the academic (or intellectual) realm as binary opposites, each providing representations of crime and law with distinctly different content and format. For example, Laurence Friedman's (1988–9: 1579) conceptualization of popular legal studies defines popular culture as the norms and values held 'by ordinary people, or at any rate, by non-intellectuals, as opposed to high culture, the culture of intellectuals and the intelligentsia.'

While scholars undertaking semiotic analyses tend to celebrate the difference between popular and academic texts, by highlighting the subversive potential of popular texts, corrective scholars acknowledge the difference by denouncing the factual inaccuracy and sensationalism of popular texts. In contrast to semiotically inclined scholars, corrective scholars also do not treat popular texts as polysemous. They do not assume that these texts contain within them multiple meanings, precisely because they presume the existence of a singular, objective reality that has been heavily distorted by media images. In taking a corrective approach, the objective of the scholarly analyst is not to highlight how a text opens up alternative possibilities for addressing issues of law and crime, but to educate 'the public' about the facts and 'reality' of law and crime. In doing so, corrective scholars cling to a popular–academic bifurcation that has the pernicious effect of assuming that they are somehow immune from the effects of cultural products that seem to so profoundly impact ordinary, 'non-intellectual' people, even though it is not immediately clear how they have formed this immunity.

Associated with the goal of mass education, the corrective impulse can be linked to recent scholarly attempts to create a 'public criminology.' Primarily conceived by American and British criminologists in the face of criminology's waning impact on the formation of public policy (Chancer and McLaughlin 2007; Currie 2007), public criminology is an umbrella term for examining the ways in which criminologists have sought to engage with and influence public responses to crime (Loader and Sparks 2011). As one of its crucial tasks, public criminology seeks to 'evaluate and reframe cultural images of the criminal' (Uggen and Inderbitzin 2010: 726), by communicating scientific research findings through mass media outlets. Given this task, public criminology is quite similar to Gregg Barak's (1994) notion of newsmaking criminology, which refers to criminologists' conscious efforts to become part of the mass-mediated production and consumption of representations of crime. In contrast to media pundits, newsmaking criminologists would provide the public with social scientific facts as a means to combat the media's 'disinformation campaigns' (Barak 1994: 270). Although criminologists would primarily educate the public through the news media, Barak (1994) condemns all forms of media, including fictional television dramas, as sources of distorted images about crime and criminal justice.

However, this corrective perspective ignores not only evidence that the general public is disinterested in reading about facts without the context of a compelling story (Feilzer 2009), but also how official statistics and academic facts are themselves social constructions. Police statistics of crime, for example, also do not mirror the reality of crime, but are cultural, legal and social constructs that the police produce for organizational purposes (Ericson 1981). Similarly, academic representations of crime are themselves social constructions that do not simply mirror reality. Scholars do not simply look through some window pane and report on the world; they write texts that help create social reality (Latour 2007: 122). As Pierre Bourdieu (1989: 53–4) argues, social reality is a representation and a reality that sociologists help create in people's minds through sociological categories of perception and division.

Cultural products as symptomatic of a culture's ideological leaning

While corrective analyses focus on factually inaccurate representations, symptomatic readings focus on connecting representations to a culture's particular ideological orientation. Generally, symptomatic readings situate mass cultural products within a trend of thought (broadly understood as ideology) assumed to be characteristic of a society within a particular time period (Bordwell and Thompson 2004: 57). Here, cultural products are treated as 'documentary,' representing the recorded body of intellectual and imaginative work of a specific historical period (Williams 1961). Often, symptomatic readings of cultural products are accompanied by normative claims about how culture (here conceptualized as the sum of cultural products) ought to develop. In these instances, mass cultural products are read as 'symptoms' of an underlying 'culture,' which the cultural critic aims to diagnose in terms of its healthy progress or unhealthy decline.

In general, criminological and sociolegal scholars have focused their symptomatic readings of cultural products on a) the messages found therein, and b) their presumed ideological effect on a mass audience. In undertaking symptomatic analyses, these scholars attend to the ideological messages being produced and distributed by the culture industry, while ignoring how the medium affects the kinds of messages that can be produced and distributed in the first place. Based on their content analysis of a cultural product, they tend to draw conclusions about a product's ideological effect on a mass audience, especially in terms of how that product might affect the formation of crime or legal consciousness.

IT'S ABOUT THE MESSAGE, NOT THE MEDIUM

Although cultural industr*ies* (i.e. various branches and genres of cultural production) are now recognized by contemporary cultural studies scholars (see Hesmondhalgh 2007), sociolegal scholars and criminologists tend to write as though there exists a singular culture industry that is similarly responsible for all kinds of cultural product regardless of medium. As I have previously discussed, popular legal studies and popular criminology assume that popular culture can be defined as a vast array of various cultural products that share a singular format, which is that of popular culture writ large. In sharing what is conceived as a uniform format across various media, these scholars assume that the culture industry creates products for mass consumption that are identical regardless of whether they appear in print, on the big screen, or on the small screen. The same presumption underlies law and film research where television is often considered film (Robson and Silbey 2012: 2). This is not to deny that television, like film, is a moving image, but to suggest that scholars take into consideration the differences in production, distribution and reception[8] between the two media.

Similarly, criminological scholars write about 'the mass media' often without disaggregating the component media that make up this 'mass.' Admittedly, there is an ambiguity inherent in the term 'mass media,' particularly when it comes to understanding how 'mass' relates to 'media.' For the most part, criminological and sociolegal scholars have read the term in the same way as one might read the term 'mass culture,' where 'mass' refers to the mass audience as addressees of the media. However, it is also possible to read 'mass media' as a description of a bundle of various media technologies and formats. This latter sense is often ignored by criminologists when they refer to *the* media in the singular and monolithic form, effectively aggregating various media technologies and formats into some uniform and homogeneous entity.

A consideration of medium specificity is typically downplayed in two particular ways. First, an analysis of medium specificity is neglected when scholars presume the existence of an overriding general logic that structures the messages produced and distributed by all kinds of mass media. For example, Aaron Doyle's (2003) *Arresting Images* focuses on television representations of policing and how these images subscribe to a cultural logic of mass media (Altheide and Snow 1979). This logic equally applies to all types of medium because it is a logic built on the commercial need to entertain mass audiences by providing the least offensive (i.e. least critical) representations possible (Doyle 2003: 21–2). Second, medium specificity is overlooked when scholars continue to use shorthand forms, such as 'crime in the media' or 'crime stories' to denote both journalistic and entertainment representations of crime.[9] The effect of using such shorthand forms is that it erases the precise distinctions that scholars should be making, not only between different media but between different genres. Even if we hold the medium constant, 'crime stories' written for television news are written with different expectations than 'crime stories' written for prime time television dramas. These diverging expectations are not only structured by different genre formats, but also by different production conditions that work to privilege particular storytelling approaches. For example, television journalists and television drama writers work under a different pace of work (e.g. deadlines for journalists occur over the course of a day whereas television writers can work on the same draft over the course of a week) as well as under different ethical obligations (e.g. journalists strive towards responsible and objective reporting of events, whereas writers of television dramas do not share this obligation).

By and large, criminological and sociolegal scholars have not attended to medium specificity, particularly a medium's distinctive format, because they have been so focused on analyzing the message(s) found in media representations. For them, the medium is *not* the message (as it was for Marshall McLuhan). Instead, what counts is the message that can be found in cultural products. Of course, this assumption is grounded in the understanding that there exists an overall dominant message to be found within various cultural products, as opposed to the plural meanings highlighted by semiotic readings of cultural representations.

As Goodman (2006: 758) highlights in his review of approaches to studying law and pop culture, this symptomatic research agenda is built on a predominantly linear model of transmission. That is, scholars assume that messages about crime are sent from producers to receivers through media, and hence media are conceptualized as mere conduits of information. The goal is not to study what makes the media distinctive in the sending of such messages, but in the informational content of the messages being sent. The research question becomes, What is the ideological influence of popular culture (primarily operationalized as content found in mass cultural products) on the formation of consciousness?[10] Specifically, criminological and sociolegal scholars have been interested in the formation of crime consciousness (Garland 2001) and legal consciousness (Ewick and Silbey 1998), respectively. Although definitions of consciousness vary (e.g. as attitude, cultural practice or conscious knowledge), both kinds of consciousness are generally theorized as being institutionalized by the media and popular culture. It is assumed that the cultural industries are a site at which scholars can examine the explicit construction of legal or crime consciousness, where such consciousness is embodied in 'messages about crime, litigation, and law' (Silbey 2005: 360).

PRESUMED IDEOLOGICAL EFFECT ON A MASS AUDIENCE

By assuming that a cultural product's ideological message can have an effect on public consciousness, criminological and sociolegal scholars have read the changing contents of cultural products as a sign of changing public attitudes towards issues of crime and law. In doing so, they treat the cultural product as symptomatic of a culture's ideological leaning during a particular historical period, often classifying the sociopolitical orientation as either conservative or liberal. Broadly speaking, a conservative orientation is also understood as a 'conventional' perspective while a liberal orientation is mapped onto a 'critical' perspective. For instance, Rafter's (2000: 165) content analysis of twentieth century American crime films identifies two kinds of film: 1) conventional films in which 'the good guys get the bad guys,' and 2) critical films that do not promise audiences that justice can be achieved.

As yet another example of a symptomatic reading, Timothy Lenz (2003) argues that changes in public attitudes towards law can be studied through an examination of images of law in film and television. What primarily concerns Lenz is the shift from the liberal view of law to a conservative one. The liberal view of law conceptualizes crime as a product of its social environment and hence amenable to individual rehabilitation and social change. It is also a view that emphasizes due process, which maintains the presumption of innocence, individual's rights and limits on the use of criminal justice discretion. In comparison, the conservative view of law primarily conceives of crime as the product of incorrigible individuals who should be punished through adherence to a crime control model (i.e. one that emphasizes the efficient administration of justice and punishment).

Other sociolegal and criminological scholars have also read into contemporary pop cultural products an increasingly conservative, law-and-order ideology. For example, Elayne Rapping (2003) uses analyses of contemporary crime television shows (e.g. *COPS*, *OZ*, and *Law and Order* among others) to argue that social problems are increasingly being transformed into legal problems. Moreover, these legal problems are being framed in conservative terms. Rapping's conceptualization of this hidden conservatism is similar to Lenz's description of the conservative view of law. Similarly, Aaron Doyle's (1998) analysis of the American reality television program *COPS* suggests that the show disseminates a law-and-order ideology that parallels the conservative law-and-order political ideology of American get-tough-on-crime policies.

Overall, this kind of academic research (e.g. Greer 2007; Haltom and McCann 2004; Jewkes 2004; Muraskin and Domash 2007) tends to conclude that films and television programs not only reflect, but more importantly disseminate a monolithic, homogeneous ideology that manipulates and deceives the audience. Here, ideology is not only understood as a system of ideas, but denotes a misrepresentation of reality. Implicitly if not explicitly, scholars working within this approach are adhering to a classical Marxist formulation of ideology, whereby ideology is conceived as a false or illusory representation that prevents people from perceiving the real (i.e. material) conditions of existence. Scholars working within this Marxist-inspired paradigm do not always elaborate on how the ideologies under study are necessarily aligned with the interests of a particular ruling class. However, they almost always imply that the media's dissemination of ideology, particularly that which is conservative and in line with the status quo, is dangerous because it has the effect of repressing alternative ways of conceiving reality. Because the media is presumed to be a powerful, schematizing force in this perspective, scholars fear that ordinary people will simply succumb and conform to the ideological position embedded in media images of crime and law.

In these symptomatic readings, however, audiences are not empirically studied, but rather theoretically conceived receivers of ideology. They are the audience constructed through the popular text's use of point-of-view identification and narrative structuring. Because the interpretation of the text is still under the power of the scholarly analyst, it is never clear how actual audiences interpret the text and its ideological underpinnings.

Studying media effects

By highlighting the conservative law-and-order ideology embedded in representations of law and order, criminological and sociolegal scholars' symptomatic readings of media representations proceed under the assumption that conformism (i.e. general approval of the state of the world) is a negative media effect, and would hinder the development of critical thinking that deviates from the status quo. While sociolegal scholars have mostly used a humanities-oriented, text-centered approach to study media representations, criminologists have used social scientific methods to examine media effects. Spurred on by a general sense that media have 'real' effects on society and criminal justice, criminologists have been attempting to document these effects for at least half a century. The study of media representations of crime and crime control has been justified by cultural criminologists because of their 'real' effects on social life: they 'shape attitudes and define policy; define the effects of crime and criminal justice; generate fear, avoidance and pleasure; and alter the lives of those involved' (Ferrell *et al.* 2004: 4).

Like most communication scholars, criminologists have focused on audience reception, presuming that the consumption of mass cultural products is primarily related to negative effects rather than positive prosocial ones (Staiger 2005). In addition to concerns about conformism, criminologists have also been traditionally preoccupied with empirically documenting two other possible consequences to viewing television images of crime: 1) criminal behaviour, especially when it is manifested as violence; and 2) fear of crime (for a review of this research, see Reiner 2007). More than any other medium (e.g. films or books) television has been constructed as the primary location of negative media effects. This continual and constant emphasis on the negative effects of television has also led media scholar John Hartley (2008: 245) to note that television studies was founded on a negative and as such resembles the study of deviance and criminality.[11] Much like the (figure of the) criminal, television has been theorized as something to be resisted or opposed.

Effects research on antisocial behaviour and fear of crime

Criminologists tend to use a positivist psychological paradigm, particularly from the cognitive-behavioural tradition, when examining whether or not children's exposure to violent television images has a detrimental effect on them. This detrimental effect is often operationalized as an increase in children's real-life aggressive behaviour. After thousands of predominantly experimental studies, researchers generally agree on the following meagre conclusion:

> [F]or some children, under some conditions, television is harmful. For some children under the same conditions or for the same children under other conditions, it may be beneficial. For most children, under most conditions, most television is probably neither particularly harmful nor particularly beneficial.
>
> (Schramm, Lyle, and Parker 1961: 11)

Despite the volume of such research since the 1920s, Livingstone (1996) suggests that there is no definitive conclusion on whether it can be empirically shown that specific mass media messages have detrimental effects on the audiences who are exposed to them. This lack of definitive conclusion also applies to empirical research on the acquisition of 'inaccurate' perceptions of the world through exposure to television. While Gerbner *et al.* (1980) have argued that heavy television viewing 'cultivates' a misleading 'mean world view' – i.e. one that represents a misleading and exaggerated understanding of violence in the real world – a reanalysis of the data has shown that these causal claims about television viewing are not sustainable once viewers' demographic variables (e.g. age, gender and income) have been statistically controlled (Hirsch 1980, 1981; Hughes 1980). While 'the mean world view' has anchored criminological research delving into the relationship between media representations and fear of crime, the empirical results of this research are mixed due to differences in research design. There has been substantial variation in the ways researchers have operationalized crime news, exposure to crime news, and fear of crime (Sacco 1995: 151). Moreover, these differences in operationalization do not always account for the ways in which crime is reported differently by different news outlets (see Ericson *et al.* 1991), by different media (e.g. print news vs. television news), or by different crime programs (e.g. news vs. reality-television vs. fictional crime programs).

Aside from methodological difficulties in operationalizing the variables under study, criminological research on media effects tends to be founded on a particular conceptualization of the mass audience. In these studies, the mass audience is assumed to be a homogeneous group of passive receivers that simply accepts the culture industry's (propagandist) message(s). Based on a simple linear model of transmission (Lasswell 1927, 1948), this conceptualization has been called the hypodermic needle theory, whereby the syringe metaphorically suggests that the mass media has a powerful, immediate and direct effect on the audience. By and large, the hypodermic needle theory has been discredited through later empirical research (Lazarsfeld *et al.* 1968).

While contemporary cultural studies scholars no longer conceive of a homogeneous audience duped by the mass media in their audience reception studies, criminologists continue to use this conceptualization in their effects research (Reiner 2007: 320; Yar 2009). While cultural studies scholars and even the media industries themselves now consider audience*s* as active and participatory (see Fiske 1989; Jenkins 1992, 2006a, 2006b), criminologists continue to view film and television meanings as monolithic and media consumers as passive receivers (e.g. Dowler *et al.* 2006). Criminologists' adherence to outmoded conceptions of the mass media and mass audience is both striking and problematic, considering that criminology's dominant mode of engagement with culture and media is through the study of media effects (Yar 2009).

Part 3: resetting the research table

Surveys of the current field of criminological and sociolegal work on media and popular culture tend to end in one of two ways. For those hoping to move sociolegal work forward (Sarat *et al.* 2005), the tendency has been to broaden the kinds of textual analysis done (e.g. to include narrative analyses) and to include questions of audience reception (e.g. to study reception among non-specialized audiences). In practice, however, studies of reception that have focused on a small group of non-specialist audience members (i.e. those who are neither lawyers nor legal scholars) have used members that happen to be specialized in other ways. For example, sociolegal scholars have studied fans (Smoodin 2005), or those with a vested interest in films generally (e.g. film critics) or in a specific law film (e.g. real-life victims of a particular crime that are fictionally represented in a film made about that crime; see Mnookin 2005; Waldman 2005). None of these groups of viewers is necessarily representative of the general population's response to a film. Instead, an emphasis on this kind of reception might overestimate a film's appeal or popularity, and certainly does not escape the scholar's interpretation of film content. In general, audience reception studies still require that the scholar interpret representations in some way in order to contextualize viewer responses to those representations (Staiger 2005).

Alternatively, for those ending a literature review of criminological research on crime, media, and culture, the tendency has been to end with the industrial production of crime news (Carrabine 2008; Reiner 2007), focusing on the questions of who makes crime news and how. However, as Greer points out in his introduction to *Crime and Media: A Reader* (2010), this kind of work on news production is not currently being done. Media criminologists are not currently conducting any sociological research in newsrooms, neither are they engaging with audiences in terms of their discursive practices. Instead, the Holy Grail of criminological research is still focused on revealing media distortions and finding media effects, especially those related to increases in antisocial behaviour or fear of crime.

In short, the research table for future criminological and sociolegal research on media and popular culture seems set for more studies based on content analysis, audience reception, or media effects. Currently, there does not seem to exist much research interest in empirically studying the culture industry, particularly the entertainment television industry, which offers us this content. Instead, it seems to be enough for scholars to infer producers' intent from perusals of a cultural product's content. For example, scholars have inferred that 'those who write and produce *CSI* sell their show by tapping into dominant contemporary ways in which we think and talk about crime, criminality and citizenship already in circulation,' which 'in turn resonate strongly with viewers as familiar and comfortable' (Byers and Johnson 2009: xx). Of course, one wonders how producers and writers are gifted with this uncanny ability to predict future commercial success. If scholars demand 'accurate' representations of the world *from* the media, it seems remiss of academic scholarship to not provide 'accurate' (i.e. empirically supported observations) representations *of* the media in return. Scholars cannot glean producers' intent or the conditions of production from content analyses alone (Doyle 2006; Johnson 1986/1987). Instead, they need to leave their comfortable armchairs and enter the field in order to study the process of production.

To that end, I propose we reset the research table in two particular ways.

First, we should come to the research table without any of the assumptions that informed the above research. We should not assume that cultural products are themselves homogeneous and stereotypical, producing negative effects when consumed by mass audiences. Instead of examining the reception of cultural products, it would be more interesting to understand how they are made 'palatable' by producers and writers. In order to do so, we need to dispense with the assumption that '*the* media' exists as some singular, monolithic, hegemonic entity.

We should be more specific about how each medium produces and distributes its products in specific ways. The aggregate and singular notion of the media does scholars no favours, especially since it tends to lump entertaining (fictional) representations together with factual ones (e.g. news representations). In doing so, the research on the accuracy of media representations, of which there is an enormous amount, evaluates entertaining representations by the same criterion as factual or scientific ones: that is, on the basis of empirical accuracy. Producers of entertaining representations do not seek accuracy, but rather verisimilitude (Frank 2003), and they are not without their own set of experts.

In creating verisimilar fiction, producers rely on technical consultants. Interestingly enough, the figure of the technical consultant entered into early discussions of popular legal studies, but has since never re-appeared despite the growing interest in such studies. In an early symposium on popular legal culture (Macaulay 1988–9), legal scholars' analyses of the popular American legal drama *LA Law* (Friedman 1988–9; Gillers 1988–9) elicited a response from the television show's legal technical consultant, Charles Rosenberg. Rosenberg (1989: 1625) begins by remarking that Gillers is a law professor writing for lawyers and assumes that *LA Law* is 'a show about law and lawyers, consciously written as a commentary on the legal system.' However, as an 'insider' of the show's production, Rosenberg asserts that the show is less a conscious attempt by writers to influence how ordinary Americans feel about the law or lawyers, than an effort to create compelling drama with law as its stage and interesting characters who happen to be lawyers. Thus, there is a discrepancy between the standards by which television writers and scholars judge the same representation: the writers do not judge the representation based on its adherence to referential or empirical reality, but rather on its dramatic potential.

The second way through which we can reset the research table is by reconsidering the cultural product itself – that is, by no longer seeing it as an already-manufactured product. There are two related theoretical consequences that occur from this re-conceptualization. One, this claim follows from Bruno Latour's (2007) rallying call to sociologists to stop considering 'society' as an already formed, homogeneous substance or domain of reality. Instead, sociologists should consider 'society' as a trail of associations between heterogeneous elements (Latour 2007: 5). Similarly, we need to give up the assumption that cultural products are homogeneous. Instead, we should consider cultural products – in this case, television shows – as trails of connections between heterogeneous elements. Specifically, we should consider a television drama as a hybrid made up of aesthetic and commercial elements. Because actor–network theory is interested in documenting the coming together of material–semiotic networks (Law 2007), we need to reject the binary distinction between art/culture and economics.

By no longer seeing the cultural product as an already-formed substance, which can then be correlated to the substance of other 'things,' such as society or culture, we can also avoid convenient symptomatic explanations that correlate the content of a television show with a particular vision of society. Because many of the criminological and sociolegal symptomatic readings treat the mass media as an ideological apparatus that maintains legal hegemony, it is problematic that their conclusions are based on content analyses, and for the very same reason that Hall et al.'s (1978) analysis of mugging was found problematic by Richard Ericson (1991: 221):

> For example, Hall and his associates based their entire analysis of coverage of a moral panic about mugging on their own reading of mass media content. In limiting themselves to content analysis these researchers failed to answer the central question they posed, namely, whether the mass media are saturated with official ideology and bourgeois sensibilities that are accepted by people and thereby effect hegemony. An adequate answer to this question requires demonstration, through the concrete activities of mass media operatives, their sources, and their readers, of how hegemony is actually accomplished. What is required is detailed analysis of the social contexts of mass media production and reception, and a view of dominant meanings as the outcome of strategies and struggles rather than as an *a priori* effect of pre-ordained privileged access to particular official sources.

Two, by no longer seeing the cultural product as an already-formed substance, we are able to shift from a product-centric perspective[12] to a *process*-centric one, which entails sniffing after the ingredients and assembling processes that allow something to be transformed into a product in the first place. Moreover, a process-centric focus involves conceptualizing the production process as an organic one rather than as rote mechanical reproduction. To that end, I propose that we conduct research on how television writers and producers 'grow a show' rather than 'set it in stone' (interview with head television writer DA 20 March 2009). Thus, television shows are not static, but growing and evolving entities. As such, this kind of analysis understands culture in its earliest use as a noun of process – specifically, the tending of natural growth (Williams 1976: 87) – rather than in its later nineteenth century usage as a product of an abstract process.

In taking a process-centric perspective, the role of the academic critic shifts from the one who debunks to the one who assembles (Latour 2004). Rather than lifting the rug to reveal the pile of dirt underneath it, the work of the academic entails examining the processes through which television shows are assembled or made up. A study of the making of television fictions then entails an appreciation of the dynamic and relatively spontaneous ways in which (television) producers and writers 'make it up as they go along' because, as one writer puts it:

> [t]hat's how we get paid. [. . .] So to make [the show] look internally coherent [as though it has meaning and import] is what makes the whole [production process] amazing. For many people, they have the idea that [the show] gets written and then made along the original plan. [But] TV is really about staying light on your feet.
>
> (Canadian television writer Adam Barken 17 August 2010)

Notes

1 This conceptualization can be traced back to Max Horkheimer and Theodor Adorno's (1972) use of 'the culture industry' as a metaphor in *Dialectic of Enlightenment*. In their formulation, 'the culture industry' can be differentiated from the term 'culture industry.' The former refers to a specific branch of cultural production, such as the Hollywood studio system. The latter refers more broadly to commodity production as the principle of a specific form of capitalist cultural production (Steinert 2003). 'Culture industry' is, in short, commodity-form culture, which stands in stark contrast to the bourgeois notion of art as intentionally devoid of all practical interest (i.e. art for art's sake). In this chapter, I will be primarily discussing 'the culture industry.'
2 For excellent and lengthier reviews of this literature, please see Reiner (2007), Carrabine (2008) and Jewkes (2009a, 2009b, 2009c).
3 It can be argued that the paradigmatic culture industry is Anglo-American, and originates in Hollywood. For example, Frankfurt School theorists Max Horkheimer and Theodor Adorno (1972) base their analysis of the culture industry on their observations of the Hollywood studio system (Muller-Doohm 2005). Similarly, Raymond Williams' thinking on television did not really occur until he also spent some time in California (O'Connor 1989).
4 All cited box office figures are from Box Office Mojo (www.boxofficemojo.com).
5 The film is remarkable because it is the first film produced by HBO to win the Palme d'Or at the Cannes Film Festival.
6 *The Wire* is now taught at some American universities, such as Harvard University and Duke University, as part of their undergraduate sociology curriculum (Bennett 24 March 2010). Harvard professor William Julius Wilson explains why he teaches the TV drama: 'Although *The Wire* is fiction, not a documentary, its depiction of [the] systemic urban inequality that constrains the lives of the urban poor is more poignant and compelling [than] that of any published [academic] study, including my own' (quoted in Bennett 24 March 2010).
7 Television studies scholars are currently re-thinking 'the masses' in order to understand mainstream media (e.g., the 2010 Flow conference). They are less concerned with understanding 'the masses' as 'cultural dupes.' Instead, some of these scholars are interested in why people come together in mass numbers to view something that speaks to them in a meaningful way. This current interest in the masses comes at a time when niche markets and new media have so transformed the television industry that the masses can be considered a surprising rather than a guaranteed phenomenon.
8 While film has been theorized as a medium that cultivates the viewer's gaze (Mulvey 1975), the medium of television has been said to work through the glance (Ellis 1982).
9 For example, Doyle's (2006) review article of 'how not to think about crime in the media' does make the argument that criminologists should start thinking about the media as diverse, while ironically using the shorthand description of 'crime in the media' and 'crime stories.'
10 This could be read as a reformulation of Emile Durkheim's (1965: 79) project of examining laws in society as a means to understand the formation of the *collective conscience* – that is, 'the totality of beliefs and sentiments common to average citizens of the same society.' While Durkheim assumed that the content and form of laws would reaffirm and *reflect* the collective (moral) consciousness of a society, more Marxist-inspired analyses would assume that the content is a misrepresentation of reality and used to *manipulate* the masses. For the scholarly work that best exemplifies the latter analysis, although it examines news media representations and not fictional ones, see Hall *et al.*'s (1978) *Policing the Crisis*.

11 In contrast, for example, 'law and literature' was founded on the study of law in 'great books' (i.e. literary classics), which was deemed a valuable exercise. Stemming from law and literature, the law and film movement also shares the assumption that film can have positive effects, and is worthy of study. Both literature and film can be conceived of as art. Because of its clearly commercial imperative, television has been a highly suspicious medium, often denied the status of art (Hartley 2008).

12 The product-centric perspective has also structured audience reception studies even in cultural studies. According to Hartley (2006), what audiences did when they read (i.e. the practice and process of reading) media texts was rarely investigated. Instead, empirical research has primarily focused on the audiences' produced texts (e.g. their responses as measured by questionnaires, diaries and focus groups). These audience responses are only made possible when members of the sample had sufficiently processed the cultural product to produce a textual account of their response.

Chapter 2

On method: trail-sniffing ants and breadcrumbs of reflexivity

SCENE: Our intrepid researcher journeys into uncharted research territory, and leaves behind a trail of breadcrumbs for other researchers to follow. The trail of breadcrumbs spells out how our researcher comes to know what she knows.

While criminological and sociolegal scholars have treated the study of texts as final products to be examined either as a matter of reception or formal analysis, they have less often studied texts as a matter of production and more importantly, of *site-specific, concrete, dynamic processes* of television production. I am particularly interested in capturing the latter in an analysis of how entertaining television representations of crime *come to be*, while also acknowledging the fast-moving, contingent nature of television production itself. To that end, this chapter outlines an actor–network theory-inspired method for studying representations made by the culture industry, here specifically understood as the television industry. In doing so, I outline a method for attending to *how* particular representations of crime are produced for television rather than to questions of *why* they were produced in the first place, or *who benefits* from their production.

Actor–network theory: on being a myopic, trail-sniffing ant

Actor–network theory (ANT) is a method that not only addresses the question of *how*, but also attends to processes of knowledge formation and representation. It stems from the growing field of Science and Technology Studies (STS), and is most commonly associated with the work of Bruno Latour, Michel Callon, and John Law. Those who use ANT do not consider science and technology as final products, but consider them *in the making* (Latour 1987: 4) or in the process of becoming. They do so by following scientists and engineers through society as they produce scientific facts or technological objects, attending in particular to the many diverse associations made between heterogeneous *actors* in *networks*. Here, network refers to a series of transformations and is 'a concept, not a thing out there' (Latour 2007: 131). It is a tool to describe a relay of actors as mediators (i.e. those who act on and transform the thing being made in contingent and unpredictable ways) and the relations between these actors.

In ANT, *actors* or *actants* are not simply people, but can also include a whole host of *things*, such as texts, ideas, objects, technological devices, information codes, etcetera. For example, Callon (1986) describes how an actor-network was deployed as a result of the scientific and economic controversy surrounding the causes of the decline in scallops at St. Brieuc Bay. He explains how a science of scallops was created only through an alliance of researchers, scientific colleagues, fishermen, and the scallops themselves. Here, it is important to note two remarkable moves made by Callon in this article. One, he analyzes people and scallops in the same terms. In doing so, he is following a methodological principle of generalized symmetry, which depends on rejecting an *a priori* separation between humans and non-humans. By using the same conceptual toolbox and vocabulary to document and analyze the relations between humans and non-humans, it allows for an inquiry into how humans and non-humans mutually constitute each other, rather than assume that they belong to different and irreconcilable material and social worlds.

Two, in Callon's description, scientific knowledge is simultaneously produced alongside the construction of a network of relationships, which makes and remakes each of the actors in the network. As part of the researchers' experimental rearing of young scallops, the fishermen change their fishing practices by not trawling near the larvae collectors. The scallops themselves are tamed when the young ones 'accept' a shelter that will enable them to proliferate and survive. As another example of the various actors that make up an actor-network, Latour (2010) examined the making of law at the Conseil d'Etat, an administrative court of the last resort in France. In doing so, he focused not only on the people who worked at the Conseil in various capacities, but on the material conditions that allowed law (here, conceptualized as legal text) to be assembled. Specifically, he focused on file folders and paper clips because he was interested in the physical organization of legal cases. Both these examples suggest that when we use ANT to describe an actor-network in television production, analyses of texts and technologies (e.g. computer software, whiteboards, folders, etc.) are just as important in the production of television representations as research on writers and producers.

In using ANT, I want to diverge from three methodological premises that underlie much of the criminological and sociolegal scholarship on representations of crime (see Chapter 1). First, because criminological and sociolegal analyses of film and television tend to centre only on content found in the final product, they tend to treat such content as not only inevitable but intentional (i.e. it was the original intention of the author), and ignore the evolution of both the product's form and content through production. In contrast, ANT acknowledges that the evolution of television texts (either taken as a whole series or individual episodes) can only be understood in retrospect or in progress because it would have been impossible to predict their final form and content from the outset.

Second, while criminological and sociolegal scholars are generally less aware of sociological production studies, they are quite cognizant of auteur theory (e.g. Greenfield *et al.* 2001; Strange 2011), which as a perspective tends to downplay the collaborative nature of film and television production by highlighting the genius of a single creator or partnership. The ANT focus on both people and things ensures that the ensuing analysis will also depart from some sociological analyses of television production. While sociological studies of production address how cultural producers frame their activities, understand the logic of production, and perceive resources and constraints (see Peterson and Anand 2004), some sociologists have narrowed these questions down to discovering who is most responsible for the final product (e.g. Thompson and Burns 1990). Whether the primary responsibility lies with the television producer (Cantor and Cantor 1992; Ravage 1978), the writer/showrunner (Mann 2009) or collaborative action between cast and crew (Sandeen and Compesi 1990), such an approach credits content only to human actors because the human actors were the only actors observed. I highlight this particular sociological perspective because it has parallels to auteur theory, whereby television shows and films are classified according to their human creators. As Latour (1988) used ANT to argue that Louis Pasteur was not a singular genius but enmeshed in an actor-network that allowed him to succeed,[1] I will similarly use ANT to acknowledge that human actors are capable of acting in the first place only because they find themselves in an actor-network of heterogeneous elements. In acknowledging that academics also work within actor-networks, Law (1992: 3) writes, 'If you took away my computer, my colleagues, my office, my books, my desk, my telephone, I wouldn't be a sociologist writing papers, delivering lectures and producing knowledge.' Similarly, for instance, if we took away a television writer's computer, her colleagues, her office, her books, and her desk, she wouldn't be capable of writing scripts, delivering pitches, and producing representations.

In addition to acknowledging the heterogeneity of actors in television production, an ANT perspective also recognizes television as a hybrid or 'contradictory' institution (Meehan 1992) because it is both a business concerned with the maximization of financial profit and a site of artistic and cultural expression. When criminological and sociolegal scholars have emphasized television as *either* a cultural art form *or* a commercial enterprise with negative consequences, they have reduced television to *either* the realm of art (the semiotic world) *or* the realm of commerce (the material world). In contrast, as a material-semiotic method of analysis, ANT operates on the principle of irreduction (Latour 2007), which holds that no object is reducible to another object or to some essential substance. Irreduction also amounts to a refusal to reduce all action to the manifestation of some agent's intentions or interests (e.g. an auteur's intent) or to some structural determinant.

Lastly, an ANT-inspired approach to the study of representations of crime will depart from the theoretical and methodological premises of some criminological and sociolegal analyses because of its emphasis on translation. Translation is a key concept in ANT, and the success of an idea, object or representation depends on its chains of translation. The concept of translation invokes both its original understanding as transportation and physical movement between places, and the notion of transposition into different languages, keys or codes. While ANT scholars refuse to reduce a thing to its core essence, they hold that something can be explained in terms of something else so long as they map the risky chain of equivalences and translations that are made by various actors.

In order to better understand the focus on translation, it might be useful to explain how the concept has been used by ANT scholars to describe the production and representation of knowledge. Because ANT was originally used to study the ways in which scientific facts come to be produced and disseminated (see Latour 1988), it has been implicated in the larger study of knowledge production and representation. For example, in describing and documenting how scientific facts are made and disseminated, Latour (1987) studies the textual work done at a scientific laboratory. In the laboratory, only the scientists can see the 'reality'[2] that they describe, a reality made possible by inscription devices, such as the microscope. The scientist then acts as the spokesperson or mouthpiece for what is inscribed on the window of the scientific instrument since bacteria, for instance, cannot speak for themselves. By being the bacteria's spokesperson, the scientist needs to translate what she has seen through her inscription devices into textual form (specifically, the scientific article) so that many other scientific readers can see her 'reality.' Thus, she might employ visual inscriptions (e.g. graphs, labels, tables and maps) and supporting texts (e.g. citations to other scientific articles in her literature review) as allies in her intellectual battle to persuade her scientific readers of this 'reality.' Hence, the production of a scientific fact or 'reality' relies on particular textual representations that are made possible by spokespeople and inscription devices. Analogously, we can consider how an entertainment television production constructs the 'reality' of crime as a particular kind of representation. Fictional characters and crimes, once conceived in the mind of a particular writer, cannot speak for themselves and need that writer to act as their mouthpiece. So an ANT-inspired approach will entail documenting how the television writer and producer *translate* these fictions into textual form and in what ways.

More importantly, ANT scholars understand that translations of representations between various spokespeople are never exact renderings, as the representations needs to be taken up by other actors in their actor–network-building activities in order to be successful. While ANT considers inexact renderings of information as translation, some Marxist-inspired criminological analyses as well as forms of corrective criticism consider them to be distortion. The notion of media distortion with all of its attendant negative connotations has been a ripe field of research inquiry (e.g. Dowler *et al.* 2006), where the key analytic moment of distortion happens at the point of reception and is understood as a media effect. Such a perspective assumes that information ought to be communicated without deformation by the media, and does not recognize, as ANT does,[3] that 'there is no in-formation, only trans-formation' (Latour 2007: 149). In undertaking an ANT approach, I am acknowledging that translations are part and parcel of the process of production, and will thereby refrain from pre-judging the quality of translations made by any actor (e.g. as good or bad, accurate or not).

The use of an ANT approach also ensures scholarly attention to particularities – specifically, attention to particular translations made at specific sites of production. In a manner of speaking, the ANT-inspired researcher is very much like an ant, 'a blind, myopic, workaholic, trail-sniffing, and collective traveler' (Latour 2007: 9). The researcher is 'myopic': she does not use ANT to create a 'big picture' of the culture industry through the provision of grand, general theoretical models about how the television industry operates, but instead empirically traces, documents and analyzes actor-networks at local sites. Like the ant, that most industrious of creatures, the researcher needs to work hard to trace translations through which television production is achieved. In the next section, I will explain how using an ANT-inspired approach might converge and diverge from previous empirical studies done under the general rubric of the 'production of culture' perspective.

Convergences and divergences: how ANT fits together with the 'production of culture' perspective

Studies about the production of television are rare in both sociology and cultural studies. When empirical work is done, it tends to be done under the general banner of the 'production of culture' perspective; I will refer to such work in shorthand as 'production studies' throughout the rest of this chapter. This is not to say that ANT has had no impact on the study of media. Some production scholars have pointed to the potential utility of ANT as part of their film and television research (Havens *et al.* 2009), although few have actually used it (for examples of ANT analyses in media/film studies, see Caldwell 2008; Couldry 2004; Mould 2009). In the few cases wherein ANT has been used, research has tended to focus on human–technology hybrids: for example, Caldwell (2008) describes the Steadicam operator as a human–technological hybrid. Hemmingway (2008) describes how the BBC news reporter uses the newsroom's various technologies to make news. These uses of ANT highlight its STS roots rather than adapting the theory to suit media research specifically (see Couldry 2004 for exception).

Because it is my intent in this chapter neither to outline a general ANT approach to doing production studies nor to advocate that its inclusion is necessary for doing such research, I will discuss how ANT has informed my own research into the television production process. In doing so, I will highlight how using an ANT approach converges and diverges with the 'production of culture' perspective's theoretical assumptions and empirical insights. In outlining these convergences and divergences, I want to clarify the ways in which ANT can be used as a complementary tool to examine television production – specifically, as a tool that embodies a methodological sensibility that is sensitive to emphasizing the complexities of actual practices and associations.

Because many studies fall into this 'production of culture' perspective, I will begin by explaining the divergences, in order to make clear what an ANT approach *cannot* do as a result of the scope of the researcher's unit of analysis. In general, the 'production of culture' perspective focuses on explaining trends in production and as such necessarily examines many cases. In contrast, ANT's use of interview and ethnographic data can provide rich description and analysis of particular case studies, and is especially well-suited to examining temporary projects, such as the making of a particular episode of a television series.

Divergences: studying 'the culture industry'

The academic origin of the term 'the culture industry' stems back to Horkheimer and Adorno's (1972) Marxist-inspired metaphor. As such, the term implicitly invokes Marx's observation that culture is rooted in the mode of production, which is arguably a general observation that grounds and underlies all production studies. However, it is in the operationalization of the 'mode of production' that production studies diverge from each other, which consequently impacts the kind of academic analysis produced. We can differentiate between three distinct operationalizations: 1) the *capitalistic* mode of production, 2) the mode of *industrial* production, and 3) *actor-networks* of production.

Capitalistic mode of production

The study of the capitalistic mode of cultural production is favoured by political economy scholars. Political economy approaches (e.g. Murdock and Golding 1973, 2005) emphasize macro-structural issues that organize the culture industry, such as the concentration of corporate media ownership and regulatory regimes. As a relatively typical example of the macro-level political economy approach, Djankov *et al.* (2001) examine patterns of media ownership in 97 countries around the world. They discover that almost all of the largest media firms are owned by government or by private families. Moreover, government ownership of the media is associated with less freedom of the press, and fewer political and economic rights. This research is representative of the political economy approach because it attempts to address the questions of 'who owns the media?' and 'who benefits from such ownership?' Often, as in this case, the research focus is on state ownership of the media and the political and economic implications of this ownership. These implications are drawn from analyses that are overwhelmingly based on ownership of the *news* media rather than entertainment media. Like other researchers working within this paradigm, Djankov *et al.* are interested in the extent to which state-owned media control the flow of information, and how this has impacted the freedom of the press to provide unbiased, objective reporting of events.

In North America, political economy scholars have traditionally dominated academic studies of the media industries, following in the footsteps of Dallas Smythe (1981) and Herbert Schiller (1989). Written within the Marxist theoretical framework, their analyses tend to tell a story in which media culture is assumed to be the ideological extension of powerful capitalist forces, serving to socialize audiences into broader economic interests (Hesmondhalgh 2006). Cast as the (underdog) protagonist, the researcher combats these capitalistic agents of false consciousness (here conceptualized as corporations), while implicitly invoking traces of Adorno and Horkheimer's conceptualization of the culture industry as inherently deceptive. As a result of this orientation, the political economy perspective has often been caricatured as 'conspiracy theory' (Schudson 1989).

Overall, political economy studies of production have something to say about the concentration and circulation of capital, particularly at the state or global level, but very little to say about the circulation of representations and meaning. Because I am particularly interested in the latter, political economy approaches are not useful for my research, especially when they tend to assume that *meaning* and textual production are predictable because they reflect only the interests of those who control the means of production. By 'meaning,' I refer to both the meaning of representations, and the meaning of processes that lead to particular representations.

In contrast to cultural studies or humanities scholars, the political economy approach does not attend to the richness of meaning(s) embedded in representations. Instead, it tends to reduce the meaning of a representation to an ideological stance that either supports a specific political position (e.g. as a conservative representation that maintains the status quo) or resists it (e.g. as an adversarial, critical representation). For example, Edward S. Herman and Noam Chomsky's (1988) 'propaganda model' of mass media reduces the meaning of news representations to how they serve the special interests of state and private activity. Because the news industry is oriented towards profit-making and depends on government officials as sources of information, they argue that the industry imbues its representations with anti-communist ideology. As Schudson (1989) notes, the 'propaganda model' is a rather blunt instrument for examining a subtle system that includes more heterogeneity and capacity for change than Herman and Chomsky give it credit for. We can understand Herman and Chomsky's neglect of heterogeneity and change within the system as part and parcel of political economy's emphasis on the 'big picture.'

By focusing on the 'big picture' (i.e. the larger political economy of society), the approach tends to miss examinations of the day-to-day practices in journalism (Schudson 1989) or television drama production. As such, a political economy approach does not attend to the everyday practices of media production, and what those processes mean to the media producers themselves. In contrast, sociological studies on the production of culture take up this perspective, by situating the making of a media product in the daily practices, local interactions, and actions of media producers. We will now turn to analyses of the modes of industrial production.

Mode(s) of industrial production

In contrast to political economy scholars who focus on the corporations that control media production, scholars who study the mode(s) of industrial production are interested in the actual work done in the culture industry. If the political economy approach often takes a macro view of the culture industry, where contradictory details are obscured by the wide focus, then those who study the mode of industrial perspective often take a 'midlevel' approach (Havens *et al.* 2009). The 'midlevel' perspective focuses on the practices of a particular culture industry. Thus, while political economy scholars would study which television channels are owned by which parent companies and how they serve the parent company's economic interests (e.g. Herman and McChesney 1997), 'midlevel' scholars would study how television networks structure their own programming content and under what logic (e.g. Gitlin 1983; Havens 2006). However, 'midlevel' scholars can themselves be differentiated[4] by the extent to which they concentrate on describing the *structure* of the culture industry under study (a predominantly sociological perspective), or on describing the *experiences* of those working within it (a recent cultural studies perspective on the media industries).

The sociological perspective on the production of culture focuses 'on how symbolic elements of culture are shaped by the systems within which they are created, distributed, evaluated, taught and preserved' (Peterson and Anand 2004: 311). In doing so, the sociological perspective tends to treat the culture industry like any other industry, and does not distinguish the making of culture from the making of factory goods. Research into the industry's structuring systems, often understood as organizational constraints, can be summarized by Peterson and Anand's (2004) six-facet model. The six facets of production are technology, law and regulation, industry structure, organization structure, occupational careers, and market. These facets are used to explain how they either facilitate major change in an industry, or constrain such change. As an example of the latter, Bielby and Bielby (2002) explain how the organizational and occupational structures of the Hollywood film and television industry sustain a systemic workplace discrimination that ensures young, white men are the most likely to be hired as screenwriters. While this sociological perspective is useful for pointing out how different symbols are made under differing production conditions, it does not examine the meaning of cultural productions (Eyerman and Ring 1998; Gottdiener 1985) since deducing meaning from reading texts is not the goal of the perspective (Peterson and Anand 2004: 327). As a result, these researchers tend to produce static snapshots of an industry's structure without necessarily attending to the representations produced by it.

In contrast, a recent cultural studies perspective on the media industries (see Caldwell 2006; Havens *et al.* 2009; Mayer *et al.* 2009) highlights the need for researchers to consider quotidian texts produced by the film and television industry as a means of sustaining its current working practices. Researchers are urged to examine how industrial texts and practices define workers' experiences. Here, meaning only figures into a researcher's analysis of industrial texts, as opposed to pop cultural texts. For example, John Caldwell (2008) examines the representational, material and symbolic practices of film and video production workers in Los Angeles because understanding their *culture of production* helps scholars understand the *production of culture*. Thus, he is interested in studying the industry's own self-representation, self-critique and self-reflection through textual analyses of trade and worker artifacts (e.g. demo tapes), interviews with film and television workers, and ethnographic field observation of production spaces and professional gatherings. Caldwell discovers that different work sectors in the industry have different kinds of self-theorizing and sense-making practice. For example, when speaking about their work, technical craftspeople (e.g. camera operators, editors, grips, etc.) traffic in war stories where they overcome overwhelming odds to succeed. This genre of self-theorizing establishes craft mastery as the result of an individual's moral character and triumph of will. In contrast, non-unionized or unregulated work sectors (e.g. assistants, agents, and clerical staff) tend to tell cautionary tales about 'making it' in the industry, which is related to their efforts to salvage careers and network in the industry. In short, Caldwell is interested in analyzing (biographically oriented) trade storytelling for what it can tell him about particular work sectors rather than on analyzing fictional storytelling.

Actor-networks of production

In taking an ANT approach to the production of television representations, the starting unit of analysis is the actor-network rather than systems or industries. In contrast to any of the previous approaches, the study of actor-networks eschews analytically bracketing different scales of analysis as a matter of course. Rather than assume that they entail fundamentally different perspectives, the micro and the macro are approached from the same analytic perspective. In contrast to vertically oriented approaches that set the level or scope of analysis from the outset, ANT advocates a horizontal or flat approach to studying things in the world. Consequently, ANT diverges from top-down approaches, such as the political economy approach, by refusing to articulate the macro as either 'above' or 'below' the interactions being observed. Instead, the macro is operationalized through the addition of more connections in the actor-network's chain of associations and interactions (Latour 2007: 177). In eliminating the division of the world between 'small' and 'big pictures,' ANT attempts to present a world where 'the micro reveals itself in and of itself the macro' (Hemmingway 2008: 15).

While systems or industries are thought to generate an entire category of text or an array of genres (e.g. the film industry produces filmic texts, which can then be subdivided by genre), a focus on the actor-network emphasizes the processes of assembling an individual work (e.g. a specific episode of a particular television drama). While ANT is not necessarily useful as a method for studying all kinds of topic, it is particularly valuable for examining new topics where things are changing quickly (Latour 2007: 142), such as the fast-paced nature of television production. In contrast to the more permanent entities of systems and industries, the actor-network is a relatively temporary entity, at least in television production. For example, the actor-network is assembled to produce a television drama series at one moment in time, and immediately disassembled once production ends.

Moreover, the unique identity of each actor in the actor-network matters, because the making of a specific television text is entangled in the making of the actor-network itself. For example, in an actor-network centred on casting screen performers for the Canadian television drama series *Cra$h & Burn*, it matters that the production company's in-house lawyer is married to the agent who represents the screen performer who will eventually play the lead protagonist in the series. Furthermore, it matters that this lead screen performer has dual citizenship – i.e. he is simultaneously both a Canadian and an American citizen – because it allows the production company to capitalize on 1) Canadian government funding for the production because funding is contingent on casting Canadian citizens in lead roles, and 2) on a potential American co-producer for the series because American producers tend to prefer American screen performers in lead roles.[5] Thus, the passport can be considered an actor in this actor-network because it not only allows its 'owner' to move between nations and different television production spaces, but translates its 'owner' in terms that are appealing to television producers. As a sign of citizenship, the Canadian passport is translated into Canadian government funding, and the American passport is translated into commercial appeal for American television producers.

Because it includes the actions of non-human actors (e.g. the passport), the actor-network is not synonymous with the social network of working relationships described as the 'culture of production' (e.g. as screenwriting groups in Macdonald 2010) by sociologists or cultural studies scholars. It also does not refer to the market network (Podolny 2001) that refracts the prestige and reputation of cast and crew onto the cultural products they produce (for Hollywood blockbusters, see Baker and Faulkner 1991; for prime-time network television series, see Bielby and Bielby 1994). These described social and market networks are stabilized entities. Their stability is what allows industry professionals to use them in fairly predictable ways and for researchers to feel comfortable in making generalizations about them. In short, they are 'black boxed.'

In ANT terminology, 'black boxing' (Latour 1987) suggests that the success of these social or market networks has had the effect of erasing the processes and circumstances under which they were produced in the first place. Thus, ANT scholars are interested in studying the formation and trans-formations of unstable things and texts, where these things and texts are understood to be formed by an actor-network. By contrast, sociologists and cultural studies scholars in the above perspective are more interested in studying the maintenance of stability of already formed industries, organizational networks and systems. Within this framework, any change or instability needs to be explained, and is often attributed to changing laws, markets or technologies. In other words, sociologists and cultural studies scholars tend to study what ANT scholars consider to be the end point of a successful actor-network, when the various heterogeneous elements making up the actor-network work together as a unified, stabilized entity. ANT scholars, on the other hand, open up the 'black box' of television production. They examine not only the starting point of the actor-network and the ways it gets assembled but also failed actor-networks.

While scholars studying television have by and large chosen successful programs[6] as the objects of their inquiry, ANT scholars do not privilege the study of successes. Successful outcomes are considered contingent upon successful translations. As such, ANT researchers also examine actor-networks that failed for lack of translation. Failed actor-networks are equally revealing in what they indicate about the processes of an actor-network's formation. For example, Latour (1996) follows scientists and engineers who worked on a French automated subway system to discover, not why it succeeded, but how it failed despite the fact that the technological innovation was commonly held to be a good idea and a symbol for the future of French transportation at its inception. He documents the time and energy spent on developing the science and technology behind this transport system, even though it never comes to fruition. Analogously, all television writers and producers believe that the show that they make is based on a good idea. However, it is never clear, even to them, whether the show will succeed. Success is an outcome that can only be understood in retrospect, and cannot be determined by observing a program's production. Whether a show is 'bad' and unsuccessful or 'good' and successful cannot be determined in advance often because such normative evaluation only occurs once television critics and audiences review the show. Thus, ANT acknowledges the uncertainty of success that characterizes the process of producing any kind of representation, be they in scientific journals or on television.

Therefore, the point of studying actor-networks, as opposed to larger units of analysis such as 'organizations,' 'systems,' or 'industries,' is to empirically examine the site-specific configurations and flows of representations, actors, translations and dynamic processes. Consequently, ANT research does not lend itself towards creating *outcome-based* general typologies or explanations of abstract (industrial) structures. In the case of studying the production of television representations, this aspect of ANT methodology is particularly desirable, because it functions as recognition that the processes of production cannot be re-constructed or inferred from scrutinizing the resulting texts.

Convergences: themes, theories and findings

Nevertheless, ANT scholars highlight three methodological themes that characterize the research on and writing about the actor-network: uncertainty, collaborative action and dynamic movement. Each of these three ANT themes can find support in previous theories and empirical findings from the sociological literature on the production of culture.

Uncertainty

Taken seriously as a starting point by ANT scholars, the theme of uncertainty converges with sociologists' empirical findings about the environment in which television network executives make their programming decisions. For example,

Gitlin (1983) studied how American broadcasting television network executives deal with uncertainty, which is considered a permanent condition of the show business industry. In the face of uncertainty, network executives make their decisions based on intuition. Their intuitive decisions are then supported by *ad hoc* rational calculations stemming from program testing focus groups, audience ratings and schedule calculations. Similarly, Bielby and Bielby (1994) suggest that for American broadcasting television network executives, 'all [prime-time] hits are flukes,' and these 'flukes' need to be rationalized and legitimated through the executives' use of rhetorical strategies. These are strategies that emphasize 1) the producers' reputations, 2) the television show's creative imitation of previously successful television programs, and 3) the show or program's genre.

In light of their research findings, sociologists have explained how network executives employ predictable organizational discourses to justify their decision-making in an uncertain, unpredictable environment. For ANT scholars, however, uncertainty is more than just a characteristic of the environmental context, but also what characterizes the formations and translations of actor-networks themselves. Contingency is always assumed and studied, even in cases of successful actor-networks. It is never certain how the actors – those various human, physical, technological, representational and discursive elements – that make up an actor-network will connect to each other and in what configuration.

Collaborative action

The study of actor-networks is always the study of collaborative action. Similarly, Becker (1982) stresses that culture is produced through sustained collective and collaborative activity (for television production, see also Gripsrud 2005; Sandeen and Compesi 1990). As I have already established that ANT is interested in studying the way things are collectively assembled by various and diverse kinds of actor, I will now discuss how collaborative *action* might be studied using ANT.

First, in order to qualify as an actor, the entity needs to *do* something, or make other entities *do* something (Latour 2007: 107). With this focus on action, ANT is premised on the study of *processes* and *practice* (the *doing* of something). With their own vocabulary, actors define for themselves and for the researcher what they do and what makes up their world (Latour 2007: 36). ANT researchers take the actors' own theories of action (e.g. why and how things happen) into serious consideration without dismissing any of their rationales and use of language, no matter how quirky and irrational they might sound. For example, during the making of the television pilot for the Canadian–American co-produced *Due South*, the cast and crew believed that a taxidermied caribou was the culprit behind the many mishaps that occurred during shooting (BO interview with author). Shot in Canada, *Due South* was a buddy cop show, in which a street smart, cynical Chicago police officer was teamed with a polite, sensitive Canadian Mountie (RCMP officer). As a recognizable symbol of Canadiana, the taxidermied caribou was used not only as part of the pilot's plot, but also as a prop metonym for the Mountie. As such, the stuffed caribou was carried to each of the shooting locations in the event that it needed to be represented on screen. However, because of the many accidents on set, including a plane accident and a special effects explosion, the cast and crew began to believe that they were cursed by the taxidermied caribou, which led to a collective desire to 'bury the 'bou.' Hearing this story, an ANT researcher does not immediately jump to the conclusion that the cast and crew of *Due South* are superstitious and delusional. Instead, she considers the taxidermied caribou an actor (after all, it moves the cast and crew to *do* certain things, such as become more cautious) in the making of the *Due South* pilot.

In taking into account actors' own theories of action, ANT-inspired research follows the current impulse of film and television production studies to provide a space for producers to 'speak for themselves' (Caldwell 2006: 118). Thus, television production studies tend to make use of data from interviews (e.g. Cantor 1971; Newcomb and Alley 1983) and participant observation. For ANT researchers, the use of ethnographic methods is centred on 'following the actors' (Latour 1987; 2007: 61), particularly on actors' translations and transformations. ANT researchers acknowledge that actors are capable of framing and contextualizing their own activity. Moreover, actors do not necessarily stick to an absolute or single frame of reference because they tend to work within multiple frames. Through their translations, actors travel from one frame of reference to another (Latour 2007: 186), and it is the movement between shifting and unstable frames that an ANT researcher wants to capture.

By capturing this movement between frames of reference, the researcher destabilizes any notion of 'the big picture' (Latour 2007: 187) as a singular and definitive frame of reference. Symptomatic textual readings of the final product implicitly operate under the notion of 'the big picture' because scholars tend to assume that the world is encapsulated in 'the picture,' and as such is wholly represented in the final text. Their analyses then compare the world in the text to the world outside the text. In doing so, these scholars assume that they can know about the text's production processes or its effects (the world outside the text) by only reading the final text. Because these researchers are not privy to all the stammering, hemming and hawing involved in the process of textual production, they also assume that representations in the final text emerged in a fully coherent form. This assumption is only possible because these researchers have never observed the incoherent, fragmentary rambling that occurs in the television writers' room when episodic stories are conceived through the collaborative action of a writing team. In this case, the shifting, multiple, unstable frames of reference are a consequence of the collaborative nature of assembling a television story.

For example, in the writers' room of the Canadian–American co-produced police drama *The Bridge*, the staff writers shift between different frames of reference in their discussion of a pivotal scene. In this scene, the main protagonist Frank,

48   Making Crime Television

President of the Police Union, discovers that someone has broken into his locked office. In the following excerpt, the writers try to determine how Frank knows that someone has been in his office:

> Writer 1: Maybe they put things back much the same way that they found them. And then later in [act] 2, Frank can realize that there's one small thing missing . . .
>
> Writer 2: And remember, he has no computer on his desk. He's completely cleaned of any trails and stuff. He doesn't leave a trail. That's what's interesting. Frank wouldn't – they could go into the room, but the real story is that [the show's technical consultant] never had a computer in his office. All the files and all the information that he needed was dispersed among three or four different terminals on the floor in other offices. So Frank comes in, he's probably going to check if other people's desks are in disarray.
>
> Writer 3: Now who exactly was [the technical consultant] worried about, anyway? I'm not really sure I understood that.
>
> Writer 2: Back then?
>
> Writer 3: Yeah, who exactly were the bad guys?
>
> Writer 2: There was that one time with the judges.
>
> Writer 4: [. . .] I think he felt that it was a non-localized thing, didn't he? He felt that there were brass who were against him, basically everyone [. . .] was against him. I don't think it was an organized cabal that he fought.
>
> Writer 2: Then the whole media had it out [coughing sound]. Definitely [any] left-wing, political entity, media [. . .] was definitely conspiring against him. I think there was also probably a faction of police that didn't agree with what was going on, that was also maybe intimidated in going against the – remember, it was a mob mentality, right?

In the above excerpt, the ANT researcher would follow the movement between the unstable frames of reference, such as a writer's incomplete thoughts. The movement between different frames is characterized by the shifting train of thought that sweeps across the writers as they discuss their dramatic problem (e.g. how does Frank know someone has been in his office?). The writers begin by noting that perhaps the culprit took something from Frank's office. Using Frank's fictional office as a frame of reference, Writer 2 notes that there is nothing of note (here defined as sensitive information) that the culprit can take, since Frank does not have file folders or a computer in his office. Moving from the material conditions that make possible information-keeping at the fictional police union, Writer 2 then jumps to a different frame of reference: what did the show's technical consultant do during his real-life tenure as President of the Police Union? It seemed clear to him that Frank would do as his real-life counterpart did: information would be dispersed among several computers in different offices on the same floor. Thus, it is not important for Frank to focus on the appearance of his own office, but on whether or not *other* offices appear in disarray. While continuing to use the technical consultant as a frame of reference, Writer 3 shifts the dramatic problem: who were the culprits that came after the technical consultant and by implication, would come after the fictional protagonist Frank? As 'bad guys' become the new frame of reference in the discussion, the writers rattle off the following: judges, police bureaucrats (the brass), media, and a faction of the police rank-and-file.

From following the movement between different frames of reference, we can note how the actors – in this case, the writers – change scale as they adopt new frames. The short discussion begins with Frank's office, grows to a floor of offices at the Police Union Headquarters, and then reaches outside Union Headquarters to include other institutions within the fictional world, such as the police, the media, and the courts. Simply by following the actors' own framing and contextualizing activities, a whole (fictional) world appears through the actors' use of different scales of reference. Because ANT highlights the scale-making activities of actors, it is different from methods that settle on the question of scale before undertaking research (e.g. midlevel research on the modes of industrial practices, or the macrolevel political economy approach), whereby the parameters of the research site are decided upon by the researcher rather than the actors themselves. Size, scale and scope, according to ANT, are not understood as given in the nature of things, but instead are treated as products and effects of actors' own activities. Since the scope or parameters of a research site are not fixed, an ANT researcher can follow actors in and out of different research sites in order to capture the dynamic movement that makes production possible.

Dynamic movement

As ANT aims to study dynamic processes, circulation, transformation and movement in general, it is similar in aim to theories about the circuit of culture. Originally conceptualized by Richard Johnson (1986/1987) and inspired by Marx's account of the circuit of capital, the circuit of culture is a theoretical model that highlights the metamorphoses (i.e. transformations or changes in form) that cultural products undergo as they pass through a cycle of four distinctive moments: production, (formal analysis of) texts, readings (i.e. reception analysis), and lived cultures. Using the case study of the Sony Walkman, Paul du Gay (1997) has also articulated a circuit model of culture. His biographical analysis of a cultural artefact focuses on five distinct processes that every such artefact must pass through. These five processes include representation, identity (constructed by representations), production, consumption and regulation. When taken together, the five processes form the complete circuit of culture. Similar to ANT, du Gay highlights the variable and contingent outcomes that result from the interactions between processes.

Moreover, he is interested in studying what he calls 'articulation' (1997: 3) – i.e. a form of connection that temporarily unifies two or more disparate elements under certain contingent conditions. Certainly, the focus on 'articulation' is quite similar to Latour's focus on examining the contingent connections that make up the actor-network. However, for du Gay, the meaning of a cultural artefact cannot be found in a single process, but in the combination of processes and their articulation. Hence, researchers need to study the entire circuit in order to understand the meaning of a cultural artefact.

Because I am interested in using ANT to study the circulation of evolving representations within a text during the moment of production, I am not attempting to examine what those representations mean in a comprehensive manner, which would also extend to moments of public and private reception (e.g. television critics and ordinary television viewers, respectively). As a result, I will not be examining the entire circuit of culture. Instead, I will be analyzing the various practices and processes that make up the moment of textual production, by following particular representations of crime as actors. In following these particular actors through their many transformations, the researcher realizes that their mouthpieces (e.g. television producers and writers) are both producers and consumers of other television texts (Caldwell 2006), and regulated by various quasi-legal entities throughout the process of creation and revision. For researchers interested in using ANT to study the entire circuit of culture, however, their research would extend from documenting the actor-networks of production to those of reception, by adding actors and actor-networks for examination just as one would add links to elongate a chain of associations.

Doing television production studies in Canada

Production studies scholars have primarily examined the creation and development of American television shows. Often cited as an exemplar of scholarship on the production of television representations, Julie D'Acci's *Defining Women* (1994) examines representations of feminism and femininity found within the police procedural *Cagney and Lacey* (1981–1988) against the backdrop of wider discussions of gender politics in US culture during the 1980s. D'Acci mixes textual analyses of the show with information gained through her access to both the show's development process and producers' meetings. As the premise for this prime-time television series, *Cagney and Lacey* followed the lives of two female New York police detectives. Interestingly enough, over the course of the series, the show transitioned from being a 'cop show' to a 'woman's program' (D'Acci 1994: 121). This transition involved 'feminizing' the female protagonists through the introduction of a new upscale wardrobe. The series' plot lines were increasingly modelled on television forms that were more closely associated with women, such as those of melodrama and soap operas. While D'Acci's research focus was on how producers (re)defined women within the context of a police procedural, Lyons (2010) examined the ways in which another 1980s cop show, *Miami Vice*, represented masculinity. Airing between 1984 and 1990, *Miami Vice* was premised on the adventures of vice squad detectives from the Miami Police Department. Unlike D'Acci, Lyons speaks of the show's production in more general terms, concentrating on describing the range of commercial and creative influences, as well as the popular trends of the 1980s, that shaped the show's identity as a premium television commodity.

From the study of American talk shows (Grindstaff 2002; Shattuc 1997) to prime-time television shows, production scholars have privileged the analysis of representations of gender, race (Gray 1995), class, and sexual orientation (Gamson 1998). However, when scholars examine the production of *Canadian* English-language[7] television shows, which happens rarely (to date, there are very few production studies on the making of Canadian television shows: e.g. Levine 2009; Tinic 2005), they tend to concentrate on how the shows facilitate or hinder Canada's nation-building project. Historically, Canadian television scholarship has been influenced by a strong communications perspective that has favoured analyses of state regulation and international (predominantly American) dependency (Druick and Kotsopoulos 2008). Consequently, the small field of Canadian television studies has tended to focus less on the meaning of cultural productions, and more on telecommunications and broadcasting policy (Beaty and Sullivan 2006: 4). This has likely been the case because of the distinct Canadian film and television production context. In the US, with the exception of public television which receives federal funding,[8] television programs are financed through partnerships between studios and privately-owned, commercial broadcasting networks, which are sometimes both owned by the same conglomerate company.[9] However, all Canadian television programs are largely financed through government initiatives, such as through the legislated tax credit system, Telefilm Canada and the Canadian Television Fund. In order to qualify for government funding, a Canadian television program needs to prove that it contains 'Canadian elements.'[10] In light of these public policy initiatives, Canadian[11] television scholars (e.g. Beaty and Sullivan 2006) have followed policymakers in attempting to answer the research question: to what extent do Canadian television programs preserve national identity and cultural sovereignty? Or alternatively, what makes a television show truly, authentically or distinctly Canadian (see Attalah 2009)?

By contrast with both American and Canadian television production studies, my research examines first and foremost representations of crime. This is not to deny the fact that representations of crime intersect with representations of identity, be they of gender, class, race, sexual orientation or of the nation state; rather, it is simply a matter of privileging a different analytic focus. That is, I am primarily interested in how crime shows get made in Canada and what they say about crime. While much has been written about Canada's national and public television broadcaster, the Canadian Broadcasting Corporation (CBC), and its explicit mandate to 'Canadianize' programming (e.g. Miller 1987), my research focuses on entertainment programs produced by and for Canadian private, commercial broadcasting networks. This came about because of research access to certain Canadian television productions.

Accessing television productions

Increasingly, the DVD releases of recent American crime television dramas have included additional 'behind-the-scenes' footage and 'making-of' documentaries, both of which provide viewers with previously unavailable access to the production process. As a result, the average layperson may already have some of the information necessary to infer the production history of a particular program's representations of crime. When discussing Canadian television shows, however, a researcher runs into two difficulties. First, unlike their American counterparts, Canadian television productions tend to operate on smaller and tighter budgets, making it unlikely that they have the additional funds required to create DVD 'extras' in the first place. As such, if Canadian television shows are even released onto DVD, they rarely provide additional content pertaining to the production of the show.

Second, when researchers rely solely on these DVD 'extras' as accurate indicators of production history, they run into the difficulty of separating the apparent industrial reflexivity (i.e. producers, writers, directors and screen performers reflect on the why and how of what they did to create the film or TV show) of such bonus material from current Hollywood marketing strategies (Caldwell 2008). It is not clear to what extent a participant's reflexivity is manufactured expressly for the purpose of the show's DVD marketing. As a form of *ad hoc* rationalization, industrial reflexivity glosses over the actual experience and 'battle' of making a television show.

> Battles do have causes and consequences, and lead to subtle reflections when they are considered years later. But none of that is available to those who take part in them. They and their comrades – and their enemies – are sealed into an experience which has no context and no comparison, a present consisting of jokes, terror, trained reactions, insane orders from above, utter exhaustion, the taste of stewed tea, the sound of incoming mortars.
>
> (Ascherson 28 November 2002: 15)

Similarly, the bonus material on DVD releases of television programs includes the reflections of cast and crew members after they have 'returned from battle' and contemplated their work over a period of time. However, these reflections do not capture the in-the-moment spontaneity and exhaustive activities of the actual production process. In the moment of production with its fragmentary and distinct stages of writing, filming and editing, cast and crew members may not be able to clearly articulate how the program comes together as a coherent whole.

In order to document those moments where knowledge about the crime-related television program is still being formed and established among its producers, ethnographic field observation is a useful method for bypassing instances of manufactured industrial reflexivity. Because ethnographic research entails doing fieldwork, the researcher needs to gain access to new or on-going entertainment television series that are in production. Researcher access then depends on 'being in the right place at the right time' in order to capitalize on as many productions (i.e. research opportunities) as possible.

'The right place and the right time': Toronto in 2008

Labeled as 'Hollywood North,' Toronto is a major Canadian production centre for film and television. As a result, the city plays host to the making of a variety of television productions. Following my ANT-inspired interest in studying the formation of crime-related television series, I began my search for original[12] Canadian television shows that were in production. In line with ANT's starting assumption that success is highly contingent, I focused on 'untried' television productions rather than successful, on-going ones. By 'untried,' I mean the first season of a television show that has not been 'tried' by any audience because it has yet to air as part of any broadcasting network's programming.

The focus on untried shows is associated with two theoretical and methodological implications. One, the study of an untried show is fundamentally tied to an exploration of the process of social construction, whereby objects are understood as not having any fixed or stable identities because they are only gradually coming into being. Documenting the first season of a television series is akin to detailing its 'unstable childhood' when the program's identity tends to be 'highly contested, volatile and open to transformation' (Mol 2002: 42), precisely because it has to fully 'grow up' to become a stabilized object. Two, as an untried series, the program's significance cannot be contextualized by a measure of its success. Having never aired, the program cannot be 'successful' since a program's 'success' tends to be measured through audience reception (e.g. ratings, television reviews and fan attachment). In practice, I also found it much easier to gain access to 'untried' shows than to 'successful' ones. With 'success,' on-going television productions gain publicists who act as gatekeepers to the production, tend to enforce confidentiality agreements and typically hold a certain amount of paranoia that one's research might tarnish the production's positive image.

In my search for 'untried' crime dramas in 2008, it so happened that Toronto was poised to become a production centre for Canadian–American co-produced police dramas, all of which would be aired in 2010. Consequently, the summer of 2010 has been hailed as the summer during which Canadian co-produced, Toronto-shot, one-hour police television dramas (e.g. *Flashpoint, The Bridge*, and *Rookie Blue*) hit television screens during prime-time in North America. In both Canada and the US, television critics marvelled at the increased amount of television programming that Canada was supplying to the North American entertainment television market (e.g. Beam 20 July 2010; Oswald 22 July 2010; Stelter 19 July 2010). Given the recent economic downturn in North America, the major American broadcasting networks needed a reduction in prime-time programming costs, due to an increasingly fragmented audience and softening advertising market (Fixmer 9 March 2009). As a result, they were particularly open to developing entertainment content in partnership with private Canadian commercial broadcasters.[13] If shot in Canada using Canadian personnel, the resulting Canadian–American co-production could benefit from funding initiatives from the Canadian government. As a result, the co-producing American broadcasting network could provide prime-time television to their audiences for a fraction of the cost it would otherwise take for a similar program to be made and shot in the US. For example, a typical episode of an American-produced police drama might cost around $1–1.5 million to make. In contrast, the American ABC network pays only a license fee of $350,000 in order to broadcast the co-produced police drama *Rookie Blue* (Adalian 12 July 2010). By the spring of 2008, the underlying economics of the North American television market were in place, but were rarely explicitly dissected by mainstream news media sources. At that time, no television critic had any clue that Toronto would become the 'mean streets' on which fictional police officers would soon patrol.

Gaining access by mobilizing cultural capital

Access depends on the structural organization of television production, which varies by country. In contrast to systems of television production in which broadcasting goes hand in hand with in-house production of programming (Ellis 2004), Canada's television dramas are produced by independent film and television production companies that sell their products to the broadcasters for distribution. In this case, access would be granted or denied by the independent production company responsible for the particular television program rather than through the television broadcaster. Having pinned down where to look for access (i.e. production company), it now became a matter of determining who at the production company would be sufficiently 'authoritative' to grant full access to observe the production process of a television crime drama.

In television production studies, much of the access has been granted through what has been called the 'producer's gate.' Unlike film where directors have the most authority, television is a producer's medium (Newcomb and Alley 1983) in which directors can come and go while executive producers remain a stabilizing force throughout a television series' entire run. However, access through the 'producer's gate' has certain implications. First, the producer dictates what the researcher can and cannot observe. Second, interviews with producers might not generate any useful insights since some producers simply 'tow the party line' by regurgitating promotional pitches for the show.[14]

Although there has been some interest in media studies to shift the focus of research (Caldwell 2008) from producers (above-the-line creative personnel) to below-the-line[15] workers (e.g. gaffers, grips, camera operators, etc.) to avoid access through the 'producer's gate,' this shift in focus would not be useful for my research. Above-the-line personnel are the only individuals tasked with deciding how images of crime and policing are created and represented; below-the-line personnel are only tasked with 'following orders' already set by above-the-line decisions. As such, my research questions required that access be granted by the television producer for spaces in which I could observe the work of above-the-line personnel.

In order to access above-the-line personnel, a researcher breaches the self-bounded, highly stratified spatial world of television drama production (Caldwell 2006, 2008), by mobilizing his or her own personal cultural capital – namely, the symbolic capital that one accumulates through education and social upbringing, and that which serves to confer distinction upon an individual (Bourdieu 1984). In short, this cultural capital may act as 'a foot in the door,' but does not necessarily guarantee entry through 'the door' into the production process. In contrast to the research choice of 'studying down,' where the cultural capital of the academic clearly outweighs that of their subjects of study, my research requires that I 'study up.' The individuals who produce television dramas (e.g. producers, writers, directors, etc.) are in high demand, and have at least as much or more capital than the academic criminologist (e.g. they have university/college degrees, are successful in their own field, are economically solvent, and are generally more popular).[16] Because cultural capital is field specific, cultural capital in the academic field does not easily translate to such capital in the field of entertainment television, and vice versa. As a result, it is hard to gain access to my particular research subjects without already being 'in the know.'

By 'in the know,' I refer to three particular sets of knowledge that act as cultural and social capital. In the first instance of being 'in the know,' knowledge is encapsulated through *who* one knows: a researcher might already be socially connected to television producers through one's personal and/or professional affiliations. Film and media/communication studies professors, particularly those who moonlight as editors of the film and television industry's trade journals, have the social and cultural capital to network themselves into researching television production sites through their professional affiliations. For example, Caldwell (2009) details how some scholars have gained access by tapping into their personal and professional circle of friends and colleagues. Rosten was a screenwriter before he wrote one of the first anthropological accounts of Hollywood, *Hollywood: The movie colony, the movie makers* (1970). Newcomb wrote screenplays before he put together his anthology of interviews with television producers in *The Producer's Medium* (1983). Dornfeld (1998) was a documentary producer and served as such while researching the production of the PBS documentary series *Childhood* (1989–1991). Other scholars have worked as production assistants (see Hill interviewed in Caldwell 2009; Grindstaff 2002) or television writers (see Henderson, interviewed in Caldwell 2009) in Hollywood.

Some researchers lacking that social and cultural capital have gained access through a second sense of being 'in the know' – namely, extensive knowledge of a particular television show derived through the researcher's personal attachment to that show (see Levine 2001; Sodano 2008). This requires that the researcher act less like a disinterested observer, and more like an enthused fan of the television show.

As a scholar without the requisite pre-existing social capital (e.g. personal connections with television creative personnel) or the capacity to be a fan because of my sample of 'untried' television dramas, I mobilized a third sense of being 'in the know' – namely, the 'expert' knowledge that I have gained through the academic study of criminology, some of which could be of use to producers and writers of crime television dramas. For example, my knowledge of insurance fraud enabled my access to the production process of a pilot for a Canadian television drama called *Cra$h & Burn*. By providing television writers with stories that could fuel their imaginations, I became part of the television program's production process. Consequently, I gained access to creative meetings as a participant observer. During the process of working with these creative personnel on the television pilot, I was also gaining cultural and social capital in the field of television production, which in Toronto is relatively small and tightly knit. This accumulation of cultural and social capital was useful for multiplying research sites and research subjects through snowball sampling. Indeed, it allowed me to later gain access into the writers' room of *The Bridge*.

Methodological limitations

Ethnographic research is extremely useful for providing new insights into the television production process, especially since the process partially operates on a level of tacit knowledge among its practitioners. That is, writers and producers know how to make television shows, but may not necessarily be able to verbally articulate their know-how. However, it should be noted that there were parts of the process that remained unobservable or inaccessible to me. For example, I was not allowed access to any financial documents, television bibles,[17] or network phone calls. Being the sole researcher on this project, I could only choose to position myself in one place at any one time for observation, while the production process necessarily continues elsewhere, beyond my reach as an observer (e.g. filming, set design, location scouting, etc.). The limits of my access and observation can be tied to ANT's acknowledgement that it is impossible to map all the components of an actor-network (Haggerty 2001).

While I highlight the generalizability of North American television production practices whenever possible, some of the research findings in this book are unique as they are irrevocably tied to scholarly access to specific productions at a particular moment in time. This uniqueness is also compounded by the use of ANT. Because the researcher decides which actors to follow and more importantly which actors make up an actor-network, no two ANT studies of the same topic, including this one, will be the same. Like most ANT stories (Law 2008), this research is told in the form of specific case studies rather than in the form of large-scale generalizations. While ANT is useful for describing and documenting the practices that occur at concrete sites, it is not useful for producing general theoretical models because of its emphasis on the contingent formation of actor-networks and their translations. Consequently, the research findings in this book are not easily replicable, which in turn might be troubling to more positivistic scholars who would prefer a method that ensures inter-rater reliability. I have tried to build in some inter-rater reliability by supplementing the data gained through field observation with interviews, textual analyses, and data from trade manuals and trade magazines.[18]

Notes

1 Latour rejects the notion that Pasteur's success was due to the fact that he was simply a great man. In a material–semiotic perspective, the actions, even of great men, are understood as relational effects. Thus, Latour charts how an actor-network of domesticated farms, technicians, veterinarians, laboratories, bacilli and statistics was generated, which served to shape and create some of its actors. For example, he documents how cattle stopped dying from anthrax because farms were turned into laboratories, and attenuated bacteria were made into vaccines.
2 Latour's (1987) work covers some of the same ground as Berger and Luckmann's (1966) *The Social Construction of Reality*. In this work, Berger and Luckmann reformulate the task of sociology to study the processes through which knowledge is constructed and comes to be socially established as 'reality.' Despite being interested in the same subject matter, Latour differs from Berger and Luckmann in terms of approach. Latour's anthropologically inspired ANT approach is not well suited to the creation of general typologies, of which Berger and Luckmann make in their work. While Berger and Luckmann (1966: 61) conclude that 'the relationship between man, the producer, and the social world, his product, is and remains a dialectical one,' Latour (2007: 169–70) would balk at the use of dialectical thinking. Instead of overcoming two (extreme) positions through dialectical thinking (e.g. actor/system, micro/macro, nature/culture, etc.), Latour follows Serres' (2007) philosophical footsteps by finding a third position. For ANT scholars, this third position comes from visualizing the world as one-dimensionally flat rather than as three-dimensional. With this premise, scholars can trace how 'reality' is assembled by diverse actors who all exist on the same flat plane.
3 It should be noted that sociological studies of news production do not all begin with the premise that news representations are necessarily distorted from some objective reality. Instead, they examine the processes by which representations of reality are manufactured as news (see Ericson *et al.* 1987, 1991; Schudson 2000). This perspective of distortion manifests most strongly in reception studies, particularly those that attempt to follow in the path laid down by Hall *et al.* (1978).
4 There is overlap between the sociological perspective and that of cultural studies, particularly through the notion of 'culture of production' (du Gay 1997; Fine 1992). This is best exemplified by Gitlin's (1983) research into the way the culture of American broadcasting network executives (with its emphases on intuition and reputation) structures the production of scheduled prime-time programming, which in turn shapes American pop culture.
5 At least this was the assumption held by the series' executive producer. If the lead role were played only by a Canadian citizen, the executive producer assumed that the role would need to be re-cast if an American co-producer came on board. The American co-producer would want an American screen performer in the role.

6   For example, academic scholarship on *CSI* did not take off until the television show itself took off and was declared the most watched show in the US and in the world. Although *CSI* premiered in 2000, it did not become the most watched show in the US (and Canada) until its third season (2002–2003). Currently, *CSI* is on a ratings decline, dropping from 26 million viewers (2002–2003) to nearly 15 million viewers (2009–2010). However, academic scholarship on *CSI* first appeared in 2005, and has been slowly accumulating despite the show's decline in popularity. This points to two observations about academic work on pop cultural texts: 1) because there is either an implicit or explicit need to justify the choice of studying pop cultural texts in academia, scholars tend to choose successful texts. This is also the case since scholarship has focused on media/textual effects on audiences, such as the so-called *CSI* effect. 2) Academic work on *CSI* peaks after the television show's own peak of success due to the different speeds at which academia and pop culture operate. Pop culture (operationalized as television) moves at a much faster pace than academia. An entire season of television can be made in the same amount of time (or less) than the time it takes to publish a peer-reviewed academic article.

7   In English Canada, the 20 most watched television prime time programs are generally American television programs. While English-language Canadian television shows need to compete with American programs for viewership, this is not the case in Quebec. In Quebec, the top 20 programs are primarily French-Canadian (Druick and Kotsopoulos 2008).

8   In 1967, the American government created and began to fund the Corporation for Public Broadcasting (CPB). Because of the economic decline in the US in 2011, there is now some debate about whether public broadcasting should go private, and forgo (CPB) federal funding altogether (deMint 4 March 2011).

9   Nearly all American television shows today are made by six conglomerate companies: GE, Viacom, Bertelsmann, TimeWarner, Disney, and NewsCorp. Independent production companies have disappeared almost entirely (Stepakoff 2007: 204). In Canada, however, television shows are primarily made by independent production companies that have formed partnerships with broadcasting networks.

10 With respect to the legislated tax credit system, 'Canadian elements' are defined by Canadian citizenship of key personnel and shooting location rather than by the content or format of the program itself.

11 When American scholars study Canadian television, they tend to ask the same research question as Canadian scholars (see Levine 2009; Tate and Allen 2003).

12 Original Canadian television programs are differentiated from American service productions. Toronto handles a substantial amount of American service productions. That is, Americans will use Toronto as a shooting location for their Hollywood productions. In service productions, Toronto tends to be disguised as an American city, because it is much cheaper to do so than to use an actual American city with American production personnel.

13 This trend is only novel in the context of creating prime-time television dramas in partnership with the major American broadcasting networks. American specialty channels (e.g. *Discovery*) have featured Canadian crime-related docudramas for North American (and global) distribution for at least a decade (e.g. *Exhibit A*, *Forensic Factor*, and *72 Hours: True Crime*).

14 I have discovered that younger, less experienced producers are more likely to 'tow the party line' than veterans in the industry. The latter tend to be more candid.

15 The above-the-line and below-the-line distinction in labour on television productions originates from the early Hollywood studio days of filmmaking, during which the

financial budget top sheet would literally have a line separating the expenditures of above-the-line and below-the-line costs. Above-the-line expenditures (e.g. salaries of the screenwriters, directors, producers and lead cast members) would have been negotiated or spent prior to the start of filming. The distinction between primary creative personnel and technical craftspeople was also held with respect to the way cast and crew were credited in the film. Above-the-line personnel were credited in the opening credits, whereas below-the-line personnel were only credited in the closing credits.

16 They are more popular in the sense that the media are interested in what they have to say, particularly on the dramas that they produce. Their work is more popular than that of any academic because more people are aware of it and potentially impacted by it.
17 A television bible is a reference guide to the (distinctive) content and form of a television series. The creators provide a description of the world in which the show takes place, as well as back stories for all of its characters. Some television bibles also function as an encyclopaedic source for all the episodic stories that have been told throughout the show's run in order to maintain narrative continuity over the course of the series. Because television bibles were considered by some of the producers as a kind of financial document, I was not given access to this source of data.
18 Here are some of the trade magazines that I have found helpful for my production research: for American film and television production, *Variety* and *The Hollywood Reporter*; for Canadian film and television, *Playback*; for television writers in particular, *Script Magazine* and *Canadian Screenwriter Magazine*.

Chapter 3

Breaking *The Bridge*: documenting the heterogeneous knowledge inputs into the laboratory of the writers' room

Entering the writers' room, a lab intent on erasing traces

While law and science make clear their sources of knowledge through the use of footnotes and citations, fiction operates by effacing its paths, its sources and its methods of knowledge, making them impossible to retrace (Latour 2010: 274). Since retracing is not an option for tracing those paths, the ethnographer needs to enter the writers' room. Here, we discover that while all matters of fact have become matters of concern in modernity (Latour 2010: 242), television writers have not succumbed, and instead matters of concern *remain* matters of concern.

In counselling aspiring television writers, industry veteran Pam Douglas (2005: 3) asserts that no scene should be written for exposition only. If facts need to be communicated, they need to be set within the emotional context of the story. As such, matters of fact are only relevant insofar as they lend an air of authenticity to matters of concern, and nothing concerns a television writer more than the dramatic story itself. While writers want to get the facts right, they also know that there will come a point when the storytelling needs to take over in order to create great drama (DA[1] 20 March 2009). For example, a memo circulated by showrunner[2] (head writer/producer) David Mamet to the writers of the now-cancelled American military drama *The Unit* (2006–2009) highlights the tension facing writers between matters of fact and matters of concern:

> Everyone in creation is screaming at us to make the show clear. We are tasked with, it seems, cramming a shitload of *information* into a little bit of time. Our friends, the penguins [read: network executives], think that we, therefore, are employed to communicate *information* – and, so, at times, it seems to us. But note: The audience will not tune in to watch information. You wouldn't, I wouldn't. No one would or will. The audience will only tune in and stay tuned to watch drama.
>
> (Mamet 23 March 2010)

If the epistemic culture of modernity, epitomized by (natural) science (Knorr-Cetina 1999), is entirely focused on the fact, often a numerical representation,[3] the culture of storytelling to which television writers belong has not reached modernity. This does not mean that there is no knowledge involved; it suggests instead that the format of knowledge is not that of the modern fact (Poovey 1998). Television writers prefer to communicate with anecdotes, often beginning with 'remember when?' stories chosen not for being statistically representative of any single phenomenon, but because they are extraordinary examples of that phenomenon. By virtue of being extraordinary, the anecdote is remembered, recounted and exchanged. It is this culture of exchanging anecdotes that underlies the storytelling culture of the television writers' room. Harkening back to enthralled audiences gathered around a fire (DA 20 March 2009; RM 22 July 2008) to hear of stories of heroes and monsters, television writers gather around a table to create the tales that will, it is hoped, engage and intrigue an imagined television audience.

The writers' room as a Latourian laboratory

While individual episodes are ultimately assigned to single (or pairs of) writers to transform into scripts behind the closed doors of their personal office, television writing begins in the writers' room[4]. In contrast to the script-writing process, the writers' room provides an outside observer with a glimpse into the collaborative storytelling process. Before describing the work done in the writers' room in greater detail, however, I want to take a moment to conceptualize the writers' room as a laboratory, albeit one that produces fiction rather than fact.

In conceptualizing actor–network theory (ANT), Bruno Latour (1979 (with Woolgar), 1987) has written extensively on how scientific labs produce scientific facts. He is interested in examining how technological instruments or inscription devices are used by lab scientists to transform natural phenomena (a material substance) into a textual figure or visual diagram featured in a scientific article (representation of scientific fact). In doing so, he emphasizes the heterogeneity of actors and instruments that produce the resulting texts and also the contingency and uncertainty during such a production. Certainty exists only after the publication of the scientific article. Latour's notion of laboratory is analogized to the newsroom in Emma Hemmingway's (2008) study of the production of news in a BBC regional television newsroom. Following Latour, Hemmingway points out that the news is not constructed extrinsic to the newsroom, even though it purportedly reports on events happening in the external world beyond the newsroom. Instead, news is constructed by the processes in place at a particular newsroom (e.g. its particular organization of personnel, equipment and inscription devices). While Hemmingway believes that ANT does not properly address issues of power, subjectivity and human agency that are integral to news processes in a way that differentiates those processes from scientific work, the concept of laboratory has been applied both in her case study and Latour's exclusively to the production of *facts*. In contrast, I want to apply the ANT-inspired concept of laboratory to a space that produces fiction as a final product.

While it was novel for Latour (1979 (with Woolgar), 1987) to point out in his early work that scientific facts are indeed constructed, it is a basic assumption that fiction is always constructed: it is assumed that fiction does not exist 'naturally' in the world, waiting to be 'discovered.' But it is also not the case that fiction exists solely in the imagination of a particular writer. Television writers, particularly those of an older generation, believe in the mantra of writing 'what they know' (DA 20 March 2009), and what they know hinges on accumulating (anecdotal, biographical, cultural, news and scientific) facts about the world through experience. That is, unlike the jurist, the television writer needs to leave the library, go beyond the books, and consequently encounter life (Goodrich 2005). The writers' encounters with life, during which they 'discover' people, events and anecdotes (DA 20 March 2009), become the ingredients for their eventual stories. As such, the laboratory of fiction-making, despite creating a consciously fictional end product, is very much the Latourian laboratory: it is a space in which things are brought in from the outside world to be assembled into a particular format before being released back into the world as a product:

> The first part (actor) reveals the narrow space in which all the grandiose ingredients of the world begin to be hatched; the second part (network) may explain through which vehicles, traces, trails, types of information, the world is being brought inside those places and then having been transformed there, are being pumped back out of its narrow walls.
>
> (Latour 2007: 179–80)

This chapter aims to reveal the traces and types of information brought from the world into the laboratory of the writers' room, particularly by a show's technical consultant, and how that information is transformed in the laboratory before being 'pumped back' into the world. When considering the notion of information, I would like to highlight the ways that it is being used in this chapter. Following Latour, it is *in formation* since I will be detailing how the knowledge is being formed and processed by television writers through a fictionalizing filter. Moreover, this knowledge is meant to *in-form* – that is, the knowledge has a particular format (form) given its communication through the medium of a television drama. The writers' room of CBS/CTV's *The Bridge* will be used as a case study for this inquiry.

Beating it out: the writers' room and breaking story

Located on the second floor of a film studio in which the television drama is being filmed, the writers' room of *The Bridge* is a sparse and utilitarian setting at the centre of the writers' own offices (Figure 3.1). The room consists of a large oval-shaped table and six office chairs. Some writers prefer to stand and pace rather than sit. There is no assigned seating because in this writers' room, all the writers' voices are equal in weight. They all, however, face the two large whiteboards that occupy two walls of the room itself. These whiteboards are the *tabula rasa*, the

Figure 3.1 The writers' room of *The Bridge*
Source: Photograph taken by author.

blank slates, on which the episode's story first takes form. Other writers' rooms might make use of bulletin boards, instead of whiteboards, filling them with index cards on which specific scenes are written. For example, the writers of the Canadian cable drama *Cra$h & Burn* (2009) employ this method, possibly because it is more conducive to the writing of its serialized narrative (Banet-Weiser *et al.* 2007). In contrast, because *The Bridge* is aired on major commercial networks, its narratives tend to represent a more episodic approach in order to attract the mass audiences desired by advertisers. Functionally, the difference between using whiteboards and bulletin boards is exemplified in what happens when scenes fail to work in the context of an episode that is being formulated. For writers using index cards in conjunction with a bulletin board, discarded scenes can be saved for use in a later episode. For writers of *The Bridge*, a scene that fails to work is erased and replaced by another scene. The content of the erased scene is lost completely, effacing from memory all of the paths not taken. While scientists document each trial and error undertaken in their labs (Latour and Woolgar 1979), the writers of *The Bridge* only document the 'successful' trials (or scenes) and wipe away from existence the 'errors.'

While one might imagine that *The Bridge*'s writers' room is 'dressed,' as film sets are, in a way meant to inspire creativity, its utilitarian office-like setting emphasizes that television writing is a primarily textual job, and that the story is something that one labours over rather than something that is merely consumed with pleasure.[5] As a job, it has a regular procedure that is used to begin formulating an episode's story: the process called 'breaking story.' A writer from *The Bridge* likens the process of breaking story to breaking a suspect (MJ 9 June 2009), which transforms the sparse, no-frills writers' room into something akin to the generic police interrogation room. In this conceptualization of the process, the story becomes a suspect to be questioned, challenged and broken down beat by beat: a fitting metaphor for a television show premised on a former beat cop-turned-police union head who is not averse to using violence to get what he wants. For television writers of scripted dramas, the dramatic beat is also the essential building block of storytelling on screen (Douglas 2005: 8). Beats are used to build scenes; scenes are used to build acts; acts are used to build episodes. As the smallest node of narrative, running about two minutes in length on the screen (Newman 2006), the beat is the first textual manifestation of an episode in formation. Used by writers to plan the sequence of relevant plot points, the beat is also the way that writers inform their audience. For viewers, following a narrative is a process of accumulating information. For writers of network television dramas, the goal is to parcel out that information in a way that will keep viewers engaged enough to watch the entire episode without changing the channel. Information needs to be continually delivered in a way that seems urgent, surprising and emotionally resonant to the viewer (Newman 2006). As such, each beat encapsulates a matter of concern – specifically, it has a motivated protagonist who wants something and will drive the action to get it, often through conflict with an opposing figure (e.g. an equally motivated antagonist).

The formula for writing an episode of dramatic (network)[6] television, and for *The Bridge* in particular, is that an episode consists of five acts,[7] each separated by a commercial break. Each act consists of plus-or-minus seven beats (Douglas 2005: 78; MP 20 March 2009). This aesthetic format – five acts with seven beats in each – is necessitated by the commercial imperative underlying network television: the rapid succession of beats keeps the audience sufficiently interested in the show to sit through the commercial breaks, which in turn pleases the advertisers whose money is partially used to fund the making of the show. Often there are fewer beats per act if there is a big action sequence, which will take time to visually develop on screen.[8]

It is this information on beats that covers the whiteboards in the writers' room. The whiteboard directly in front of the writers' round table is divided into five acts, and the process of breaking story will then fill those acts with the appropriate beats. In 'boarding' the episode (Stepakoff 2007: 136), the writers are able to visualize how the plot of an entire story will play out before writing the episode's script. The whiteboard is used to break the story down into its component parts, to quite literally plot the events that make up the story. In the process of 'boarding,' the episode's story is transformed into an easily visible five-act plot[9] structure when it is laid flat across the space of the whiteboard.

Before discussing the writers' room in action and the making of fiction, it would be worthwhile to explain the logic of the television drama *The Bridge*, which both underpins and generates the show's particular storytelling.

The Bridge: from here and now to anywhere and to anytime

Airing in Canada as of early March 2010 and shot in Toronto, *The Bridge* is a Canadian (CTV)/American (CBS) co-production[10] that is premised on revealing the politics behind a big-city police force. After Frank Leo, former beat cop, is unanimously voted into office as head of the police union by the rank-and-file, he begins his 'quest to put street cops first and clean up the force from the ground up' (CTV 2010a). As 'Frank walks a thin blue line' (CTV 2010a) in his quest, he encounters the 'brass wall' (DA 20 March 2009), made up of the old boys' network running the police force and the city's self-serving politicians, who try to bring him down. Given this premise, the logic of the show already privileges particular representations of the police. It privileges the perspective of a street cop over the perspective of the bureaucrat ('brass wall'). More importantly, the logic of the show is built around the producers' premise that it tells 'universal' stories about policing, where this assumption of universality is a matter of both commercial and aesthetic concern. Any knowledge claims or factual information used by the television production need to align with these twin matters of concern. The show's universality will be discussed in terms of the following four elements: 1) it tells stories about *anywhere*, which 2) is partially a legal requirement for the production's purchase of *Errors and Omissions insurance* coverage. 3) The show also tells stories that ought to resonate at *any time*, and telling these 'universal' stories is part of 4) the *showrunner's preference and artistic vision of the show*.

Anywhere

First and foremost, *The Bridge* is a television drama concerned about representations of professional policing, precisely because it revolves around the investigative work done by the police union, an entity that is only brought about by the professionalization of the police force. The show is also preoccupied with the concerns that preoccupy a modern, urban, professional police force – specifically, police misconduct and corruption (DA 20 March 2009). This focus has certain effects that work to the television writers' advantage. By telling the stories of a professional police force, the writers are essentially telling 'universal stories' in the sense that virtually every developed country has one, resulting in explicit or implicit concerns about police corruption. Because *The Bridge* is premised on stories in which cops get into trouble, it should be noted that there are only a finite number of ways in which this can happen. As such, the show can be set in the archetypal Big City rather than the specific location of Toronto because 'what happens to a cop somewhere happens to a cop anywhere' (DA 2 June 2009). As the showrunner explains, the show's stories are:

> not specific [to Toronto]. We are not hiding the fact that it's Toronto, but we're not saying that it's Toronto. There's a reason for that. [. . .] It helps with the universality of the story because these stories come from everywhere,

from every police department. It's exactly the same all over the world. It's not any different in France than it is in Canada, than it is in Los Angeles, as far as how the brass, the power structure,[11] and the rank-and-file work. It's all the same.[12]

(DA 20 March 2009)

In reaching for universality rather than a sociocultural/local particularity, the showrunner ensures that the show has the 'legs' to be transported into different television markets in different countries. For Canadian television programs, particularly scripted fictional ones, it is assumed by most Canadian producers that success in the US market is a pre-requisite for eventual commercial success in the international market (Tinic 2005). Because *The Bridge* is partially an American production, its success in the US is especially important. Consequently, naming the city in which the series takes place is unnecessary, and:

actually hampers us [. . .]. When I was meeting with CBS, they asked me, 'where is this city?' And I said, 'where do you think it is?' They said, 'it could be anywhere.' And I said, 'exactly.' That's where it is. Anywhere. That's much more important for universal storytelling than you know … That's what reaches the audience. Well, they may ask themselves, 'what city am I in?' But it's not going to matter if the story's great and they love the characters.

(DA 20 March 2009)

Errors and Omissions insurance

The setting of 'Anywhere' also 'saves [the producers'] ass' (DA 20 March 2009), by satisfying the show's Errors and Omissions (E&O) insurance requirements. All television productions in North America need to purchase E&O insurance as part of their distribution deal on a large broadcast network.[13] However, E&O is not the only insurance[14] coverage that film and television productions need to purchase. All film and television productions need to also purchase comprehensive general liability insurance in order to shoot on location. For example, the city of Toronto, as is the case in all other North American cities, requires that production companies provide a certificate of insurance as part of their application package in order to get a film permit to shoot in the city's streets, parks, and buildings. The certificate is evidence that the production company is insured, and has named the City as an additional insured. The latter ensures that the City will be properly compensated in the event of third party claims for property damage, and/or bodily injury.

While general liability insurance protects producers from claims of property damage or bodily injuries incurred during production, E&O insurance protects them from the risk of future lawsuits arising out of claims about the content of their production. Upon notification of such a lawsuit, the insurance company will cover the cost of the producers' legal defence for one legal case. These lawsuits might arise out of claims alleging copyright and trademark infringement, libel or slander of persons and/or trademarked products, invasion of privacy, and plagiarism. Television productions are particularly concerned about representations that might be potentially construed as trade libel. For example in the making of the pilot of Cra$h & Burn, the showrunner was particularly excited about having a scene where a character drops a trademarked beer bottle from the balcony of an apartment onto the protagonist's company car below. While the smashing of the beer bottle was assumed to have great dramatic effect by the showrunner, the non-writing executive producer removed the scene as a means to remove the possibility of any trade libel. It was deemed possible that the beer company would see the smashing of its product as a representation that harms its product's reputation.

In addition to trade libel, producers and insurers are concerned that some of the production's content might be construed as defamation. In order to avoid defamation lawsuits, E&O requires that television writers source their knowledge claims, although what counts as factual accuracy varies with each television production.

In the case of crime docudramas, in which documentary storytelling of a 'true crime' case plays a significant role, journalistic standards of fact-checking tend to be used because many of the docudramas employ former journalists as researchers or story producers. Thus, every fact brought up in the documentary narration is sourced, either from the court records of a particular criminal case, or from interviews done with police officers or forensic scientists (BL 22 August 2008). However, crime docudramas themselves vary in terms of the amount of effort put into fact-checking. Some productions ensure that there is a convergence of information from three different sources, such as from interview data, academic sources, news sources, court records, etc. (GK 3 July 2008). Other productions are more lax: as long as an interviewee proclaims something to be true on camera, it is considered a fact (RB 8 August 2008). Despite these differences in fact-checking practices, all crime docudramas select cases with (legal) closure because of E&O insurance requirements. That is, producers deliberately choose criminal cases that have a conclusion, in which the accused is either convicted or exonerated (RM 22 July 2008). Producers cannot choose cases that are on-going or under appeal, because they would be putting the production and the broadcaster in a situation where they might be sued for suggesting someone is guilty before she has been declared so in a court of law (FF 7 July 2008; RM 22 July 2008; SJ 26 June 2008). Working in conjunction with the production's efforts to recruit police officers as interviewees, the latter E&O insurance requirement skews story selection in a particular way: producers pick cases in which the police successfully solve crime and get offenders convicted.

In the case of fictional television dramas, facts that underlie a particular fictional story are also sourced, often to newspaper articles or to the show's technical consultant. Because of their particular technical consultant's involvement in the production, the producers of *The Bridge* are particularly concerned about preventing particular kinds of lawsuit: invasion of privacy, and defamation (libel or slander).

Because *The Bridge* is inspired by insights from BC, the show's technical consultant/executive producer, setting the series in Toronto would have opened the production up to potential lawsuits by third parties claiming to have been depicted in the show because of their previous interaction with the show's high-profile technical consultant. The show's protagonist, Frank Leo, is the president of a police union, which makes for a simple comparison with BC, who was himself a controversial former president of the Toronto Police Union. As such, the Toronto-based producers feared that local (Toronto) viewers would make this connection between Frank Leo and BC, especially if the show was explicitly set in Toronto:

> It's if we make this [setting] Toronto, then they immediately think it's BC. And if it's BC, then we're in this situation where everybody and their brother can say that 'that happened – that must be me in that story!' Even though it isn't. I made it up. That could happen, so we can't say specifically we are in Toronto.
>
> (DA 20 March 2009)

Thus, *The Bridge*'s stories need to be written in such a way that viewers cannot reasonably identify a real, living person based on the information observed in any particular television episode (Donaldson 1996). To that end, identifiable names and likenesses are removed over the course of writing the script as a preventative measure to avoid potential lawsuits concerning invasion of privacy.

Given that the show is premised on telling stories about crime and police corruption, in which many of the peripheral characters are morally questionable, the move to generalize the characterization of persons, by removing any personally identifiable and unique elements, is one that also prevents potential lawsuits regarding character defamation. As an additional means of dissociating viewers from seeing themselves as depicted in the television series (i.e. as the real, living persons who have previously interacted with BC while he was employed as a police officer in Toronto), the producers have generalized the setting. Some Canadian communication scholars (e.g. Tinic 2005) and Canadian viewers[15] consider this generalization of setting to 'Anywhere' as de-Canadianizing the content of a Canadian television show. They deem it particularly galling because Canadian film and television shows are largely supported by government funding and legislated tax credits. However, in the case of *The Bridge*, it is neither a financially nor legally[16] wise decision to explicitly show Toronto as the setting for representations of what one writer has called 'the worst police force in history' (MG 2 June 2009). Because *The Bridge* is a Canadian–American co-production, it is also not immediately clear how legal jurisdiction will be determined in the event of defamation lawsuits. In fact, one cynical story producer of crime docudramas (FF 7 July 2008) claims that this confusion in jurisdiction is precisely what makes Canadian–American co-productions appealing:

It's harder [for Americans to sue Canadian production companies] and it's just more of a hassle and it's kind of dislocated. Apparently, at [this one crime docudrama production] that I worked at, people threatened to sue all the time, but it was an American lawyer. We were instructed that until you get a letter from a Canadian lawyer, 'don't worry about it.'

To avoid lawsuits from both American and Canadian viewers, *The Bridge*'s showrunner makes generalizations, which operate to transform particulars into universals, not only with respect to the setting but also with respect to the stories that the writers want to tell. As the showrunner puts it:

You're insured so [...] there are certain stories that you cannot tell. So how do you tell those stories if you want to? Well, you look for the universal element within that story. And you can find it anywhere. I can find it in Vancouver; I can find it in Los Angeles; I can find it in New York; I can find it in Toronto – wherever. I can find that same story virtually somewhere else, because they're so similar. Cops are going to get into trouble in certain ways.

(DA 20 March 2009)

However, it should be noted that the ways in which cops get into trouble are to a certain extent culturally specific, and not necessarily universal. *The Bridge* represents a predominantly North American-centric vision of police corruption. In the episode titled 'Painted Ladies,' Frank Leo uncovers a prostitution ring run by a vice cop. While the episode's story was inspired by a *Toronto Star* news article about a Toronto Police 'morality officer who ran a sex-for-pay service' (Story 7 April 1990: A1), this kind of police corruption can only occur in places where prostitution-related activities are illegal, and the police have a specific vice control department. In the Netherlands, for example, the Dutch police would be less inclined to engage in this particular kind of police corruption because voluntary prostitution is not a criminal activity. While it is not empirically accurate to suggest that all police officers get into trouble in similar ways, irrespective of a consideration of cultural context, what is important to note is how E&O insurance requirements facilitate the showrunner's assumptions of universality, and consequently his generalizations.

As science's use of induction transforms a limited set of observations into generalizing conclusions about a phenomenon, the showrunner's method of generalization can also be understood as inductive. He chooses a particular incident about police corruption that he wants to tell. Under the assumption that the particular incident is generalizable to other police forces in different cultural contexts, the showrunner multiplies the number of stories told about a similar incident from various independent sources. Typically, the writers will need to be able to point to three publicly available (news) stories about a similar kind of police incident to not overly particularize and subsequently identify a police force with the selected incident.

In using news stories, the writers are using knowledge from the public domain. This also saves the production money, since producers do not need to purchase copyright permission from the relevant owners in order to use such knowledge in the crafting of *The Bridge*'s stories. Such copyright permission is necessary for E&O coverage and to prevent potential lawsuits concerning copyright infringement. Intellectual property rights are not attached to knowledge in the public domain, especially if the writers simply use the underlying facts of the police incident reported in the news article.[17] Later, we will examine how these sources of knowledge are run through a 'fiction filter' as an additional means for transforming particulars into universals in the formulating of an actual episode.

Anytime

By setting the series in 'Anytime' – that is, by '*not* specify[ing] exactly the time that you're in' (DA 20 March 2009) – the showrunner ensures the show stays 'fresh' despite time lags in its release (e.g. initial airing and potential syndication), including a time lag of at least a year. For example, I first interviewed the show's executive producer and showrunner in March 2009 when it was first announced that the show would also be picked up by the American network CBS. It was assumed at that time that both networks (CBS and CTV) would begin airing the show during the summer of 2009. When that did not occur, it was assumed that the networks would put the show on their midseason schedule in early 2010. When CBS could not find any available time slot in their midseason program schedule (CBC News 10 January 2010) and CTV was still operating under the assumption that it would simulcast the show with CBS (i.e. air the show simultaneously at the same time and same date), the show's airing was pushed back indefinitely. However, CTV finally decided to not wait for a simulcasting opportunity with CBS, and premiered *The Bridge* immediately after its coverage of the 2010 Winter Olympics (Vlessing 3 February 2010). CTV used the Winter Olympics as an opportunity to advertise its original Canadian television shows to a larger-than-average Canadian audience, by promoting the series to Canadians who tune in to watch the Olympics, but otherwise do not tune in to CTV's other televisual offerings. On the American front, CBS finally aired the first two episodes of *The Bridge* in July 2010 before cancelling the show.

Showrunner's storytelling preference and artistic vision for the show

Lastly, the universal quality of the stories told on *The Bridge* is a result of the showrunner's own preference in storytelling, which in turn sets the tone of storytelling for the rest of the writing team. For the showrunner, his:

> whole thing is I want to tell universal stories. [. . .] I'm more of a Jungian than a Freudian in that way. I mean, I'm always looking for those classic

elements. [...] So once I find [the archetypes] in a story, I can then use [them] because drama is – we make sense of the world by telling ourselves the stories of our lives. And that's what drama is. That's what writing is, or that's what storytelling is. You want to tell the story because people cannot necessarily process this information in another way. And this goes way back to people sitting around a fire saying 'hey, today I ran into this situation, and I'm traumatized...' But by creating this and putting mythical elements to it, I can make it so that everyone can understand it who is sitting around that fire and also *process* it. We not only give it credibility, but we also give it, what's the word I'm looking for? Palatability, I suppose. I mean, the ability that we can now share it. By sharing it, we can breathe a sigh of relief. We make sense of it now. Even if it doesn't make sense, it makes sense because we've shared it. 'Cause we can all look at each other and go 'I've been there. I *know* that feeling.'

(DA 20 March 2009)

The showrunner's understanding of his storytelling method is interesting for two reasons. First, his preference for telling stories with a universal form and with universal themes (e.g. love, loss or brother against brother) is one that has been espoused by filmwriting guru Robert McKee. McKee (1997: 4) asserts that the archetypal story is able to travel across different audience contexts because it reveals a universally human experience, even though it might take the form of a culturally specific expression. As this showrunner also equates universal stories with myths (DA 22 July 2012), he concerns himself with revealing the similarities and parallels in policing experiences from around the world rather than their differences. Under the notion of universality, the showrunner's storytelling preference aligns with a distributor's concerns about selling the series on the international market.

Second, the showrunner conceives of storytelling as a means through which people process and make sense of information. As John Ellis (2000) has theorized, television provides viewers with a process of 'working through' the raw material of everyday life, by offering various definitions, explanations and narratives to make intelligible such material. Similarly, the showrunner understands good television as 'telling ourselves stories so that we can make sense of tragedy, of success, of joy, of all those things in our lives' (DA 22 July 2012). Television is embroiled in the process of 'working through' precisely because of its position as witness. Since the twentieth century, watching television is a way of bearing witness to newsworthy and noteworthy events (Ellis 2000). As the showrunner clarifies, the viewers have a shared experience of being a witness, whereby they can all feel as though they have 'been there [and] know that feeling.'

Working within this particular understanding of television storytelling, the showrunner envisions *The Bridge* as a series revolving around a dramatic biography that resonates with an audience. The series takes the form of a biography rather than a cultural story per se (i.e. a story we tell ourselves about ourselves; Geertz

1973), and it is the biography of Frank Leo where the facts about his life are only significant if they form an emotional context that can be shared by the audience. In archetypal terms, Frank Leo's life is the Honest Lion's quest, a heroic journey during which he battles what appears to be never-ending corruption. In short, his quest is to 'clean house,' by purging it of dirty cops 'from the ground up,' because the foundations of the 'house' are themselves dirty.

Given this quest, the networks also issued some guidelines about how the series ought to be formatted: it ought to generate 'satisfying cop stories' where Frank takes an active role in all of the stories being told (MJ 2 June 2009). In order to take an active role in the writers' stories, Frank is given all the investigative powers of a police officer without actually being one. Although Frank Leo insists that 'he is not a cop' (as in the episode 'Painted Ladies'), the writers have basically made him out to be one as a response to audience testing results (DA 22 July 2012). Before being picked up by CBS as a series, the first few episodes were tested by an audience in Las Vegas. From the test audience's feedback, it became clear that viewers were confused about the work done by the head of a police union as the following questions were constantly raised: 'who is this guy [Frank Leo]? Why does he do what he does? He doesn't carry a badge? Oh, he does carry a badge but he's not a cop? Who is he? What does he do?' (DA 22 July 2012). While the series was novel because it centred on the exploits of a police union president, its innovation became a double-edged sword because there was no 'codified language' or images associated with police union officials, as in the case of crime-solving police officers, to help the audience understand the work that they did (DA 22 July 2012). To lessen viewers' confusion, the showrunner transformed the work of a police union head into the general kinds of investigative work performed by police detectives.

For example, Frank is not actually a cop when employed full time as the head of the local police union. However, he is not so different from the crime-solving cop that populates television crime dramas because he, too, solves crimes on a weekly basis, albeit crimes allegedly committed by police officers. His investigation into these crimes is aimed at helping the officers in cases of alleged misconduct and corruption by eventually accumulating enough evidence to clear their names. In order to explain the scope of Frank's investigative powers, the writers spend some time justifying under what authority Frank can investigate the alleged corruption of other police officers. Having turned in his police badge, he now carries the badge of the Police Association. He rationalizes the legitimacy of his investigations under the power of the Police Association and its mandate of protecting (street) cops. His investigative work tends to involve delegating the actual investigating to active police detectives, particularly those from the division in which he previously worked as a beat cop.

By making Frank an investigator in cases of police misconduct and corruption, the writers translated the network demand for 'satisfying cop stories' into stories where Frank actively solved crimes. Thus, the show transformed from its original premise of revealing the political machinations behind police forces to the more standardized format of a police procedural, such as those series (e.g. *CSI*) currently airing on its coproducing networks CTV and CBS. As one writer puts it:

> [Frank]'s in on a lot of investigations, out in the field giving orders to cops, so on and so forth. So there's not much realistic about that. It's funny. What we've done in some respects is the way that the *CSI* guys, the forensics guys dig for fingerprints and so on; but they're out tailing suspects and doing investigations [. . .]. We solve crimes. It's an interesting progression we've taken here.
>
> (MP 2 June 2009)

As a result of this series translation into the standard format of a CBS police procedural, the relevant part of Frank's story becomes his work life, which in turn becomes defined by a series of episodic investigations into crimes – specifically, crimes conducted primarily by dirty cops rather than civilian criminals. Because *The Bridge*'s main character is a former cop now working to protect the cops (the mottos of this fictional Police Protective Agency include 'We protect those who protect us,' and 'It's like we're 911 for cops'), the show's representation of police corruption does not suggest that all cops are corrupt.

The nature of the show's narrative determines which approach to representing police corruption – either the 'bad apples' or systemic approach – is taken in a given episode. When the show takes on the narrative of 'modular episodes' (Douglas 2005) – new situations, such as a criminal investigation, that conclude at the end of an episode – the show takes the 'bad apples' approach to representing police corruption. Here, the show takes great pains to *not* represent the police as a monolithic entity, but as a constellation of discrete police units and departments, some of which include individuals or teams that are corrupt. When the show takes on a more serialized narrative – a long narrative where the stories continue across many episodes (e.g. soap operas or HBO television dramas) – it represents a more systemic form of corruption, one that runs from the old boys' network that anchors the police force to city politicians (mayor), criminals (organized crime) and other criminal justice figures (attorney general).

The remainder of this chapter will examine the 'bad apples' approach through the way writers discussed the corruption of an Emergency Task Force (or SWAT) team in the writers' room. This examination will also take into account the way in which information from the technical consultant inspires the writing team, and the way it gets translated into the conceptualization of the episode. It is also an inquiry into how television writers act in the face of doubt. When experiencing doubt about procedural technicalities, they call in their technical consultant. When scientists are faced with doubt, they leave the lab and go back into the field for more research (Latour 2010); when television writers are faced with factual doubt, they do not leave their 'laboratory' but instead call their expert in from the field to deliver a recounting of the relevant facts as he knows it.[18] As a result, the technical consultant brings the world as he knows it, from personal experience on the job, into the writers' room.

Making 'bad apples' in Toronto: breaking 'Injured Cop'

On June 2, 2009, *The Bridge*'s writing team, made up of five writers, broke the story of 'Injured Cop' (episode 12 in an order of 13 episodes). In broad strokes, the story begins with a hostage situation at a restaurant involving two drug-addicted thugs, during which a police officer is injured and taken hostage. Frank Leo rushes to the scene. Although he finds Good Sergeant[19] cooperative, Frank is prevented by Bad Sergeant from going in to the restaurant to take down the hostage takers. In doing some of the negotiating with the hostage takers, which primarily involves providing the thugs with their drug of choice, Frank discovers that there is more crime than first meets the eye. Above and beyond the current theft and hostage taking by the thugs, the restaurant is a place for a money laundering operation that is somehow facilitated by Bad Sergeant. Unlike reality television shows about policing, such as *COPS*, the shooting of a fictional police television drama requires a script premised on a plot that delivers certain dramatic sequences.[20] Because the appeal of reality television is said to be related to its capacity to show unscripted 'reality' or the 'raw, unvarnished truth' (Doyle 2003), it suggests a dichotomy between fiction and what Latour (2010: 241) calls 'raw facts,' that strange hybrid of law and science. In practice, however, the distinction between fact and fiction is not so easily drawn. *The Bridge*'s writers begin with 'reality' in the form of anecdotal 'true stories' about police incidents across North America. For example, the writers acquire these anecdotal stories about policing from an online website called Officer.com. Police officers across North America discuss their particular policing concerns on the site's message boards. In the Information Age, the Internet has become an important means through which the world of policing is brought inside the writers' room. The search engine function provided on the Officer.com website is also a convenient way through which writers can find different stories about the same kind of police incident, which is useful for satisfying the E&O insurance requirements of the episode.

These anecdotal stories are then passed through a 'fiction filter' (DA 20 March 2009). Although conventionally one would assume that this filter gives writers total creative license, it is primarily understood to be a filter that transforms matters of anecdotal fact into matters of dramatic concern (e.g. what are the stakes involved in telling this story and for whom?), because the filter is just:

> drama [or] the building of the drama within [the story]. Because you have to ask yourself, what's at stake for everybody? Where's the conflict? What are people's – what do they want? How are they going to get it? And at the same time, I combine elements from this story and I put it with this story. And these stories are all published and public domain. They're based on things in newspapers, or published somewhere that makes them public domain. So then you take those stories, you can combine them, work them, do what you want with them.
>
> (DA 20 March 2009)

In combining previously published and publicly available stories about police corruption, the fiction filter functions to erase the sources of the writers' knowledge about the police. Unlike scientists or academics, television writers do not need to cite the sources of their knowledge, particularly if they are claiming that their story, and the knowledge encapsulated within it, is a universal one. As such, the fiction filter makes the story familiar in the sense that the audience is likely to have encountered it before, albeit as news or in filmic representations of the police; however, this familiarity also implies that the story is likely to resonate with its audience. Even though the fiction filter erases the sources of the writers' knowledge in the crafting of the script, the filter can also be understood as a legal requirement from the E&O department. In this case, writers get the facts deliberately wrong in order to avoid future lawsuits.[21]

So what are some of the ways in which television writers come to know about the police? For the showrunner, this general question is met with the vague answer that he 'hears stories' about the police, but could not tell you from where or from whom in any exact, precise identification of the source of his knowledge. Sometimes, these are from news stories about the police that he has read over the years, anecdotal stories told by former technical (police) consultants on other crime-related television dramas that he has worked on, anecdotal stories told by friends that were or are still police officers, or anecdotal stories told by *The Bridge*'s technical consultant. As I alluded to earlier in this chapter, retracing how television writers know about the police or an incident of police corruption is rather impossible after the fact. It is, however, possible to trace what writers know and how they know it while they are still breaking an episode's story in the writers' room. The questions for the remainder of the chapter are as follows: how do the writers come to know about the episode's 'bad apple'? What kinds of source of knowledge allow them to imagine and represent the 'bad apple' in a particular way? How does that knowledge inform the story? In addressing these questions, I will be examining heterogeneous sources of knowledge, including factual (e.g. newspaper articles), anecdotal (from the technical consultant) and fictional (e.g. fictional police shows) sources. It is important to note that the making of fiction does not rely on any singular kind of knowledge source, but is the result of combining various kinds of knowledges together. As Latour (2007) claims that society is not simply made up of 'social' stuff, but is itself a heterogeneous mixture of social, political, technological, psychological matter, fiction – like society – is also notably not made up purely of fictional stuff.

Local knowledge: the technical consultant's anecdotes and competing representations of policing

Although *The Bridge* is said to be set in 'Nowhere's Ville' (writer MJ 2 June 2009), local knowledge is an important ingredient and input into the writers' storytelling process. What writers know about policing and police corruption originates relatively close to home. In the case of *The Bridge*, its writers know first and foremost about Toronto policing, either through reading the local newspapers, watching locally made police procedurals (specifically, *Flashpoint*) or through the show's technical consultant. Thus, the relevant knowledge claims that anchor the universal story told in this episode of *The Bridge* are local ones. In detailing these knowledge claims, this case study illustrates that although the writers and producers – much like scientists (Latour and Woolgar 1979) – attempt to represent their account of the world as 'universal,' such an account is inextricably tied to various local, contingent, semiotic and material elements.

Newspaper articles

While breaking story for this episode, the writers had initially conceived of this particular episode's 'bad apple' as a member of the police drug squad unit. As one writer explains to his fellow writers, 'Think of the drug squad in Toronto. It was said that they stole [drug dealers'] drugs and their money' (MJ 2 June 2009). As such, this 'bad apple' was consciously modeled after members of the Toronto Central Field Command's drug squad unit. In 2004, major Toronto newspapers informed the public about this particular squad's wrongdoings. Allegations included charging a 'tax' on drug dealers, stealing over $400,000 from safety deposit boxes and beating up drug dealers (Seglins 28 April 2008). However, over the course of breaking episode 12's story in the writers' room, it was decided that the 'bad apple' would be primarily represented by a sergeant from the Emergency Task Force (ETF). The decision to have a bad ETF sergeant was inspired by anecdotes told by the show's technical consultant.

The technical consultant

The use of technical consultants in television dramas, particularly procedurals, is fairly standard practice in North America.[22] For the most part, technical consultants for crime dramas are local experts, where their procedural expertise is anchored to the setting in which the fictional series takes place. For example, *Hawaii 5-0* (2010–present) uses police consultants from the Honolulu police force. The police consultant for the American fantasy-crime drama *Grimm* (2011–present), in which fairy tale monsters are criminals that need to be understood and caught, is from Portland, Oregon, precisely because the drama is set in Portland. As a result, these police consultants input their localized knowledge about police cases and police procedure into the writing of the series.

In the case of police procedurals, it appears that local technical consultants have been used since the American television production of *Dragnet* in 1951. As North American television's first hit crime television series, *Dragnet* featured a hard-working cop as its hero, and in doing so, provided some of the first favourable representations of police on television (Stark 1987–8). As a series, *Dragnet* was notable for its dramatization of real cases from the Los Angeles police files and its use of a technical advisor. Described as 'a rotund, cheerful Los Angeles detective sergeant' (Anonymous 15 March 1954), the show's technical advisor challenged its creator to make a 'real show about policemen.' The series creator rose to his consultant's challenge as *Dragnet* was lauded for its realistic portrayal of the police. However, the show's realism was 'simply a byproduct of [its creator's] lust to entertain' (Anonymous 15 March 1954).

Today, filmmakers and television showrunners continue to treat realism or verisimilitude as a means through which to better entertain audiences (Kirby 2011: 10–11). In crafting an entertaining representation of policing, creators of crime dramas often turn to police consultants in order to ensure that their representation of police procedure is inconspicuously correct. As the showrunner of *The Bridge* further explains, 'you want [the police series] to be procedurally correct so you can work drama within it. [. . .] You want the procedure to be just as correct as possible so that it just slips by. It shouldn't stand out in any way, shape or form' (DA 22 July 2012). Representations of inaccurate police practices or incorrect procedures may have the effect of taking viewers out of the show's stories, interrupting their willing suspension of disbelief. According to Coleridge's (1817) formulation, audiences are willing to suspend their disbelief about the implausibility of a narrative, so long as the writer infuses 'a human interest and a semblance of truth' into the story. While television writers are tasked with providing their stories with 'human interest,' technical consultants are expected to provide writers with 'a semblance of truth.' Specifically, the presence of police consultants provides an air of authenticity[23] to the stories being told by writers in four ways.

First, the police consultant provides writers with the technical details about the way things are done by police officers, including the relevant professional jargon. In a police series, this might include explaining to writers about proper police procedure, or showing screen performers how to hold a gun.

Second, a police consultant is expected to review the script during production to ensure that there are no glaringly incorrect representations of police protocol. However, there is flexibility as to what counts as an accurate representation (Kirby 2011) and whether accuracy is the goal of a particular representation. Writers might deviate from the so-called facts of policing if they want to include certain 'gags' that reference images of policing from previous entertainment films or television series. As writers and showrunners are ultimately 'not making a documentary' (DA 22 July 2012), the goal of representing such 'gags' lies in their entertainment value. For example, as a general rule, real-life police detectives should not handcuff themselves to a suspect. A technical consultant's input would have highlighted how such an action would be against proper police protocol. Nevertheless, writers might choose to ignore their police consultant's input in this particular instance in order to highlight a gag that involves handcuffing two antagonists together, bringing to mind the handcuffed characters in the crime film *The Defiant Ones* (1958). Because the writers have followed the consultant's suggestions in other instances, the consultant might simply allow the inaccurate representation because 'it's just TV' and not reality (CM 7 June 2012). In making a distinction between 'TV' and 'reality,' the technical consultant acknowledges that 'reality doesn't always work best for television' (police consultant quoted in Watercutter 20 September 2011) because reality does not necessarily come with the entertaining and dramatic flourishes that are expected of television dramas.

Occasionally, the police consultant might also deliberately allow inaccurate representations of policing because they are thought to indirectly aid real-life policing. For example, the CBS reboot of the American police series *Hawaii 5-0* employs a police consultant from the Honolulu Police Department (HPD) who describes himself as 'only a guy with a big mouth who knows a lot of people' (CM 7 June 2012). The consultant is aware that the show's writers, perhaps following in the footsteps of most writers of detective fiction (Thomas 1999), have imagined technological devices that are far in advance of those owned and used by the local police department. As he remarks:

> The bad guys think that every phone is tapped. That's the hardest thing in the world to get. That's a good thing for us [HPD]. The bad guys think that we have these flare things that [the main characters use], that's a good thing. And if the bad guys think that we have [advanced technological tools to detect crime and identify criminals]? Good. What they don't know won't hurt [the HPD]. It's funny – [the bad guys] watch TV, too.
>
> (CM 7 June 2012)

Despite exercising a certain amount of flexibility in terms of representing police work and police tools, the presence of a police consultant is part of a production's proactive approach to navigating and avoiding criticism. In the case of making a police series, production seeks to avoid having some '*CSI* guy' or police officer calling the network to complain about any inaccuracies associated with their images of police procedure (DA 22 July 2012). In addition, the production seeks to avoid a situation where lay audiences become aware of their procedural inaccuracies and take to voicing their complaints through social media. As the showrunner of *The Bridge* notes:

> We exist now in a world where it's an instant[ly] critical world where within a matter of minutes a million people can have the mistake that you made on your show on their Twitter. And they could be going, 'fuck that; that's bullshit.' So it's like you have to kind of police yourself in an odd way. There's certain things that you have to be careful of.
>
> (DA 22 July 2012)

Thus, a police consultant is expected to help showrunners and writers police the representations they create, in order to avoid criticism from lay audiences as well as law enforcement audiences.

Third, the presence of a police consultant can also be considered useful to showrunners for navigating criticism or feedback from the network itself. Upon review of an episode, a network executive generally has notes to give to the showrunner, often highlighting areas of confusion for potential viewers. In response to network notes, showrunners can use their consultant as part of a strategy for justifying their particular representation of policing. As one of the showrunners of the Canadian–American co-produced police procedural *Flashpoint* explains:

> CBS is very respectful of research and authenticity. Any time you had a creative discussion [such as questions about 'why would the police protagonist do this?'], I would say 'no, I'd talked to a cop and this is what they would say about that.' And almost instantly, 99 times out of a 100, you would get a 'great.'
>
> (Ellis 10 May 2011)

Here, we can see that the network tends to accept a representation that has been supported by the showrunner's research. For the most part, television writers conceptualize 'research' on policing as an activity that involves talking to their police consultant or to other police officers. By highlighting how their research supports their particular representation, showrunners are able to fulfill their creative vision of the series with the support of network executives.

Lastly and perhaps most importantly, police consultants are crucial to the storytelling process because they might be the one to provide the story idea in the first place. Technical consultants tend to provide their story ideas in the form of anecdotal retelling of actual cases (e.g. the case of the 'dirty' judge or the case of the 'dirty' cop). In retelling their previous cases as stories, police consultants are articulating their past experiences in the speech format preferred by the entertainment industry: the anecdote (Gitlin 1985).

In our following case study of the story-making process of an episode of *The Bridge*, we will examine how the technical consultant contributes to the making of an episodic 'bad apple' through the provision of an anecdotal story. Before we dive into our case study, I will provide some background information about this particular episode's story.

Because episode 12 was meant to give viewers closure by resolving its discrete investigation of a case of police corruption, the writers broke the story into its component parts using a mystery structure. To conceptualize the mystery, they needed to answer two questions: whodunit and 'howdunit' (how was the crime committed)? The crime in question would be theft – specifically, police officers stealing money from drug dealers. However, in the episode, these corrupt police officers would be represented by ETF Sergeant Coombs ('Bad Sergeant') and Deputy Chief Cafferty. So the remaining question for the writers was: how can Coombs smuggle the money out of the restaurant if police officers are constrained by a chain of evidence that holds them accountable and prevents them from confiscating criminals' possessions (money, drugs or weapons) from a crime scene? As the writers were in doubt as to the correct police procedures to be followed in such a scenario, they called their technical consultant in from the field.

An hour after receiving a text message from one of the writers, the technical consultant ambles into the writers' room in a Hawaiian T-shirt. Here, expertise is not manifested in a professional dress code, unlike the formal attire of court or the white lab coats of science. Instead, in many cases, technical consultants for television shows are divested of such professional attire through retirement[24] or a career change. In other cases, professional attire is symbolically left at home, so that the technical consultants are speaking off the record in their own name, and not in the name of their company or profession. This allows them to disassociate from the obligations of confidentiality and potential conflicts of interest that tend to otherwise characterize their jobs as lawyers or police officers. The informal attire also mirrors the way in which information is shared between technical consultant and the (almost always informally and comfortably attired) writers. In their casual clothing, the technical consultant can speak freely about various anecdotal 'war stories' encountered on their former job, which function as case studies for the writers. They can also speak from experiential knowledge (e.g. the technical knowledge of how particular procedures are carried out and under what logic) without self-censoring.

The initial question posed to the technical consultant is provided in the following excerpt, serving also as recap of the relevant scenes that the writers had been imagining up to this particular point in their process of breaking episode 12. Following the initial question, I have also provided a relatively lengthy excerpt of the exchange between the writers and their technical consultant in order to reveal the changing questions and dynamics of reasoning that occur over a single conversational exchange, as well as the collaborative nature of the writing team. Although this episode is written by and credited to only two writers on the team (KD and MJ), the process of breaking story requires that the entire team be mobilized into thinking through the formation of the story and its characters prior to the script-writing stage. The following excerpt demonstrates the transitional moment during which the writers' conceptualization of the episode's crime is transformed by new pieces of information provided by their technical consultant.

Writer MG: What's the process when either money or weapons or drugs are confiscated at the scene of the crime? The scenario is SWAT team goes in and busts big drug dealers' money . . . A big pile of money. And the next scene, the lockup officer or whoever is in charge once [the money] gets to the station, comes to Frank and says, 'I know money and those photographs from the crime scene show that it's clearly five million dollars, and when it came in it was only three.' So what's the process of getting the money from the crime scene to lock up?

Technical consultant BC: This much money you'll have an escort. And it goes to what we call the property bureau. This is cash, it's logged. Firearms go to Forensic. Anything with blood or DNA goes to Forensic; here down on Grosvenor Street [Toronto]. Cash just goes to the property bureau. That much money would be escorted with an ETF truck. [. . .]

MG: Who photographs the scene?
BC: Your Forensic.
MG: We sort of need that initial photograph of the money for the guy at the property bureau to say, 'The money that came in doesn't match the crime scene.'
BC: Yeah, without counting anything, you just want them to stack it. The way that coppers would do it is not just counting it all, but stack it. Say, four equal stacks [of money]. Line it up against the wall or something, right? Okay, take a quick picture if you don't want to count. If the stack is lower in the next picture . . . [. . .] They [then] transport [the money] in these big cans that look like hockey bags. They can seal it. The one thing that you're going to have to get around is that there's a property seal that goes on that can't be broken. At the scene.
MJ: But the idea is that not all the bags make it to property. Somewhere between the . . .
Writer MP: Yeah, but they've logged those when they put the seal on.
BC: For what you're talking about, they seal the bags at the scene so it can't go missing. I don't know how you're going to get around that 'cause those seals are not broken.
MJ: Well, it will have to be before it goes into the bag.
KD: That's a lot of money to take though.
MP: We started out with a lower number [monetary figure] but we've gone up to [five million dollars]. But if it's a couple of hundred thousand . . . The thing is we're saying it's this SWAT team that's gone in [to bust] this heavy duty group of drug dealers. Before forensic photos are even taken, they could have made some of the money disappear, right?
BC: Yeah, there's a huge investigation up in York region right now. It was just in the papers two days ago. They went and did it. It was in the *Toronto Sun*. [. . .] ETF went at 4:30 in the morning, kicked the door [open], beat the people and there are pictures of the beating. There's an internal investigation . . .
MJ: So depending on how you want to lay out the crime scene – there's shooting and stuff going on – if more than one of the SWAT guys is in on this, they can separate themselves [. . .] from the rest of the people [especially] if there's bodies on the ground and you know, people getting cuffed and all that kind of stuff going on. But one guy's job, they know going in, [is to] get the money [. . .].
BC: There's one answer to all that. It's the amount of money that you're using. I don't think you can pull this off. If it was less money . . . nobody comes into a search warrant until the ETF clears the scene. Nobody is allowed in.
MP: There you go. That's great.
KD: What if we make it half-a-mill[ion]?
MG: What if we make it two? Somehow a [couple of] thousands doesn't make it interesting like that.

BC: The only way to get around that . . . I would say that if you want to add to this story, make it less but that these guys have been doing it for [a while].
MG: So that's why [this] has gone unnoticed for so long.
BC: 'Cause it's such a small amount. And the bad guys aren't going to say, 'Hey,' you know, in court, 'where's the rest of it? [. . .] Well, I had more drug money!'

Over the course of eight minutes, the technical consultant has changed the dynamics of the crime committed by the corrupt police officers: they have stolen less money in this particular instance, but the crime is still severe because it suggests a pattern of stealing money from drug-dealing criminals over time. It is likely that an entire ETF unit rather than a singular officer is guilty of such a crime since it requires collaboration between members to pull these thefts off. The moment of criminal opportunity is built into the police procedure itself: the crime scene must be cleared by ETF before any other police team (e.g. forensics) can enter the scene, which allows a corrupt ETF unit to confiscate evidence prior to it being logged. This in turn would 'get around' the obstacle of having large sums of money being logged into sealed containers by the forensics unit, particularly since the seal cannot be easily broken. If the writers need inspiration or a news reference for such a scenario, the technical consultant also pinpoints a publicly available news story about such corrupt cops in the nearby York region.

In changing the dynamics of the crime, the evidence of the crime itself changes. No longer can a forensic photograph suggest wrongdoing by corrupt officers in a before-and-after comparison of the amount of confiscated money. After all, forensics is only allowed into the crime scene after ETF has done their work 'clearing it.' What the writers now need is a whistle-blower (e.g. an undercover narcotics cop or a *Serpico*-like member of the ETF unit), or an informant (e.g. a criminal who rats out the bad cops) that can tell them of this difference in money, and subsequently implicate the ETF unit. The technical consultant leaves this problem with the writers.

Having established how the crime can play out in this episode, the technical consultant goes on instead to provide some information about Toronto's ETF, or more precisely, the ETF as he knew it based on his former interactions with some of the members of its unit. Through an anecdotal story[25] about a particularly memorable member of the ETF, the technical consultant fuels the writers' imagination about how to represent ETF Sergeant Coombs, especially in contrast to the representations of the ETF on *Flashpoint*. Filmed in Toronto, *Flashpoint* is a procedural about an elite tactical police force, the Strategic Response Unit (SRU), which is modelled on Toronto's ETF.

BC: When I ran the [Toronto police] union, the second biggest union clients was ETF. I had one [that] was shoplifting, stealing from the station, you know. These guys were unbelievable. They just thought that they were so protected. Domestic assaults, everything like that . . .

MJ: And they're not the second biggest [police] unit, are they?
BC: There's only – when I was there, there was only 75 of them. It's a very small unit, but they're fucking crazy these guys! One guy would wear a turtleneck all the time. And he got shit [on it once . . .] so he had to go to his house, it was me and X. We go to the house, [. . .] and it's like in the summer, he's got this turtleneck on. The house is really heated 'cause he had three really big boa constrictors running around the house – 30 feet long. You know why he wore the turtleneck? He had 'Hatred' [tattooed] across here [gestures to the neck]. He was a complete skinhead, white supremacy. I'd walk in and there are fucking snakes curled up in the corner! We got to get this guy cleared!
MP: What was his . . .?
BC: And the boa snake had just [fed on] a pig or something!
MP: What was the issue that brought you there?
BC: It was involving a shooting. He shot a guy. I won't give you names. He's still on the job . . . See, the problem is that on [ETF] detail, they're there for years. They could be there for ten years, you know. [. . .] And they had a different set of rules in shootings; they had their own breakdown times, their own rules.
KD: That's how Coombs has functioned like this, almost above [the law] . . .
MJ: Yeah, there could be a turtleneck.
KD: Yeah, or for his snakes to try to strangle him. [CB in background: I don't know what he was feeding those snakes.]
MG: Should we do that? That same thing?
BC: I don't care. [. . .] *Flashpoint* . . . You got to be kidding me! Please! Little girls running around with guns.

'Little girls running around with guns' is a summation of how the technical consultant perceives representations of the ETF unit in *Flashpoint*. Femininity is attributed to male ETF members represented in *Flashpoint* who articulate the psychological stresses of their work through any form of emoting. According to BC's perception, real-life ETF men do not show any psychological or emotional cracks. In his example, the ETF man does not feel emotions deeply, but instead only manifests them, such as feelings of hatred, as tattoos on the physical surface of his skin. Still, such emotion is generally hidden underneath clothing, especially on a professional basis. At home, the described ETF member enjoys only the companionship of large snakes. As the archetypal Adam who has chosen the Serpent over any Eve, he also metonymically takes on the characteristics of his favoured pets: dangerous, predatory, cold blooded, unemotional, and deceitful. Here, deceit comes in the form of betraying the professional code of being a police officer insofar as one is expected to uphold the law and not commit any crimes while doing so. Instead, this ETF member is himself a snake who will eat pigs (also a metonym for the police) when necessary.

In providing the anecdotal story about the unforgettable ETF member, the technical consultant does two things simultaneously. First, in his description of the particular ETF member, there is no mention of that member's affiliation to other members of the police brass and/or municipal politicians. As such, the technical consultant offers up to the writers a discrete police unit that can be represented as corrupt, playing into the 'bad apples' approach to representations of police corruption. In writing about 'the guy that you call to stop guys like him' (MP 2 June 2009), the writers are intrigued by the possibility of representing the most conventionally heroic of the police as also potentially the most corrupt. Moreover, the writers understand this particular ETF member as an exemplar of ETF culture 'as it really is' (in contrast to its representation in *Flashpoint*). As the writers are getting deeper into conceptualizing the character of ETF Sergeant Coombs (FT 2 June 2009), the more they are simultaneously delving into ETF culture as a police subculture that frequently works above the law. Here, culture is understood as depth of character. Although TV writers love writing complex characters (DA 20 March 2009; Douglas 2005), some characters (e.g. Bad Sergeant Coombs) come to personify an entire (sub)culture in the writers' minds, becoming a character *type* rather than a fully *individualized* character. In the following excerpt, note how a single individual ('he') becomes generalized into a type ('they').

MJ: [A potential whistle-blowing cop could say,] 'it's somebody on the SWAT team, I think. I don't really know them. They're all crazy. They wear turtlenecks in the summer and have giant snakes in their house. We don't really hang around with them. No one does.'

MP: There's this guy, this famous ETF guy. He's the cowboy of the [ETF] department and everybody looks up to him. He's right out there. He does have snakes. The crazy tats that are hidden, covered with clothing. Does Frank have to get into his life somehow? Set him up for something? Or find out who he is connected to somehow? [. . .] Is there a way that they can get to this guy? [. . .]

KD: Well, we got to keep it small [for production purposes], right? We could visit a paintball place and this guy is well-known 'cause he'll go and take on a team of eight [paint-ballers]. It's non-stop with these [ETF] guys. They're adrenaline seekers.

At this point, the writers are visibly excited about representing a relatively small, insular police unit, comprised of tough and 'crazy' members that can be characterized by an adrenaline-seeking, tattooed, turtleneck-wearing subculture. In their spare time, the ETF members continue to practice their shooting and tactical skills by playing paintball. As a group, they are best exemplified by their leader, Sergeant Coombs, the biggest and 'baddest' of them all.

Second, the technical consultant's anecdotal story of 'the ETF guy' is a clear example of how technical consultants from different police television dramas offer different kinds of knowledge to television writers. Their knowledge in turn shades the kinds of stories that can be potentially told by the writers. *The Bridge*'s technical consultant is, like Frank Leo, a former beat-cop-turned-union head who is not a stranger to controversy. As a former beat cop in Toronto, BC made a name for himself by 1) allegedly assaulting a homeless man (CBC News 24 January 2003), and 2) leading a wildcat strike with officers from Toronto's 51st Division. The strike was the first of its kind in local Toronto police history (Fine 15 February 1999), and was later dramatized in the first episode of *The Bridge*. During his tenure as President of the Toronto Police Association, BC was most well known for launching a telemarketing campaign called Operation True Blue. For their financial support, donors were given a windshield sticker for their cars, which seemingly exempted them from being held responsible for minor traffic infractions. Critics believed that BC was using the funds from Operation True Blue to target his own political opponents (Duncanson 4 February 2000). Since his retirement from the police force, BC has become a radio personality, and is interested in working in the television industry. He clearly enjoys his work in the television industry as much as his work on the police force. After all, he decided to become a police officer 'after getting hooked on television cop shows like *Police Story* and movies such as *Bullitt* and *The French Connection*' (BC 10 May 2007: R08). This penchant for drama comes through in the way he tells his anecdotes, telling them with a sense of emphasizing the extraordinary example that will captivate his audience (e.g. the very tough 'ETF guy').

From his former employment, BC knows about the complaints filed against certain police officers and still keeps in touch with former police buddies so that he is aware of current Internal Affairs investigations. Both his former work and current police gossip keep him abreast of anecdotal stories about police corruption in Toronto. More importantly, he is willing to speak about cases of police corruption and misconduct, which can then be translated into episodic stories on *The Bridge*. In contrast to *The Bridge*'s high-profile technical consultant, the anonymous technical consultants for *Flashpoint* were 'gentle souls' (FT 2 June 2009). Prior to working on *The Bridge*, one of the writers had worked on *Flashpoint* and asserts that the *Flashpoint* writing team had never talked about police 'dirtiness' with their technical consultants, possibly because the consultants themselves never bring up or say anything dirty about the ETF unit.

Unlike *The Bridge*, which has a single consultant, *Flashpoint* had several technical consultants over its first two seasons. During her time on *Flashpoint*, the writer is aware that the show had 'two older guys' (FT 2 June 2009) as consultants who spoke from their personal experience. One was a retired negotiator who speaks about the need for police psychologists on the international police lecture circuit, while the other was a team psychologist for Toronto's ETF unit. The technical consultants primarily talked to the show's writers about post-traumatic stress disorder and the psychology behind being an ETF member. When the *Flashpoint* writers toured the Toronto ETF unit, the writer notes that the ETF members 'were sort of young looking guys, but well spoken' (FT 2 June 2009). Both the touring of the facility and the provision of technical consultants suggest that the production of *Flashpoint* was made possible through cooperation with the Toronto Police Service (Moscovitch 2008). This in turn suggests that the Toronto Police Service at least tacitly approves of the representations of the ETF on *Flashpoint*. In order for any police service to cooperate with television writers and tacitly approve of their representation of policing, the production needs to represent the police in a positive light.

Similar police cooperation is extended in the making of crime docudramas, such as *Forensic Factor*, on the condition that writers and producers will not make the police officers or the department look bad, even in cases when the writers themselves suspect the officers of some wrongdoing. This production condition not only allows the police to police their own media image, but also acknowledges the necessity of police cooperation in the production process. As a *Forensic Factor* story producer notes (FF 7 July 2008), they need the police officer as an interviewee to tell part of the 'true crime' story, by setting the scene and explaining to viewers how the dead bodies were found and processed.

Generally, the police cooperate with these kinds of television productions because they 'like the fact that they're getting cast as the good guys' (FF 7 July 2008). Additionally, it serves the police well as a 'fantastic, free marketing tool' (SK 17 November 2008) at a time when the North American police have become increasingly proactive in harnessing the media to their own advantage (Ericson 1989). Since at least the late 1980s, senior police officers have recognized a 'need for the police force to sell themselves [or to] put an attractive image before the public about what the police force was trying to do, and how they were trying to do it' (senior police officer quoted in Ericson 1989: 208). For example, *Forensic Factor* was easily able to recruit police interviewees from the US Bureau of Alcohol, Tobacco and Firearms (ATF) because the law enforcement department wanted to change its image. For the most part, the ATF had been unfavourably compared to the Federal Bureau of Investigation (FBI), which was the more well known and acclaimed agency. The ATF perceived their participation in *Forensic Factor* as an easy way to get public recognition for the work that they do, because their agents would be represented as heroes (SK 17 November 2008).

Thus, the necessity of police cooperation in the production process of both fictional and docudrama television series tends to suppress negative representations of police officers. The need for police cooperation, in order to acquire 'inside knowledge' to create a television show about the police, whether fictional or not, has the effect of privileging the police officer as heroic protagonist (see also the making of *COPS*, Doyle 2003). In contrast, because of BC's galvanizing history in Toronto, *The Bridge* did not receive police approval, formal police cooperation, or clearance from the City of Toronto to name it and show it as such. From this analysis, it is clear that the technical consultant's standpoint is crucial, since it determines what kind of knowledge enters into the show's production and whether that knowledge encourages writers to take a more or less critical perspective on policing.

Flashpoint

Following ANT, television shows can become actors in the production of other television shows. As a television show, *Flashpoint* becomes an actor in the production of *The Bridge*. *Flashpoint* is a Canadian–American co-produced prime time television drama that debuted in the summer of 2008 on CTV and CBS. It was produced as a result of the Writers Guild of America strike in 2007 and 2008. Because American television writers were striking, no television dramas were being written in the US. As a strategy, American broadcasters teamed up with Canadian broadcasting networks in order to put content on the air (Adalian 28 January 2008; Stelter 29 January 2008). The show's debut was deemed a commercial success by both broadcasting networks. Since 2008, *Flashpoint* has also been cited as proof that Canadian–American co-productions are a viable business model for the future of North American television production. More importantly, *Flashpoint* is the reason that CTV and CBS teamed up again for the production of *The Bridge*.

As the show's premise, *Flashpoint* focuses on how an elite policing squad handles highly dangerous situations that cannot be handled by regular public police officers. In showing these officers as particularly competent, *Flashpoint* traffics in the image of the heroic ETF officer. Given that both series are written and shot in Toronto, *The Bridge* writers are fully aware of *Flashpoint*'s starting premise. In creating a contrasting representation of the ETF, *The Bridge* writers are making an argument that their particular series is not afraid to show the ETF as they actually are in 'real life.' Here, 'real life' is captured by anecdotes from the show's technical consultant who is conceived by writers as a direct line to insider police knowledge and the 'reality' of policing.

Because television dramas achieve their own unique identity through demonstrating semiotic differences from other shows of the same genre, we can see the writers' desire for this semiotic difference in the following exchange, whereby making a 'bad apple' is part and parcel of *The Bridge*'s distinction.

MP: BC was telling us about a real ETF guy who always wore turtlenecks 'cause he had 'Hatred' tattooed on his [neck], 'cause he was a white power-head. He had huge boa constrictors all around his house. [BC] said it was like one [boa] just ate a pig. Don't know if it's *that* guy, but it's an interesting character.
Showrunner DA: Well, we can't use anybody real, so . . .
MP: [BC] said all of the ETF guys were all crazy . . .
DA: . . . which is something we can use, since we've never seen that. We've always seen them as the straight-laced, you know, like on that show you [FT] used to work on.
FT: They're just gentle souls.
DA: Yeah, let's make them hard motherfuckers. Let's stick it to [*Flashpoint*].

In the above exchange, we can note that authority in the writers' room is embodied by two people: the showrunner and the technical consultant. While BC might be the authoritative source of knowledge that is used to add authenticity to the story by providing matters of anecdotal fact, the showrunner is the authority on if and how that knowledge is used in the serialized narrative of the show. Unlike the writing team, the showrunner has a sense of the 'big picture' – that is, where the show begins and where it is ultimately headed as a serialized narrative. The writing team lacks this precise knowledge, and tends to be asked to think episodically. As a result, the writing team tends to only write the stories for modular episodes.

In his capacity as producer, the showrunner also has the last word on how the writing team will graft the technical consultant's matters of fact onto matters of concern. While BC did not care whether the writers wrote his ETF example into the episode, the showrunner is much more concerned about the potential insurance implications of doing so, cautioning the writers that they cannot use 'anybody real.' He offers, however, a way to graft the anecdotal example onto a matter of dramatic concern: character type. That is, the ETF guys can be characterized as generally crazy, and this would be an innovative characterization in the genre of network police shows. Thus, the showrunner directs his writing staff to translate a particular, 'real-life' officer into a general character type through the use of the 'fiction filter' (DA 20 March 2009).

After a day of breaking 'Injured Cop,' the writers are satisfied with their conceptualization of Bad ETF Sergeant Coombs. In the first beat of the episode, Coombs is shown stealing drug dealers' money while 'clearing the scene' with his ETF team after a big drug bust. Frank learns of Coombs' theft through a whistle-blowing undercover drug squad officer. Frank tells his team to look into Coombs. His assistant comments that while there are only 75 of them on the force, the ETF account for over 50 per cent of the police infractions and citizen complaints handled by the police union (beat sheet[26] 8 June 2009). Recall that this is an insight gleaned from the show's technical consultant, right down to the number of ETF officers. Such a factual comment is meant to build authenticity into the representation of the ETF, by providing viewers with a sense of 'insider' police knowledge. Frank's team, however, cannot pin anything on this particular ETF team: there have been no big bank deposits or unexplained cases of large personal expenditures. Coombs is a 'cowboy who's been in trouble a lot, [l]ike all the nutcases on ETF, [b]ut there's no hint of corruption on this scale' (beat sheet 8 June 2009). The rest of the beats involve Frank's investigation into Coombs' suspected misconduct.

Conclusion

In this chapter, I have documented the heterogeneous sources of knowledge that become inputs into the writers' room of a fictional crime drama. Because the writers' room is conceptualized along the lines of a Latourian laboratory, I have juxtaposed the making of (television) fiction against the making of scientific and legal facts. While the laboratories of science and law are interested in processing and establishing factual knowledge claims, the laboratory of the writers' room is primarily concerned with translating matters of fact into matters of aesthetic and commercial concern. Specifically, *The Bridge* showrunner needs to ensure that the logics of the following matters of concern align with one another: legal E&O insurance requirements, the commercial interests of CBS network executives, and his own creative vision for the series.

In doing so, this chapter illustrates that there does not exist a single over-riding media logic that regulates the production of media representations. As such, it departs from the conclusions drawn by some television production studies scholars, particularly those who have reduced aesthetic decisions to a matter of economics. For example, Gray (1995: 68) asserts that the proliferation of black-oriented situation comedies on American television in the mid to late 1980s was not driven by some noble aesthetic goals on the part of network executives, but simply by economics. These shows were put on the air because they could attract audiences, and consequently could deliver a new category of audience – i.e. the black audience – to advertisers. By reducing the programming content of a television program to its ability to attract audiences, the dramatic series is reduced to the commercial status of an infomercial. Its programming value depends on making audiences sit still long enough to watch the advertisers' commercials. Here, writers' aesthetic concerns are reduced to commercial concerns (as exclusively defined by network executives)[27] as though there were no important discrepancies between them.

In the case of *The Bridge*, there were clear differences: the showrunner originally envisioned a serialized narrative about systemic police corruption and political machination. Presumably, Canadian network executives (CTV) were onboard with this premise, because the series was not re-conceptualized until the inclusion of American network executives (CBS). My point is not to deny the significance of commercial imperatives as important influences on the content and form of a television series. Instead, it is to highlight how the production of a television series is not reducible to a single logic. Although multiple logics are at work within the production process and can be in tension with each other, the act of balancing these logics is not understood by television writers, producers and showrunners as a zero-sum game. As *The Bridge* showrunner (20 March 2009) notes, the balancing of a broadcaster's commercial concerns and a writer's aesthetic concerns is 'a negotiation to a certain extent; but it's not a war, [especially] if you're smart enough as a writer to be able to incorporate those [broadcaster] ideas and go "how do I make that work for what *I* want to do?"'

Thus, in this chapter, I document how an assemblage of multiple logics comes together in the production of a specific episode of a television series. In my analysis, each of the logics – whether legal, creative, or commercial – is from a different actor-network, and more importantly, is considered more than just a different perspective on the production of a single episode. Instead, each logic describes a different reality altogether. This observation is similar to Annemarie Mol's conclusion in her book *The Body Multiple* (2002).

Using an ANT approach, Mol describes the diagnostic and treatment practices for lower limb atherosclerosis. This medical condition is represented differently by different medical practices: it presents as a walking pain in surgery, as narrow or blocked blood vessels in X-ray photos, as white paste scraped out of blood vessels in operation procedures, and as Doppler readings (e.g. representations of increased blood speed) in ultrasounds. From this research, Mol suggests that while the body may be singular in theory, it is multiple in practice. Because there are many body practices, there are many bodies created and imaged from these practices.

Similarly, the emerging 'body' of an episode of *The Bridge* might appear singular in theory, but it is actually multiple in practice. It presents itself as anecdotal facts in the knowledge actor-network (consisting of the technical consultant, newspapers, Internet websites, and fictional texts), as beats in the writing actor-network (consisting of the writing team, the showrunner, the whiteboard, and network executives), and as risky errors and omissions in the legal-insurance actor-network (consisting of insurers, lawyers, and bureaucratic technologies). The episode is made to appear as though it were a singular entity only through the coordinating work done by the showrunner and writing team, in which they assemble and translate these different realities and logics into a single reality. For example, they translate anecdotal stories about police misconduct into plot points in the form of beats. As the reader will recall, beats are the commercial-aesthetic building blocks of storytelling on network television. When taken together, the beats form an episodic story, which is then made to withstand the scrutiny of the showrunner's creative vision, the broadcaster's commercial demands and legal considerations.

As part of this assemblage of logics and realities, law plays a significant role in shaping the content of television representations. While production of culture scholars examine law and regulation as one of the six facets of the production nexus, they have tended to focus on how law provides the ground rules that shape the development of creative fields (Peterson and Anand 2004: 315). In general, these scholars have focused on copyright laws and the notion of intellectual property (e.g. Marshall 2004; Scafidi 2005; Vaidhyanathan 2002; Woodmansee 1998). For example, Griswold (1981) has demonstrated how changes in copyright law influence the kinds of novel that are published. Literary critics tend to remark upon the differences between British and American fictional novels: while American novels focused on the theme of Man against Nature in the nineteenth century, British novels focused on examining domestic manners. While critics saw these differences as representative of enduring differences between American and British culture, Griswold discovered that this was a consequence of nineteenth century American copyright law. Under that copyright law, American publishers preferred works by English authors because they could be sold in the US without paying author's copyright fees. To sell their work, American authors turned to distinctive topics, such as the Man against Nature theme. When the American copyright law of 1909 put American and English authors on the same footing, American authors increasingly published 'English-style' novels successfully.

In television studies, scholars have focused less on copyright laws and more on broadcasting laws. For example, Cantor and Cantor (1992) discuss how the

American Federal Communications Commission's (FCC) de-regulation of the cable industry allowed cable television to develop programming that the broadcasting networks, still chained to FCC regulations, could not. Scholarship on Canadian television has also tended to focus on telecommunications and broadcasting policy (e.g. Babe 1990; Raboy 1990), although it does not usually connect these public policies to actual production practices of specific television programs (Beaty and Sullivan 2006). For example, Raboy (1990) examines the history of Canadian broadcasting policy from 1928 to 1988, but does not provide an account of broadcast programming during this period. Instead, from this history of successive public policies, he argues that the tendency to confuse 'national' and 'public' interests turns Canadian broadcasting into an instrument of state policy.

In contrast to the scholarly focus on copyright law and broadcasting policy, this chapter examines how legal concerns enter into the everyday television production process through insurance. As such, this chapter does not examine how these legal concerns have shaped the development of an entire creative field, but the development of content and form in a particular fictional crime procedural. In the case of *The Bridge*, the legal requirements of E&O insurance influence how writers represent crime and policing in the series. Specifically, representations of police misconduct and corruption need to be situated in a generalized setting and involve archetypal characters. Because this E&O requirement stems from the specific identity of the program's technical consultant, it protects the show's producers from the legal risks associated with the production processes of knowing and representing, such as potential litigation against the production company from viewers. In particular, it allows *The Bridge* writers to use knowledge about police corruption from a high-profile technical consultant as long as they represent that knowledge in universal, fictional terms and get some of the facts of the real-life case deliberately wrong. While criminological and sociolegal scholars tend to complain about what television writers and producers get wrong in their representations of law, this corrective criticism ignores the role law plays in the television writing process. Ironically, law – here understood as a combination of E&O insurance requirements and potential lawsuits – requires television writers to occasionally be factually inaccurate, even when it comes to representations of law itself.

Furthermore, my ANT analysis of the work done in the writers' room suggests that writers know about law and crime in ways that fit with the kind of storytelling format required by network television. In order to create a story that will fit the modular format of storytelling, only certain sources of knowledge are privileged. Particular 'knowledge moves' (Valverde 2007: 83) are required to translate matters of factual knowledge into matters of dramatic concern. Because the technical consultant is the primary means through which *The Bridge* writers know about the world of policing, he inputs his knowledge into the writers' room. Depending on who is playing the role of technical consultant, the kind of knowledge inputted into the television show already has a distinctive content and format: for example, while he discusses procedural technicalities in a matter-of-fact kind of way, BC formats his anecdotal knowledge of discrete and corrupt police units as extraordinary exemplars. This is already a particular knowledge move that begins the process of applying the 'fiction filter' (DA 20 March 2009) to the writers' sources of knowledge, making local (Torontonian) insights into universal stories. While the fiction filter is a legal requirement, its knowledge moves also effectively transport viewers into another time and place (Latour 2010: 273): the contemporary Big Urban City where the characters and settings are meant to be generic and archetypal. Specifically, the filter transforms local, 'real' individuals into character types (Bad ETF Sergeant), which is made possible because the specific facts about the individual (tattooed, white supremacist) only matter if they are conceptualized as essential to the story being told (*the* matter of concern). In this case, the tattoos become a symbolic shorthand for the rogue, risk-taking subculture of an ETF unit, which is itself a matter of dramatic concern precisely because the unit's sergeant is the prime suspect and antagonist in Frank Leo's investigation.

In studying the knowledge actor-networks of science and law, these actor-networks can be reconstructed because both of these modern institutions create permanent traces of their knowledge inputs through their production of texts and use of citations. These permanent traces are available to scholars because law and science 'remember' primarily through pen and paper. In contrast, the knowledge of television writers takes the form of orally told anecdotes. As the 'style of [television] industry speech' (Gitlin 1985: 14), anecdotes circulate without leaving permanent traces. As a result of this lack of documentation, television writers do not always know or remember the exact sources of their own knowledge. Although texts are eventually produced by television writers, they only serve to further distance the show's knowledge from its sources, as the fiction filter is applied repeatedly on each draft of the script. As such, modular episodes of network television dramas have a memory analogous to the whiteboard: the beats and stories written upon it are destroyed as soon as they cease to concern the writers. For each new episode, the slate is wiped clean and each story needs to be broken anew.

Notes

1 All references to initials refer to comments made by the showrunner (DA), writers (MP, FT, MG, KD, and MJ) and the technical consultant (BC) of *The Bridge*.
2 The showrunner appears to be a role that is specific to North American television production, as it is still an unfamiliar term in other countries, such as England (Cornea 2009: 121). As a recognized role in scripted television production, it appeared much earlier in the US than it did in Canada. While the showrunner first appeared in the late 1980s as the writing executive producer on an American television series (Stepakoff 2007), it was not until 2007 that the Writers Guild of Canada finally created the Showrunner Award. The award is meant to celebrate the writer/producer who holds the creative vision for a television series and who oversees the creative decisions for the production from development to post-production. This is in contrast to executive producers who primarily oversee the production's financial decisions. If the showrunner is understood to simply be the person who 'runs the show' – that is, is responsible for

the day-to-day operations of a television series – then the term is still being disputed between writer-producers and non-writer producers in the Canadian television industry. More importantly for this chapter, the showrunner runs the writers' room.
3 Numbers also count in the television industry, both in terms of the production's financial budget and television ratings. However, the latter does not count in the writers' room, especially for a television show that has not yet aired. While the production budget needs to be taken into account, its influence is most clearly felt in revisions of the production draft of the script (i.e. a script that is primarily read in terms of the production budget).
4 The staff-writing process of episodic television is primarily an American innovation. In contrast to film scriptwriters, television writers cannot be solitary creatures, and are forced instead to work with one another. For more information on the writers' room in terms of practical advice on being a staff writer, see Laurence Meyers' *Inside the Writers' Room* (2010). From interviews with established network TV writers, Meyers provides aspiring television writers with answers to the following questions: how does one become a staff writer? How does one become a better writer? How does one break into the business? For a more academic account of the dynamics in the writers' room, the reader will have to wait since there is no published research on this matter to date.
5 Similarly, the writers' room of *24*, a popular American television drama about how special agent Jack Bauer deals with multiple terrorist plots, is described as a room that resembles a 'suburban basement' in a 'building [that] provides no clue that *24* is one of the most successful – and profitable – shows on television' (Berenson 2 April 2010).
6 'Network' is my shorthand reference to a commercial broadcasting network that airs episodes for a mass audience. The narrative for television shows on these networks is cut up by commercial breaks. This is in contrast to the television format of shows on premium cable networks, where the uninterrupted narrative is meant to intrigue a narrow, niche audience market.
7 Some shows, like Joss Whedon's *Dollhouse* (2009–2010), have been written with fewer than five acts. According to Golick (2008), the show has a four-act structure whereby an opening teaser is followed by three acts. Recently, however, there have been more commercial breaks inserted into network television dramas to counter the cost of their production due to the overall decline in advertising revenue faced by most large American and Canadian commercial television networks. As a result, it has become conventional for shows to have five to six acts per episode.
8 This is particularly the case with police shows, like *The Bridge*. As a result, these shows tend to have shorter scripts overall. For example, *The Bridge*'s scripts tend to be around 50–55 pages long. More lawyer-based shows tend to have longer scripts because the additional dialogue compensates for the fewer number of action sequences. In fact, *Law and Order* is reported to have longer than average scripts, running 60–70 pages long.
9 This is in keeping with Bordwell and Thompson's (2004: 71) story-plot distinction. They define the episode's plot as all the scenes that will be visibly and audibly presented to television viewers. The episode's story is the chronological reconstruction of all the events in the narrative, both explicitly and implicitly alluded to by the plot. Thus, there can be more to the story than is represented in the plot.
10 Being an American/Canadian co-production, *The Bridge* has potentially two sets of audiences to please – one American, the other Canadian – as well as a potentially larger audience than if it were simply a Canadian show. For Canadian television dramas, it is considered successful if the Canadian viewing audience is above one million. For an American television drama on CBS, the American viewing audience ranges from

12 to 15 million viewers. Being a co-production, *The Bridge*'s producers and writers also need to satisfy two 'masters' – CBS and CTV, but in exchange for this 'dilemma,' the show has much better production values than most Canadian programs.

11 *The Bridge*'s representation of a power structure in which the 'brass' of the local police force is closely embroiled in local, municipal politics is a particularly North American one. Mawby (1990) highlights how the development of other police forces (e.g., under the European continental model) was organized under the direction of a centralized, monarchical system of government. For example, in Denmark, the Commissioner of police and the chief constables are not appointed by the mayor or local municipal council, but appointed by the Queen or on recommendation from the Department of Justice. These appointments are strictly on the basis of merit and seniority. However, *The Bridge* producers' assumption of universality in their representation of the policing organization, despite its North American bias, mirrors that of academic researchers. Brogden (1987) finds academic explanations the the development of policing to be similarly ethnocentric with their almost exclusive focus on Anglo-American patterns of policing.

12 It is possible and plausible that there is a set of similar policing practices and organizations that circulate between the police forces of various countries, making them 'universal' in the sense that they are no longer tied to a particular context of practice. While the American police have sought to teach other countries' police forces about their specific policing tactics, they have also imitated strategies of policing developed in other countries. More recently, North America has embraced the notion of community policing, which was originally a policing practice particular to East Asian countries (Marenin 1996). The circulation (import and export) of various 'successful' police practices between countries is made possible by international conferences held by police chiefs (International Association of Chiefs of Police) and other police executives.

13 In contrast to purchasing E&O insurance during the pre-production phase of making a television series, film productions might wait to purchase E&O prior to making their distribution deal, particularly if it is a low-budget, independently made film. The need for E&O is also often ignored in films made for Europe, but is demanded by North American film purchasers (Rosenthal 2007: 136–7).

14 Film and television production is a risky venture that is heavily regulated by insurance, which is not surprising since insurance emerged as an institution that governs risks with financial implications (Ericson, Doyle, and Barry 2003).

15 For example, a viewer's response to the premiere of *The Bridge*'s pilot was posted on the Internet Movie Database (imdb.com), emphasizing how tired he/she was of the de-Canadianization of Canadian television shows. The viewer urges producers to get some 'Canuck pride' and to accept Canada on both sides of the camera.

16 If the show's producers had decided to represent police corruption in the specific city of Toronto, it might have incited a lawsuit from the city itself. If the City of Toronto (as a municipal corporation) decides to sue the Toronto-based production company, it might be possible for the City to sue on the grounds of pecuniary losses suffered as a result of damage to the city's business reputation (e.g. downturn in tourism in Toronto as a result of foreign tourists no longer seeing the city as safe due to representations of the city's police corruption). However, two recent Ontario trial court decisions suggest that freedom of expression, as protected by the Canadian Charter of Rights and Freedoms, also protects citizens' criticism of government bodies as an absolute privilege (*Halton Hills (Town) v. Kerouac* 2006; *Montague (Township) v. Page* 2006). In short, municipal corporations do not have a right to sue their critics for defamation. It is not

clear, though, how these court decisions, triggered by complaints from private citizens about their local public officials, applies to a television/entertainment production company.

17 If writers are using a news story with an editorial bent, in which the journalist has asserted a particular argument and re-arranged the facts to illustrate that argument, intellectual property rights might be violated if writers use exactly the same telling of the facts.

18 For some American television series (e.g. *Hawaii 5-0*) where filming occurs at some distance (e.g. in a different state) from the writers' room, the technical consultants receive calls or emails from writers. Production meetings are held through Skype conferences.

19 These are the initial names given to this episode's guest characters (i.e. characters that are integral to the episode's plot, but are not going to continually appear in the series).

20 The ethics of creating reality TV or docudramas (see Nichols 2001), premised on events in actual 'reality,' are very different from those used to create a fictional television drama. The latter does not concern itself with the potential issue of exploiting or further harming victims (e.g. interviewing the families of a murder victim for the purpose of entertaining a mass audience) since all victims are fictional. As a result, the writers of *The Bridge* have 'killed' and 'injured' many police officers, averaging about one to two officers per episode.

21 While the sources of knowledge are never explicitly acknowledged in the episode's story, the sources are retained by the writers for insurance purposes.

22 To date, there has been no published paper on police technical consultants used in the making of television drama series. It is not clear how frequently technical consultants are used in crime procedurals, although almost every (entertainment) news report about a crime procedural on North American television tends to include some mention of a technical consultant. Attempts to determine the number of technical consultants might be hindered by the consultants' anonymity, particularly since some of them choose to remain uncredited for their work. In contrast, some researchers have been able to determine the identity of scientific technical consultants involved in the making of Hollywood science fiction films precisely because they are credited (see Frank 2003; Kirby 2003).

23 To become script consultants of TV medical dramas, the American Medical Association (AMA) teamed up with producers of such shows (e.g. *Dr Kildare*, and *Ben Casey*) in the early 1960s. While the AMA used this liaison to secure popular consent for its profession during a time of growing national debate over the merits of private health care, the producers of medical dramas used the AMA's 'seal of approval' to legitimate their program as a form of high 'science' with pedagogical value (Turow 1997).

24 Crime docudrama producers also tend to favour retired police officers as interviewees because there is less conflict of interest in their participation in the program's production (JH 16 June 2008). In contrast to police consultants, science consultants are still working in their field of expertise (Frank 2003) because their expertise is derived from continued scientific practice. Moreover, scientific practice is not bound by the same obligation of confidentiality that tends to characterize on-going police work.

25 I have fictionalized and modified the excerpted anecdotal story so as to avoid implicating any particular active-duty ETF officer. This story was fictionalized in a slightly different way in Lam (2012), although both fictionalized accounts retain the original gist of the anecdote.

26 The beat sheet contains all the beats from the whiteboard in a single word-processing document.

27 Such a perspective buys into the idea that network executives know their audiences, and know what they want. As Ohmann (1996b) notes, marketers can know who consumes a product and in what contexts, and if the consumer liked or disliked the product. However, they do not empirically know anything about people's deeper desires, needs and values. For that kind of knowledge, they rely on intuition (for a similar argument about network executives, see Gitlin 1983).

Chapter 4

The case of the missing 'bad apples': transforming 'Injured Cop' into the 'Unguarded Moment'

As the last chapter was interested in documenting the writers' room as a laboratory in which the world was brought into its narrow walls in particular ways, this chapter is interested in following the ways in which the writers pump that transformed world back out of their offices through the production of texts. While the last chapter documented an episode's formation, this chapter examines its *transformations* across multiple story documents. In so doing, we will embark on the case of the missing 'bad apples.' In tracing the transformations of the episode, the 'bad apples' – Bad Sergeant Coombs and Bad Deputy Chief Cafferty – disappear in the process of revising the story documents for the episode: Where did they go? When did they go missing and how? Were they 'killed' and if so, by whom or what? We will discover that Coombs and Cafferty were collectively assassinated. Their 'deaths' were 'built right into the nature of things' (M. Giraud quoted in Latour 1996: 10).

By pursuing the case of the missing 'bad apples,' I will demonstrate that neither observation in the writers' room nor of the final product (here, the final revised script and actual episode, both entitled 'The Unguarded Moment') captures all of the details and elements that characterize the story at various stages of development and revision. A large part of writing a television episode involves re-writing. Each phase of re-writing is yet another experiment in how to conceive of the story, its characters and the plot. Some of these experiments fail while others succeed. Here, 'success' is measured by the revision's ability to withstand various stages of approval by various stakeholders, such as other writers, the showrunner(s), networks, producers, etc. As such, the final product gives perhaps a better sense of all the initial labour – especially in terms of conceptualizing police corruption in the writers' room – that was lost in subsequent revisions and the amount of labour needed for making those revisions, both of which are also missing from content analyses of the final product. These content analyses fail to capture changes in representations of crime because they proceed under several erroneous assumptions. First and foremost, there is the underlying assumption that the initial conceptualization *is* an accurate reflection of the finished product (e.g. Byers and Johnson 2009: xxi; Rapping 2003: 264–6), which is itself related to the presumption that the created texts are much more stable than they actually are. However, the televisual text does not stabilize until it is fixed by the final cut of the episode that airs on a broadcast television network, and is consequently consumed by a mass audience.

In making assumptions of representational stability, scholars who undertake such content analyses implicitly treat the script as though it were an *intermediary*. That is, they treat it as something that transports meaning without transformation, such that the inputs can be used to define the outputs (Latour 2007: 39). Despite a conceptual separation between a story's conception and execution, the script is treated like a product that doubles as an accurate blueprint for shooting (see Maras 2009: 22) when the scholar assumes that the script is written and shot as planned (i.e. the television episode is accurately rendered in images as originally rendered in words by the script).

Instead of concentrating on a single script or final product, it would be more accurate to recognize that writers create not a single script but multiple story documents over the course of writing and re-writing a single television episode. Moreover, it would be more fruitful to treat these multiple story documents as *mediators* (Latour 2007: 39). In contrast to static or definitive texts, these story documents are conceptualized as transitional texts that transform and modify the meanings of representations over the course of the production process (Maras, 2009: 6). By understanding story documents as mediators, it will give us a better sense of how textual transformations are connected to the different audiences that are mobilized at each stage of the revision process. While television writers and producers do create texts for an audience, that audience is not ultimately the consumer audience,[1] as supposed by academics undertaking content analyses of the final product. Instead, as Muriel Cantor (1971) argues, television dramas are created for an initial and actual (as opposed to imagined) audience composed of network officials, insurers and the show's writers and producers.

For an untried show like *The Bridge*, the consumer audience is, as the showrunner puts it:

> always a crapshoot. You don't know what the audience wants. No one – you know [. . .], William Goldman wrote [. . .] [in the book *Adventures in the Screen Trade*], 'the first thing you have to remember about Hollywood or television is [. . .] that nobody knows anything; but they all believe they know what they're doing.' So when a broadcaster tells me 'well, I know my audience,' it's not [true]. You only know them by luck, by 'I lucked into that.' But if you were to ask them what were the elements that you put together to create that, that you knew the audience would love that, they can't answer that question.
>
> (DA 20 March 2009)

Unlike the unknowable consumer audience, it is quite clear what the audience of network executives, insurers, writers and producers want. For such an audience, the story documents are mediators because they are meant to mediate between the different (commercial/artistic/legal) contexts and (writing/production/broadcasting) processes in and through which they work.

The study of an episode's textual transformations is also important because they illustrate that the ideological[2] underpinning of an episode – in this case, what it means to make 'bad apples' and 'criminals' – is not decided upon by a single authorial actor. While some television studies have focused on the genius of specific showrunners and their creative ideas (e.g. Mann 2009), it is not the case that the showrunner is able to create and rewrite an episodic story without an actor-network composed of other writers, network executives, producers and screenwriting software. While the last chapter documented the assembling of an episodic story, this chapter examines the processes of re-assembling such a story, by extending the writing actor-network of the last chapter to include a story-revision actor-network.

During the process of *re-aligning* interests among various actors, the meaning of a 'bad apple' becomes the outcome of behind-the-scene negotiations between various stakeholders. In taking this perspective, the process of conceptualization is not reduced to a single moment, but instead spread over the entire production process as various and multiple 'authors' are asked to weigh in on the meaning of the 'bad apple.' While there have been scholarly studies on Hollywood storytelling (e.g. Maras 2009; Thompson 1999) and hundreds of manuals on screenwriting (e.g. Douglas 2005), these studies only privilege the process of writing. In contrast, we will be focusing on *re*-writing as a significant meaning-making practice in television production.

As a means of documenting the process of revision, what follows is a frame-by-frame analysis of the transformations in story documents associated with a single episode of *The Bridge*. Such an analysis stands in stark contrast to both the academic literature on crime, media and culture, and DVD extras that feature writers and producers reflecting upon their work. These academic analyses and DVD special features are able to provide a 'big picture' of the television series and its creative and ideological direction, precisely because they are created at both a spatial and temporal distance from the production process. Once removed from the production process, writers and producers are able to act like academic critics by providing detached contemplation and rationalizations for why production events happened in the way that they did. They are able to comment on an over-arching progression of ideas and representations, which appears to them primarily in retrospect. What these *ad hoc* discussions fail to capture, however, is the messiness – that is, the myopic, complex, fragmentary and sometimes incoherent processes – of rewriting and revising.

A frame-by-frame analysis, however, captures part of the messiness by recognizing that writers think in terms of momentary frames, whereby they create 'in the moment' and are asked to revise various story documents under tight deadlines. As the showrunner of *The Bridge* (22 July 2012) explains:

> I was in a situation where things were changing so quickly [. . .] because of network notes, because of where [network executives] wanted to take the

show, because we were rushed into production. I didn't have time to rework things the way I wanted to.

As a result of the fast pace of production and revision, a neat and tidy, pre-existing and stable 'big picture' for an episodic story does not necessarily exist while in the midst of the production process. It does not exist because there is often not enough time for writers and producers to engage in in-depth contemplation of the changes that are being made on the fly.

The messiness of the story revision process is also a by-product of the collaborative nature of television production, which entails the coordination of activities of hundreds of people. Consequently, such messiness reflects the fluidity of both the fictional world being created as well as the real-life production world: the fictional world is constantly being modified according to changes stemming from production concerns raised by various actors in the story-revision actor-network. Through a frame-by-frame analysis of numerous revisions made during the storytelling process, we can acknowledge that the story's final configuration came into being only through a particular assemblage of specific concerns and actors. With another assemblage, the story could have taken another course and representations could have been differently imagined and realized.

What follows is a documentation of the changes made to an episode of *The Bridge* whereby the representation of 'bad apples' is amended with each subsequent revision. In following the trail of these 'bad apples' and their ultimate fate, I have written this chapter in a way that approximates the experience of the revision process for writers, one in which writers do not know from the outset where the story will take them because the story is constantly being adjusted to the demands made by various actors. As a result, I have refused to reduce and simplify the sometimes tedious changes to the story through the provision of a clean overview. Instead, I have built the experience of surprise, often felt by writers, into the narrative of how the story of 'Injured Cop' was eventually transformed into 'The Unguarded Moment.'

Investigative procedure

Before we undertake our investigation into the case of the missing 'bad apples,' I would like to delineate our investigative procedure. In the last chapter, we observed the *thinking workshop* of the writers' room, where the oral storytelling of anecdotes and collective thinking through the story beat-by-beat characterized the work done in that space. As we move into the *writing workshop* embodied by the writers' offices in this chapter, we need to be mindful that we cannot actually lurk behind the writers as they silently type away at their computers. Instead, our investigation requires that we enter the textual universe created by these writers, where we trace the broken story of 'Injured Cop' through its written story documents. Here, a story document is simply a written text that documents the episode's story at a particular stage of revision. Specifically, we will trace the disappearance of the 'bad apples' through the paper trail left by beat sheets, drafts, outlines, memos, and production drafts. In so doing, we will treat the representation of police corruption as an 'actor' that we can follow through the writers' imagination and through story documents.

As we carry out our investigation, we will learn about these different story documents and examine how these different texts, operating as actants (Latour 1987), interact with each other. In actor–network theory, an actant is a material entity (or a human person or group) that takes on form, definition and facticity only under the following conditions: 1) it enters into an alliance with a spokesperson since actants cannot represent themselves; and 2) this alliance is able to withstand 'trials of strength,' which might include hostile attacks meant to bring about its dissolution (Latour 1987, 2007). In this chapter, we will consider the story documents as actants, represented by particular spokespersons (writers), and made to withstand trials (various stages of approval) during which they might be transformed by various 'attackers' (network executives, producers, etc.). Because Latour (2007: 54) borrows the term 'actant' from Greimas' narrative theory (Greimas and Courtés 1982), the term is especially relevant when we apply it to a study of narrative through our examination of *story* documents. For Greimas (1982: 5), 'actants' were idealized or generalized characters (e.g. the 'hero' or 'villain') that were used to construct stories. These actants went through different ordeals (or trials) in the stories, and were consequently transformed by the process. In our case, our archetypal 'bad apples' did not survive all the ordeals that came their way.

While all but one of these story documents (the final revised production draft on which the aired episode is based) will remain unknown to the public, we have the privilege of sorting through these various documents. Although story documents for a single episode accumulate and are stored in a file during the show's production, this accumulation is very different from that of the 'ripening file' in (French) administrative law. To understand this difference, it might be useful to first explain what Latour means by 'the ripening file.'

In his study of the Conseil d'Etat, Latour (2010) immersed himself in the textual universe in which administrative counsellors/lawyers produce legal writings from other non-legal writings, and he does so by following the process through which legal files are made (i.e. how documents become legal and are arranged in a file folder). The file is a visible, material thing that the ethnographer can locate and trace, and is used to organize all the activity of the Conseil d'Etat (Latour 2010: 70). By beginning with 'the stamps, elastic bands, paper clips, and other office paraphernalia which are the indispensable tools of cases,' Latour (2010: 71) follows the (sometimes quite literal and material) making of such a file, in order to examine the particular movement of legal work, a movement that includes the arrangement of quotations (textual conditions) and folders (material conditions). For example, he follows the inauspicious beginning of a citizen's complaint arriving as a letter at the Conseil d'Etat in the mailroom to the letter's passage into the Conseil's office where it is given a number for office use. He details how much of the

Conseil's initial labour is devoted to gathering evidence to transform various documents into a legal case. Not all the documents in the file, however, are legal in nature, even though they allow for legal judgment to be rendered (Latour 2010: 76). For example, in the case of a skiing accident, police reports, witness statements, medical reports, geographical reports of the ski hill, insurance reports, and meteorological reports need to be gathered and put into a file before the legal case can proceed to court. Yet this process of gathering documents takes time, and the files need to 'ripen' (i.e. thicken with the relevant documents) on wooden shelves until they are ready for use in court. Latour (2010: 82) likens this 'ripening' process to 'the same way that our grandmothers slowly let their apples turn ripe – and sometimes go bad – during winter on wooden racks.'

Although we are interested in 'bad apples' in the sense of representations of corrupt police officers, we are not interested in the 'ripened' files of administrative law, but the idea of 'ripening.' While files are left to 'ripen' through accumulation in the Conseil d'Etat, story files in television production 'ripen' through the process of revision. What we can also learn from the above example is Latour's method of investigation. He studies the material basis of making law, which initially requires an examination of how its files are made and transported throughout the Conseil d'Etat. Similarly, we will treat story documents as the visible, material bases of making television dramas, and a police drama in particular. We will examine how they are 'transported' or circulated to various stakeholders in the show's production for comment and/or approval.

However, unlike the physical file of administrative law, the file of story documents is primarily electronic[3] as the story documents themselves often take the form of either a word-processing document (.doc) or a portable document format (.pdf). While these formats allow for convenient document exchange between various collaborators and stakeholders, particularly ones that are spatially distant from the actual production site (e.g. CBS network executives are located in Los Angeles), we cannot follow these computer-based documents around the production site as Latour follows the documents that make up a file across the physical space of the Conseil d'Etat. While Latour traces the multiple 'inputs' needed to create a legal file, story documents in television production are better understood as successive and multiple storytelling 'outputs' of a single episode. At any given moment, there is only one definitive draft of the script used for production discussions, and as such can be said to operate as the document on which all decision-making is based. However, as we will soon see, scripts are revised at a much faster pace than legal precedents, which is yet another reason why the script revision process dispenses with any sluggish means for document circulation, such as any time-consuming attempts to mail documents between production sites. In the linear and sequential revision process, the story itself 'ripens' as each subsequent story document replaces, supersedes, and renders obsolete all of the previous story documents in their entirety.

In pursuing our investigation into the disappearance of our particular 'bad apples,' we will treat the story documents as our primary informants. They will provide us with clues to the 'passions and politics and [. . .] calculations' (Latour 1996: viii) of *The Bridge* production's human actors.[4] We will also consider these story documents as suspects, because they 'know' how and when our 'bad apples' went missing and are partially complicit in their disappearance. They are considered suspect because each story document *is* an opportunity for our 'bad apples' to go missing, capturing some of the means and motives behind their disappearance.

Before we line up our textual 'suspects' for a series of in-depth interrogations, it would be helpful to briefly introduce each of them as we establish a timeline for the appearance and disappearance of our 'bad apples.' By 'disappearance,' I mean the point at which the characters in question, specifically Bad ETF Sergeant Coombs and Deputy Chief Cafferty, are either removed from the episode completely, or transformed to such an extent that they are rendered unrecognizable during the rewriting process. It should also be noted that we will not discuss the entire collection of story documents for the episode, but only those that contain significant changes in the representation of police corruption.

Suspect #1: The Beat Sheet Entitled 'Hostage' (released 8 June 2009)

Written after the process of breaking story, the beat sheet is a short word-processing document (eight pages in length) that breaks the episode down to its essential beats across five acts. Its telegraphic descriptions of each beat are meant to convey the basic information needed to comprehend what action happens when, in order to properly plot the events in the episode. There is no dialogue, only brief descriptions of setting. According to the beat sheet, Deputy Chief Cafferty was seen having dinner one night in a restaurant that later becomes the setting of a robbery and hostage taking. Under the Deputy Chief's command, Bad ETF Sergeant Coombs arrives on the scene and was last seen attempting to salvage their money laundering operation at the restaurant.

Suspect #2: Network Outline Entitled 'The Unguarded Moment' (released 17 June 2009)

The network outline is a slightly longer word-processing document (14 pages in length) that outlines all the scenes in the episode, elaborating on the descriptions provided in the beat sheet with full sentences. The first inklings of dialogue appear amongst the described scenes. This story document is circulated to network executives for approval, and should give the executives a sense of the content and shape of the episode. In the network outline, Coombs and Cafferty are first spotted exchanging dirty money in an isolated area of the city. Both are spotted at one point or another at the same restaurant, worrying about their money-laundering operation.

Suspect #3: Network Draft Entitled 'The Unguarded Moment' (released 12 July 2009)

As a draft of the entire script (58 pages), each character's dialogue is now scripted, and descriptions are now made brief and confined to describing setting and non-verbal actions performed by screen actors. This draft is also circulated to network executives for approval of the episode, and for inspection of 'problematic' representations. In the network draft, Cafferty goes missing. Without Cafferty, Sergeant Coombs has transformed into a good, morally upright sergeant. No longer working as a 'bad apple,' he arrives at the restaurant hostage-taking scenario and strategically plans a way to get the hostages out.

Suspect #4: Full Pink Production Draft Entitled 'The Unguarded Moment' (released 26 July 2009)

The full pink production draft can be considered a shooting script (54 pages in length). As a production draft, it has been read by producers for budgetary constraints and approved. In this draft, Coombs also goes missing.

From this reconstructed timeline, it appears that our first step would be to investigate the restaurant at which both Cafferty and Coombs were last seen. Were they doing anything that precipitated their disappearance? Did they leave any clues as to their whereabouts at the scene of their disappearance? In order to answer these questions, we need to visit this restaurant before the trail goes cold.

Getting a clue: entering the kitchen

In *The Making of Law*, Bruno Latour (2010: 22) enters 'one of the kitchens of law, not in the manner of a health and safety inspector checking on hygiene standards, but like a gourmet keen to understand the recipes of the chefs.' In our last chapter, we entered one of the 'kitchens' of television production, in order to understand the chefs' recipes (e.g. the beat/act formula for a modular episode of television). We considered what local ingredients, such as the technical consultant's procedural and anecdotal knowledge, were used to inform the 'universal' recipe that ought to be made 'palatable' for mass consumption (DA 20 March 2009). In this chapter, we examine the chefs' (writers') actual 'recipes' and how they are governed by the practice of 'health and safety inspectors.' As actual health and safety inspectors enter the space of the kitchen to ensure that it meets certain hygiene standards, network 'inspectors' ensure that any 'dirt' (in the form of graphic images or language) are scrubbed from the space of the 'recipe' (script). Because *The Bridge* is an American (CBS)/Canadian (CTV) co-production,[5] the show has potentially two sets of 'inspectors,' and we will examine the 'recipes' that they have inspected and to what effect. But I digress from the actual reason why our investigation begins at the restaurant's kitchen: we are here to discover why Coombs and Cafferty were at the restaurant. They were not here in search of recipes, but of money.

As 'head chef' of *The Bridge*'s recipe-making kitchen, showrunner DA explains why Deputy Chief Cafferty would periodically visit the restaurant:

> [The] restaurant is a money drop-off place for a banker, likely a foreign banker. It used to be Hong Kong, but no more. It's now more likely to be Brussels.

> The restaurant is a way-station for money. It cannot itself launder the money, which is why a bank is needed. At a restaurant, [hypothetically speaking,] I [would] be able to put a few grand in the till to launder but not the million dollar sums in the episode. The Deputy Chief gets $10 grand; the suitcase carriers each get $20 grand. The money goes out of the country in suitcases of $1–2 million each. It's not illegal to do this, [though] you can get into a fuckload of trouble now. Because of 9/11, this has gotten more difficult. [The money] could be headed towards Singapore. After the money is delivered to the restaurant, the money is taken through the restaurant's back-way and into a van, where it eventually is taken to a fancy hotel room. Don't ask me how I know this. It was once described to me.
>
> (DA 2 June 2009)

Thus, the showrunner explains the restaurant setting to the other writers in a functional sense: the restaurant's function is to serve as a transitional holding space for 'dirty' money before it is transported elsewhere. From this perspective, it makes little difference whether this way-station for money needs to be set at a restaurant or whatever other shooting location the producers can afford. As such, one writer cautions the other writers to be prepared if producers want to later change the location from a restaurant to a real-estate office (MG 2 June 2009), as money can just as easily be laundered through the real estate business. Yet something about setting the crime at a restaurant captures the writers' imagination, and this setting provides shape and content to the crime itself. The restaurant-as-crime-scene, as much as motives, perpetrators and circumstances, plays an important role in the construction of (fictional) crime realities (Kalifa 2004: 175), by making crime intelligible to the writers in a particular way.

Through the writing and rewriting process, three different kinds of restaurant are imagined by the writers as the crime scene setting, each making the crimes of police corruption and money laundering intelligible in different ways. We will examine each of these restaurants in turn as they are envisioned through various story documents in order to analyze how these settings are related to the appearance and disappearance of our 'bad apples': 1) the 'nice' Italian steakhouse restaurant, 2) the Mediterranean restaurant, and 3) the breakfast diner.

The 'nice' Italian steakhouse restaurant: the beat sheet (8 June 2009)

The beat sheet is the first written story document produced immediately after breaking story in the writers' room, making it a textual version of the writers' collaborative imagining of the story and crime in question. If we recall from the previous chapter, the episode's story is as follows: police union boss Frank Leo attempts to rescue a police officer who is injured and taken hostage in a restaurant during a robbery by two drug-addicted thugs. During his intervention into this restaurant hostage-taking scenario, Frank learns that the restaurant is the setting for a money-laundering operation whereby Bad Sergeant ETF Coombs and Deputy Chief Cafferty launder confiscated drug money. There are two crimes in this story, both of which converge at the restaurant setting, partially as a result of serendipity and partially as a result of the complicity of restaurant staff: 1) robbery and hostage-taking done by civilian thugs with some help from a restaurant server, and 2) police corruption facilitated by the restaurateur.

For the rest of the episode, much of Frank's investigation involves following the trail of 'dirty money.' This trail is conceived as linear, providing Frank with 'investigative lines' to pursue (MJ[6] 2 June 2009) and 'lines of information' to corroborate (MP 2 June 2009) through interrogation. The linearity of investigation parallels the linearity of the evidentiary chain of continuity, which needs to be maintained as part of typical police procedure (MP 2 June 2009). As a consequence of this linearity, the chain of knowledge linking suspects together, be they police or civilian, is also assumed to be linear, which in turn has certain effects. That is, the writers' assumption of linearity is quite useful in the context of investigating police corruption because it highlights how the police are hierarchically organized in a linear chain of command. For example, Frank's investigation into Bad ETF Sergeant Coombs unearths the fact that he was sent to the restaurant hostage-taking scenario by 'somebody in the [police] brass [which allows Frank] to track [the direct order for Coombs' presence on scene] to who sent him in' (MP 2 June 2009).

Moreover, the conceptualization of investigative linearity highlights its implicit analogy to the act of fishing through the notion of fishing lines cast into a stream of suspects, here envisioned as embodiments of particular kinds of information that allow the writers to structure their mystery plot. While Frank is not embarking on a 'fishing expedition' through an open-ended, unlawful investigation of suspects for the purpose of discovering damaging or embarrassing information, the writers want to create an investigative line that allows him to go 'upstream and into the police department, to the deputy chief or whoever dropped [the money] off' (MP 2 June 2009) at the restaurant, rather than 'downstream' to low-level money-laundering civilian operatives. Within the framework of a fishing analogy, Frank's investigation initially nets him Bad Sergeant Coombs in order to bait the 'bigger fish' (beat sheet 8 June 2009: 6) embodied by the Deputy Chief. Consequently, Frank's investigative line in this particular episode provides a set-up for a larger serialized narrative about police corruption. As episode 12, the penultimate episode in an ordered lot of 13, the writers want to pursue an inquiry that would implicate a high-ranking police administrator (i.e. Deputy Chief Cafferty), rather than the corrupt frontline police officers that have been featured in the majority of the season's episodes. By ensuring that Frank finally realizes that corruption within the police force is 'bigger than [he] thinks' (MJ 2 June 2009), the writers turn their protagonist's attention towards the 'brass wall' itself. In attempting to take down both Coombs and Cafferty in this episode, Frank has antagonized the entire 'brass wall,' which will come after him in full force in the season finale.

As previously mentioned, the 'brass wall' refers to an old boys' network that connects together high-ranking police administrators (police department), city politicians (the mayor's office), and prosecutors (the Attorney General's office). In this episode, viewers would finally get to see a corrupt member of the 'brass wall,' and this sighting is tied to the restaurant setting. At the top of Act Two, in the interior of a 'nice restaurant' (beat sheet 8 June 2009), writers establish the character of Deputy Chief Cafferty as a grey-haired man eating dinner with a companion. He excuses himself and heads to the restaurant's back room with a large briefcase, handing it over to the restaurateur. The briefcase is opened, and shown to viewers as being full of 'hundreds of thousands of dollars' (beat sheet 8 June 2009). Cafferty is dropping off the drug money for it to be transported out of the country by the restaurateur. So, how does the 'nice restaurant' as crime scene contextualize the crime of money-laundering?

The 'nice restaurant' is imagined in the writers' room as an Italian restaurant, which is still standing in Harlem, New York City:

> This is from way back in the day. [. . .] For many years before it was gentrified [. . .] it was an Italian restaurant in the middle of this real rough gang area. [. . .] Every night there was this major political figure, legislator, major showbiz figure, major crime figure and major police figure, too, I think [dining in the restaurant]. What happened was one night these two guys come in and hold the place up: 'Give me your fucking money!' And they're going behind the cash register, and [restaurateur Frankie] says, 'Hey, I got a box full of money here behind the counter. You might want to take it.' He [robber] says, 'Are you crazy?' Frankie says, 'Spend it fast, though.' They found these guys [robbers] all over the five boroughs the next morning.
>
> (MP 2 June 2009)

From the anecdote, we get a better sense of what the imagined Italian restaurant means to the writers and to the story. It is a hobnobbing place for various members of the 'brass wall,' which extends beyond criminal justice and political figures and into associations with organized crime. It is imagined as an explicitly Italian restaurant in which powerful figures gather because their safety is guaranteed, despite the restaurant's location in a 'rough gang area,' by the restaurateur's ties to the Italian Mafia. While robbers might steal money from diners and the restaurateur, the Mafia punishes such theft with execution, sending a clear message of general deterrence to other would-be robbers. More importantly, the Mafia's connection to the 'brass wall' is highlighted by writers through restaurant setting. The setting of the Italian restaurant implicitly suggests that Deputy Chief Cafferty's money-laundering operation is partially facilitated by the Italian mob. By choosing an ethnic restaurant as crime scene, the writers implicate a particular kind of 'ethnic' criminality, drawing on the familiar pop cultural association between Italians and organized crime that was most famously constituted and disseminated in Francis Ford Coppola's (1972) film *The Godfather*.[7]

In addition to imagining an ethnic restaurant as the setting for the crime scene, the writers conceive of the restaurant as being a 'steakhouse' (KD 8 June 2009). The writers' choice of steakhouse[8] serves to highlight a certain kind of masculinity[9] that underlies both the conceptualization of the 'brass wall' and the ETF police subculture. The steakhouse is imagined as an elite dining club primarily for an old boys' network, thereby allowing the writers to draw on the link between (hegemonic) masculinity and meat consumption already found in pop culture (Adams 2000). Semiotically, 'meat eating' has two additional connotations that are specific to the world of policing. First, 'meat eating' refers to severe, systemic police corruption, including deviant behaviour and cover-ups within a police agency. The term 'meat eaters' was introduced in the *Knapp Commission Report on Police Corruption* (1972: 65) to refer to police officers who aggressively seek out situations that they can exploit for financial gain during most of their working hours. In contrast to 'grass eaters' who engage in petty corruption by accepting gratuities or relatively minor payoffs, meat eaters engage in premeditated corruption, such as keeping for themselves drugs or money confiscated during a police raid or arrest. In this episode of *The Bridge*, Cafferty and Coombs exhibit a meat eating pattern of police corruption.

Second, the phrase 'meat and potatoes'[10] also describes aggressive, 'in-your-face' policing (Street 2008), which characterizes how the writers have conceived of ETF policing. In the context of the episode's story, for instance, hyper-masculine ETF officers as best exemplified by Coombs are tasked with 'taking down' drug lords (Act One), hostage-taking thugs (Act Three) and potentially Frank (Act Four) through physical force. This proactive police use of physical force tends to elicit citizen complaints against officers who engage in this 'meat and potatoes' type of policing (Street 2008). Interestingly enough, *The Bridge* writers also incorporate information about such complaints against the ETF squad into their story. Anonymously citing their technical consultant, the writers put the following words into the mouth of Frank's police union assistant/partner: '[t]here are only 75 [ETF officers] on the police force, but they account for over 50 per cent of the police infractions and citizen complaints' (beat sheet 8 June 2009: 2). ETF Sergeant Coombs, in particular, is a 'cowboy who's been in trouble a lot' (beat sheet 8 June 2009: 2).

Thus, by setting the crime scene in a steakhouse restaurant, the writers seem to acknowledge that although a 'meat and potatoes' policing tactic can be problematic and linked to police corruption, meat consumption is a normalized aspect of interrelated representations (and understandings) of police culture and masculinity. More importantly, the old boys' network, conceived by the writers as including prominent members of Italian crime families, can only appear in this imagined Italian steakhouse. The restaurant provides a common meeting place for law enforcement personnel, such as the Deputy Chief, and for mobsters, such as the unknown Mafioso controlling the money-laundering operation from afar. As a crime scene, this particular restaurant setting puts the spotlight on the illicit activity of the old boys' network, and their larger corruption implies a serialized narrative that will continue and culminate in the season finale. In this episode, Bad Sergeant Coombs is only useful to the plot (and to Frank) if he can implicate Deputy Chief Cafferty. Cafferty then becomes the target for Frank's investigation in the next episode, revealing to him the extensive nature of the old boys' network and all of its attendant law enforcing and criminal associates.

The Mediterranean restaurant: the network outline (17 June 2009)

After the beat sheet, writers are asked to produce a longer story document known as an outline, fleshing out the telegraphic beats with longer descriptions of characters and story action. The outline[11] serves as yet another attempt at fine-tuning the story prior to the writing of full drafts (i.e. scripts complete with dialogue).

In our discussion of the outline stage, we will bypass the writers' outline, which can be considered the first trial of strength. Released on 11 June 2009, the writers' outline is an internal document that circulates among the writing team. The showrunner and other members of the writing team (who remain uncredited as writers for the episode) read the outline and provide feedback to the writers (in this case, MJ and KD). Based on that feedback, the writers will make the suggested story adjustments, if any, prior to sending the document to the networks for review. Because the writers' outline follows the beat sheet closely without any major alterations in story or character, it can be said to have withstood its first trial quite successfully. Instead, we will focus our attention on the network outline, which is the first[12] opportunity for external reviewers (i.e. external to the writing team) in the form of American and Canadian network executives to inspect the episode's story. We will note that the network outline survived any network 'attack' because it was approved without any major changes in story. However, the network outline contains a different representation of the restaurant setting in comparison to the beat sheet or the writers' outline, which in turn modifies the meaning of the crimes committed within that setting.

In the network outline, the writers take seriously the idea of making the 'restaurant [look like] where the [dirty] money is going to [*sic*]' (MG 2 June 2009). In lieu of the 'nice' Italian steakhouse represented in the beat sheet with its 'upstream' associations to the 'brass wall' and Italian Mafia, the writers focus on making the restaurant the spatial manifestation of the intermediate criminal figure: the middleman in the money laundering operation (i.e. the transporter of laundered money). Instead of an Italian restaurateur disappearing with the laundered money in the Bahamas, as in the beat sheet, the network outline ends with a Mediterranean restaurateur taking the money to Cyprus (17 June 2009: 13). As the restaurateur has transformed into a Greek, the restaurant setting has also been re-imagined as Mediterranean. In so doing, this change in restaurant setting has two effects. First, it suggests that the writers have backed away from connecting the Italian Mafia to instances of police corruption committed by the 'brass wall.' Second, the writers continue to associate a certain kind of ethnicity with criminality, and do so through the representation of the ethnic restaurant.

So how did the writers make the conceptual leap towards representing a Mediterranean restaurant, given their earlier attachment to the idea of an Italian steakhouse? Writer KD (8 June 2009) considered casting the restaurant as Carman's Dining Club, a well-known Toronto steakhouse. Some reviews of the restaurant, which opened its doors in 1959, noted the faded glory of its interior, which in turn inspired *The Bridge* writers to describe the 'old fashioned surroundings' of the fictional restaurant interior in the network outline as follows: 'The dining room is twenty years past its prime' (17 June 2009: 1). More importantly, on Carman's walls, '[t]here are photos of previous prime ministers and attorney generals dining in the restaurant [. . .] and it was a cop hangout' (KD 8 June 2009). Because real-life members of the 'brass wall' normally dined in the restaurant, it is easy to assume that powerful members of the fictional 'brass wall,' both political and criminal justice figures, would also dine in such a place. The old boys' network would feel at home in a restaurant described as a 'boys' club hangout' (Liu 19 November 2009). However, Carman's is named after its owner Carman (born Athanasios Karamano), an immigrant from Greece and not Italy (Chatto 1998). In keeping with the logic of making the restaurant an ethnic mirror of its owner, the restaurant in the network outline became Mediterranean as its owner is now described as 'Cassandra [note the Greek origins of the name], early thirties, Mediterranean looking, attractive' (network outline 17 June 2009: 1).

As a character, Cassandra changes the dynamics of both crimes – robbery/hostage-taking and money-laundering – that take place in her restaurant. She arises as a result of both production and creative concerns. Production wise, she is an attempt to cut down on the number of separate characters in the episode, by amalgamating the beat sheet characters of restaurant server and restaurateur into a single figure. As a result, producers would only need to cast one guest screen performer rather than two performers. It would also be easier for viewers to keep track of fewer 'new' (i.e. one-off and non-regular) characters in the episode, and allow a chance for the writers to more fully develop these characters. Creatively speaking, the writers wanted to include more female characters in their episode, having noted the overwhelming number of male characters that populated the episode.

The single character of Cassandra also allows the writers to streamline the plot because she becomes the reason for why both crimes happen at the same place on the same night in contrast to the happenstance version of criminal events in the beat sheet. In the beat sheet, male restaurateur Varda facilitates the money-laundering operation in which Coombs and Cafferty take part. Restaurant server Veronica happens to notice the money coming through the restaurant and calls her boyfriend Thug 1[13] and his brother Thug 2. The thugs come to rob the restaurant of this to-be-laundered money, which triggers Coombs and Cafferty's money rescue mission. Coombs and Cafferty assert their presence and control at the restaurant as police officers in charge of the ETF operation to bring these thugs to 'justice.' In their attempt to rob, the thugs had accidentally injured a police officer, and were holding him hostage along with restaurant patrons and staff in order to negotiate their escape from the restaurant.

In the network outline, however, Cassandra becomes the connection point for both crimes: Cafferty drops off the drug money specifically for her to launder in Greece, and she plans to rob him of this money with help from her boyfriend and his brother. In fact, she is so pivotal to the plot that the episode has been re-titled from 'Hostage' to 'The Unguarded Moment,' shifting the episode's focus from rescuing the injured police hostage to the 'unguarded moment' during which Frank (and viewers) see Cassandra react to her boyfriend's death at the hands of Coombs. To rescue the stolen money, Cafferty orders an ETF raid of the restaurant ostensibly to save the injured officer. This, however, is actually an opportunity for ETF Sergeant Coombs to take back the stolen money and justifiably[14] execute both thugs for knowing about the existence of such money. Even though Cassandra's thug boyfriend 'drops his gun and gives up' during the ETF takedown, 'Coombs shoots him' (network outline 17 June 2009: 8). She reacts to his death by bringing about the downfall of the Deputy Chief.

In his attempt to wipe clean any clues of his involvement in the money-laundering operation, Cafferty kills Coombs before the ETF Sergeant can confess his crimes and the names of his 'brass wall' associates to Frank. Previous versions of the story have ended with the killing of Coombs and Frank's investigation into Cafferty presumably still open but without any leads. In the network outline, however, an additional scene is added at the end of the episode to provide viewers with a greater sense of narrative (and investigative) closure, in which the Deputy Chief is himself brought to justice. Viewers learn about the fate of both 'bad apples' by the end of the episode. As a result, the episode's narrative has become increasingly modular: the episode introduces the 'bad apples of the week' as the foci for Frank's investigation and ends with the 'bad apples' essentially being punished for their crimes. While the writers had initially envisioned the episode's story as a set-up for the season finale, the story has increasingly taken on the narrative format of a standalone episode, closing off the potential to show a serialized representation of systemic police corruption among high-ranking police officials by instead showing the arrest of the Deputy Chief.

In the final scene of the episode, Cafferty is persuaded by Cassandra to come to the now closed restaurant during the day. He arrives and is confronted not only by Cassandra but also by Frank. After Cafferty is taken away in handcuffs, saying that 'they'll never get any charges to stick against him' (network outline 17 June 2009: 13), Cassandra:

> hands Frank an envelope and says it's the banking records from the last three times she took money to Cypress [sic] and then had it transferred to Cafferty's offshore account. Should be enough for a conviction.
>
> (Network outline 17 June 2009: 14)

By nightfall, both Frank and viewers learn that the banking records are sufficiently condemning because Cafferty has accepted a plea bargain and will be going to jail. With a change in restaurant setting, the episode's story now serves up a plate of justice instead of providing a serialized bone of contention on which viewers can continually chew.

The breakfast diner: network draft to full pink production draft

After the outline stage, the rewriting process enters the draft stage. Rather than being rendered in prose, each scene's action is expressed through dialogue and stage directions. Three different sets of 'inspectors' review different versions of the draft, requiring that our 'bad apples' pass through three trials of strength. Like the writers' outline, the writers' draft is first written for feedback from other members of the writing team. Because it is essentially an elaboration of the network outline, we will not examine the writers' draft in detail, but proceed in our investigation to the examination of the network draft and the production draft. The network draft (second draft stage) is written for review of content by the network executives; the production draft (third draft stage) is written for review in light of budgetary and location constraints by the show's producers.[15] While we will discuss each of these drafts in greater detail in a moment, we will first note their significance for several reasons.

First, Deputy Chief Cafferty, our 'bad apple' that was ultimately punished by Frank's good police work in the network outline, goes missing in the network draft. Also, ETF Sergeant Coombs transforms from 'bad apple' to 'good apple' in the network draft, and completely disappears in one of the production drafts.

Second, the disappearance of both our 'bad apples' coincides with a change in the episode's time scheme. Film scholar David Bordwell (1985) writes about time scheme as an audiovisual cue that allows viewers to unify the action. The time scheme establishes temporal unity of narrative action, a requirement for film and television continuity, so that characters' actions are seen to continue over the course of time. For example, in the case of representing a lengthy, ongoing police investigation, the investigative action is seen to continue over the course of a day (day turns to night), or over the course of several days (with the appropriate demarcations of day and night separating each day of investigation). In the script, the time of action is written in the scene heading, which is itself written in all capital letters. For example, if the scene is set in a restaurant, the scene heading might look as follows: INT. (interior) RESTAURANT – DINING ROOM – DAY. If the action continues in the restaurant setting, the writers will add 'continuous' to the scene heading as an adjective that modifies the time of action (e.g. CONTINUOUS – DAY). Productionwise, a determination of time scheme is especially significant for exterior shots and for lighting schemes, both of which impact the cost of the episode's production.

In our particular episode, the story was initially set at night and over the course of two days, but in the network draft stage, the story now only occurs over the course of a single day during daylight hours (from morning to presumably afternoon). As a result of this change in time scheme, the restaurant setting has also been changed. The fine dining experience provided by the 'nice' Italian restaurant or the Mediterranean restaurant can no longer be offered to 'a dead slow breakfast crowd' (network draft 12 July 2009: 3). From a production perspective, the number of diners that make up the early breakfast crowd is no different from that which made up the late dinner crowd[16] in previous story versions. In both cases, writers were thinking of using four to five diners to keep production costs relatively low. Aesthetically, however, the breakfast diner represented in the draft stage is quite different from previous restaurant settings, and comes about initially as a consequence of simply changing the episode's time scheme.

Thus, these production considerations have inadvertently changed the semiotic meaning associated with the setting's chronotope.[17] Chronotope refers to a particular way of combining temporality and spatiality, such that 'each space appears to us not abstractly [. . .] but rather embedded in a particular temporality' (Valverde 2006: 138). The notion of breakfast diner is already embedded in a particular temporal setting, since it tends to serve food intended for consumption in the daytime. As a result, the episode's robbery now happens in the morning, and is perhaps made more shocking by the fact it happens in broad daylight rather than under the conventional cover of darkness,[18] where criminal activities are imagined to generally occur. Moreover, by transforming the restaurant into a breakfast-serving diner, the implications of the previous ethnic incarnations of the restaurant setting no longer apply. We will now examine the network draft and production drafts in greater detail.

Network draft (12 July 2009)

The network draft is a full-length script treatment of the episode, which is sent to both sets of (CBS and CTV) network executives for feedback. While the network outline provided the first opportunity for network review, the network draft is yet another opportunity for network executives to provide their input, if any, to the writers. Network feedback generally does not take the form of production considerations, but instead their notes 'view everything through the prism of what [the network executives] think their audience wants, and what will get them excited, and what will get them to NOT [*sic*] change the channel' (McGrath 13 August 2009). In practice, the network notes tend to remark on areas in the story that need to be clarified for (at this point, imagined) viewers and the executives' emotional reactions to certain characters and/or scenes. In the case of *The Bridge*, network notes are given over a telephone call to the writers of the particular episode and the showrunner. As a co-production, *The Bridge* ought to receive two sets of notes, one from each network. In practice, the showrunner receives a collated set of notes from both networks, although members of the writing staff have primarily considered notes received from CBS. We will now examine the draft of the episode sent to the networks for review.

In the network draft, the restaurant setting has once again changed, such that all ethnic implications have now been erased in its description. The restaurant is generically described as:

> [a] nice place, quiet. A young couple in their 20's, sits at a table near the front. Two older women, 50's, sit at another table. And a [sic] older man, late 60's, alone at another table. A waitress delivers food. And a bus boy cleans the table.
>
> (Network draft 12 July 2009: 2)

Cassandra, owner of a Mediterranean restaurant, has now been transformed into 'Ella, 28, the restaurant manager' (network draft 12 July 2009: 2). While Ella assumes much of the role originally written as Cassandra (e.g. she transports drug money and calls her boyfriend to rob said money), she no longer deals with Deputy Chief Cafferty who has remarkably vanished from the story. As the restaurant setting has changed from high-class steakhouse to breakfast diner, it is no longer a setting for the city's elite, including members of the 'brass wall,' to hobnob. Instead, the diner is a place for ordinary people to grab a quick and cheap meal during the day. As a result of this change in restaurant setting, Ella transports laundered money for Munson who is a 'big time hash importer, real old school' (network draft 12 July 2009: 40). While the laundered money remains 'drug money,' its source is no longer police confiscated drug money but rather the money accumulated through the selling of hash. The knowledge gained from long conversations in the writers' room about how police officers can steal money from the crime scene no longer informs the episode's story in any way. Moreover, Ella will not be transporting the drug money to Cyprus but to Singapore, which is deemed a less friendly place for money-laundering since '[t]hey've got soldiers with machine guns and signs all over, death to drug dealers' (network draft 12 July 2009: 4). Notably, in contrast to the logic that underpinned the choice of restaurant setting in the network outline, the restaurant setting in the network draft is not made to epitomize the foreign place to which the drug money will be transported. Instead, we can consider the diner setting to be a relatively typical North American fast-food dining experience, and hence is associated with notions of ordinariness and the everyday. Even the appearance of hash dealer Munson in the restaurant can be deemed normal within the context of the restaurant business, in which 'drugs are rampant' (DA 2 June 2009).

With Cafferty's disappearance, Coombs undergoes a moral transformation into a morally upright Good ETF Sergeant. This transformation is highlighted by a conversation between Frank and Coombs during which Frank is trying to persuade Coombs and his ETF squad to enter the restaurant and take down the thugs. In reply, Coombs calls Frank a 'cowboy.' Thus, the designation of 'cowboy'

– here understood as a dangerous, reckless risk-taker – is no longer applied to Coombs (as in the beat sheet) but to Frank *by* Coombs (network draft 12 July 2009: 50). No longer the embodiment of the 'bad apple,' Coombs arrives at the restaurant hostage-taking scenario and strategically plans a way to get the hostages out. He even generously collaborates with Frank on this endeavour. However, Good Sergeant Coombs is a peripheral character in the episode's story in comparison to Bad Sergeant Coombs who was the focal point of Frank's investigation in previous story documents. Whatever insights into ETF culture the writers initially thought could be explored through the character of Coombs have been removed.

It is possible that Coombs' moral transformation was a pre-emptive measure to ensure network approval. Both CTV and CBS air the successful television program *Flashpoint*, and it is not clear that the networks would appreciate any of its shows, especially new untried ones, to tarnish the conceit of their other established and popular programs – in this case, the conceit of exceptionally heroic ETF officers. According to one of *Flashpoint*'s co-creators (Ellis 10 May 2011) 'people love heroes in network television and procedurals, and we made a conscious choice to view every member on that [ETF] team as heroic.' While *Flashpoint* was deliberately conceived to fit into CBS' line-up of police procedurals both in tone and content (Barken 17 August 2010), *The Bridge* was not initially conceived to fit into such a mould. Even when following network guidelines, *The Bridge* writers continued to pursue some stories about police corruption that made both CTV and CBS, as one writer of *The Bridge* puts it, 'nervous' (MJ 21 July 2010). The story of a corrupt ETF force can be considered an example of one such story.

With the complete removal of the corrupt Deputy Chief and the moral transformation of Coombs, however, the original representation of police corruption has been removed from the episode's story. In its place, the writers tell a story about 1) serialized police politics and 2) episodic civilian crime.

In telling a story about police politics, the writers continue to attempt a serialized representation of the 'brass wall' as suspect, although the 'brass wall' is no longer suspected of outright crime but of questionable motives that will negatively impact Frank in both this particular episode and the next. Police Chief Wycoff replaces Deputy Chief Cafferty as simultaneously the episodic 'bad guy' as well as the member of the 'brass wall' featured in this episode's story. Making his first appearance in the conceptualization of this story as a result of network notes, Wycoff arrives at the hostage-taking scene in order to provide an obstacle to Frank's attempt to save the injured police hostage. Outranked by Wycoff, Frank needs to call in a favour from the city's mayor. She also shows up at the scene to place Frank in charge of the hostage rescue mission, and to inform him that Wycoff has been talking to the Attorney General, both of whom want Frank removed from his post as police union chief. In putting Wycoff in the episode in this manner, the writers foreshadow the revelation of the police chief as completely corrupt in the season finale.

While the episode includes a side-story about police politics, its primary story line explores the commission of money laundering by civilian criminals, rather than by Cafferty and Coombs. The removal of Cafferty and attendant simplification of Coombs' characterization left a void in storytelling that was filled by fleshing out the characterization of the civilian criminals: Ella, Thug 1 and Thug 2. While the titular reference to the 'unguarded moment' in the network outline referred to Cassandra's reaction to the death of her boyfriend Thug 1, the moment of note in the network draft is Ella's realization that Thug 1 is not the man that she thought he was, and is instead capable of hostage-taking and potentially murder. She realizes that her plan to steal the drug money has gone horribly wrong because her co-conspirators are unable to stay on task, having been made unpredictable and irrational by their heroin addiction. While Cassandra survived the robbery and hostage-taking and brought Cafferty to justice, Ella and both thugs die in the final act of the episode, partially as a result of mutual self-destruction (e.g. Thug 1 shoots Ella with his gun and she later retaliates by shooting his brother Thug 2) and partially as a result of an ETF takedown of the civilian criminals (e.g. Frank shoots Thug 1).

The networks generally 'approved' of the major changes in the episode's narrative, as the pattern of representation set down by the network draft – specifically, the removal of 'bad apples' Coombs and Cafferty, and the fleshing out of civilian criminals – continues to be elaborated upon in the following production drafts. As we will soon see, some of these changes can be read as pre-emptive measures to ensure that the script will easily pass through the networks' Standards and Practices department.

Full white production draft (16 July 2009)

The production draft signals the draft's transformation from a purely creative story document (script) to a practical blueprint for production (shooting script). It is read by producers for budgetary constraints, which will have an impact on the story through limitations imposed on the number of characters that can appear (this is constrained by the number of guest/additional screen performers that can be hired) and the setting of the episode itself (this is constrained by the affordability of the chosen location). It is not the case, however, that a single production draft governs the entire shooting of the episode. Instead, production drafts are themselves revised during production as both writers and producers figure out what will and will not work for the episode.

To delineate the sequence of revised drafts, production drafts are produced following a colour revision system, and every production company has its own order of coloured revisions. When production drafts are printed, they are printed on a particular colour of paper in line with the colour revision system. *The Bridge*'s colour revision system is as follows: white, blue, pink, yellow and green. For example, a production draft labelled 'double pink' means that it has gone through an entire cycle of ('full') colour revisions and is now on its second cycle ('double'): in layperson's terms, it is the eighth production draft for the episode. The 'full white' production draft that we will first examine is the first production draft written. Before we discuss the producers as 'inspectors,' we will discuss the networks as the episode's 'health and safety inspectors.'

Health and safety inspectors: standards and practices

While the networks review the network draft for what they think their audience wants or expects to see in their programming, they inspect the 'full white' production draft in terms of eliminating 'dirt.' That is, the network's Broadcasting Standards and Practices (S&P) department scrutinizes the draft for the story's moral, ethical and legal implications, where 'dirty words' and 'dirty acts' (graphic depictions of sexual intercourse and/or excretion) are assumed to offend moral sensibilities and the 'dirt' of potential trade libel is imagined to offend advertisers. To my knowledge, *The Bridge* receives all of its S&P memos from CBS rather than CTV, and as such the episode's content is indirectly regulated by the American Federal Communications Commission (FCC). Implicated in the governance of (pop) culture, the FCC rules are applied by S&P executives as a means for the American broadcast networks to self-regulate and self-police the content that they broadcast. In short, these executives are charged with keeping their television network 'clean,' by flagging lewd jokes, errant curse words and provocative sexual elements in any of their scripted television programs prior to public dissemination. In doing this work, the executives use the FCC indecency and obscenity[19] rules to regulate the boundaries of acceptable television programming, although these boundaries might vary among American broadcast networks as S&P executives also take into consideration what is acceptable for their particular network brand (Rice 2 May 2007). Anecdotally, for example, the FOX network allows more 'edgy' (i.e. sexier and more violent) representations than CBS, which is considered the most conservative of the big four American broadcast networks.

After their scrutiny of the full white production draft, the S&P department produces a memo to the showrunner enumerating 'issues' that need to be properly dealt with during production. Some of these 'issues' are related to the network's general programming practice policy, and will apply to the entire series. For example, dialogue in any television series may not, per CBS' Program Practices, contain the words 'pissed on' or 'pissed,' both of which refer to urination, but may contain the phrase 'pissed off' (i.e. angry). Similarly, writers cannot use the term 'nuts' to describe male genitals, but may use the alternative terms 'nads' or 'sack.' References to fecal matter ('crap' or 'shit') or blasphemous references to God ('Jesus,' 'Christ,' 'Jesus Christ,' 'God' or 'Goddamn') are never permitted. In short, an S&P executive needs to consider a CBS television program as though it were a 'guest in the home [where i]t is expected to entertain and enlighten but not to offend or advocate' (CBS/Broadcast Group 1988: 133). As a guest, the entertainment program needs to conform to 'generally accepted boundaries of public taste and decorum' (CBS/Broadcast Group 1988: 133), indicating that audience expectations of the network's programming will be taken into consideration.

In order to discipline a potentially unruly 'guest' before it arrives in the homes of the CBS audience, S&P executives also pinpoint specific 'issues' in an episode that need to be managed by the showrunner and producers before the episode can be broadcast. These specific 'issues,' however, are derived from general program practice principles, such as a ban on nudity and the unauthorized use of product placement. For example, in this particular episode, the S&P response to the image of an inebriated waitress in panties and a torn-open blouse is to have the showrunner ensure that 'she is sufficiently covered for broadcast' (CBS Program Practices 20 July 2009: 1). The S&P executive will review a rough cut of the episode to ensure that this is the case. Scenes shot in the restaurant should also avoid having 'nationally recognizable commercially identifiable product signs and props' in the background (CBS Program Practices 20 July 2009: 1). The last S&P note is in reference to the specification of the episode's restaurant setting as the motel diner, the False Bay Bistro (full white production draft 16 July 2009: 19). These S&P notes highlight the economic imperative that underlies what can be shown on screen: it must not cause a loss of viewership or of advertisers.

More importantly for the plot of our particular episode, we will consider how CBS S&P executives might react to a potential 'guest' that speaks of large-scale police corruption and civilian drug use. While these topics might be explored and explored well by television writers and producers of shows on American pay cable channels (e.g. *The Wire* and *The Shield*), those shows do not need to conform to the same level of standards and practices maintained by network broadcasting channels such as CBS. Network S&P executives consider their job to be 'pro-social,' and this translates into an unwritten mandate whereby they 'don't want evil to triumph' (head of ABC's Standards department, quoted in Friend 19 November 2001). In maintaining the idea of 'good triumphing over evil,' the executives ensure that their shows do not break 'the covenant to not surprise the audience' (NBC Standards executive, quoted in Friend 19 November 2001). How does upholding this covenant affect this particular episode of *The Bridge* and in what ways does it herald the disappearance of our 'bad apples?'

Although the S&P memo is released in response to the full white production draft, the S&P executives generally work closely with writers and producers throughout production (Henderson and Doktori 1988) and are likely to have an effect on representations of people and places prior to the production draft stage. In the past two decades, network S&P executives have been especially vigilant about stereotyping and role portrayals (Henderson and Doktori 1988; Rice 2 May 2007), particularly with respect to the representation of ethnic minorities. For instance:

> [i]n 1994, the producers of the Fox sitcom 'Monty' were told that a character in the [television] pilot could not get food poisoning from a Chinese restaurant. He also could not get it from an Italian restaurant. He could, however, get it from *a* restaurant.
>
> (Friend 19 November 2001: 6, author's emphasis added)

In considering the above anecdote as a precedent for the American networks' treatment of representations of ethnic restaurants, the removal of ethnic connotations of the restaurant setting in this episode of *The Bridge* seems related to current standards and practices. Although the episode does not deal with food poisoning in an ethnic restaurant, early story versions implicate a given ethnic group with criminal activity (e.g. the Mafia are associated with the Italian restaurant, or Greek launderers with the Mediterranean restaurant). By making the restaurant generic (i.e. non-ethnic) in this episode, the writers fulfill a particular S&P guideline, yet in doing so need to make changes to the way they conceive of the 'brass wall.' Because Deputy Chief Cafferty can no longer dine in an upscale ethnic restaurant, he disappears in the network draft since the restaurant setting is no longer conceived as conducive to the wining and dining of the brass wall's various movers and shakers. While Cafferty could theoretically appear in the diner, his appearance is no longer necessary since the writers are no longer pursuing a serialized narrative about how certain police bureaucrats facilitate ethnically related organized criminal activity. Because unnecessary characters inflate an episode's production budgets without contributing any dramatic pay-off, they tend to be removed. Consequently, the removal of Cafferty facilitates the moral transformation of Coombs.

With the disappearance of the 'bad apples,' the writers focus on fleshing out the civilian criminals. When considering overall changes to the story, we can note a shift away from telling a story about 'bad apples' and towards a story about 'bad seeds.' Because the civilian 'bad seeds' are heroin addicts, the thugs' substance abuse comes under review by CBS' S&P executives. The CBS guideline for representations of substance abuse states that:

> it must be thoughtfully considered, essential to plot and role development, and not glamorized. When the line is crossed between normal, responsible consumption of a particular substance and abuse, the distinction must be clear and the adverse consequences of abuse specifically noted and explored.
> (CBS/Broadcast Group 1988: 135)

Compared to the network draft, the full white production draft characterizes the thugs as morally irredeemable. The 'adverse consequences' of their heroin addiction are noted and explored. During the robbery and hostage-taking, they experience painful withdrawal symptoms, but once high on drugs, they engage in morally reprehensible acts that only appear in the full white production draft. While both thugs take pleasure in torturing their injured police hostage, one of the thugs drugs and rapes a waitress off screen. The thugs are also given a criminal record, having previously hijacked cars and nearly beaten an old lady to death. In short, they are described as being 'as mean as they come' (full white 16 July 2009: 21), and their meanness is implicitly attributed to a tightly drawn nexus of crime and drug addiction. Given the CBS Program Practices guideline, their drug addiction is also what causes their inevitable downfall. High on drugs, the thugs are unable to properly plan their escape from the restaurant and hence evade the law. Instead, Frank outwits the thugs and they are killed during the ETF takedown in the restaurant.

With this particular revised ending, the case of the drug-addicted thugs is resolved by the end of the episode, providing the audience with narrative closure. Narrative resolution is also:

> what broadcasters love. That's the kind of programming people want to watch and it's neat and tidy. It's resolved at the end and the public is satisfied. And that's the simple way that [popular] television works [because network broadcasters uniformly believe that] their audiences need to feel comforted, and the whole idea of the bad guy being put away was really important. The right bad guy!
>
> (BL 22 August 2008)

Conceived as a guest in the audience's home, the episode is rewritten to maximize the comfort it can give to audiences, by not only removing the possibility of corruption among police officers but also by emphasizing that the drug-addicted thugs are unmistakably 'the right bad guys.'

Practical inspectors: the producers

While some revisions were prompted by S&P executives, other revisions to the episode were the result of production concerns, especially because most of this particular episode needed to be shot on location and in real time. While many Canadian television shows are shot on standing sets (i.e. stable sets that are built inside a studio) because it is cheaper to do so, shooting on location tends to tax the series' budget.

In taking into consideration production concerns, part of the transformation of the script into a blueprint for shooting entails the addition of two new textual entities, both of which signal to the producer ways in which the episode's budget can be spent or saved: the asterisk and the list. Although the addition of sets and characters lists first appeared appended to the beginning of the network draft, these lists have been modified by the addition of the asterisk in the full white production draft. To aid producers in their practical inspection of the production draft, writers highlight revisions to location, characters and story with the asterisk, which is a small star-shaped symbol that first appears in the page margins of the production draft itself.

THE ASTERISK

We will pause in our investigation into the missing 'bad apples' to examine how a simple typographical symbol enters into the making of a particular type of story document (i.e. the production draft) and facilitates its evaluation by our practical inspectors. While the *Oxford English Dictionary* defines the asterisk as a symbol used in text as a pointer to a footnote or annotation, the textual genre of screenplay writing implies a different use of the asterisk. Rather than act as a reference mark, the asterisk in the screenplay is a revision mark made possible through the writer's use of Final Draft, which is a screenwriting software program that bills itself as 'the industry standard' for film and television writers. While early story documents, such as the beat sheet, are written with word-processing software (i.e. Microsoft Word), the draft stage entails the use of Final Draft. Because Final Draft is programmed to provide the appropriate scriptwriting format, writers do not need to concern themselves with the mechanics of proper formatting and can instead concentrate on the content of the script. The software's automatic programming includes the standardized use of the asterisk to indicate revisions and changes in the script, which is particularly important when the screenplay needs to be read and worked on collaboratively. Similarly, Microsoft Word has a 'track changes' function, intended originally for the legal profession (Basch 2006), that allows writers to note additions, deletions and modifications to the text when they are writing the text collaboratively. Textual changes are tracked through underlining to denote added text, or using strike-throughs to denote deleted text. Final Draft, however, tracks textual changes – only additions and not deletions – with the placement of an asterisk beside the new or modified text in the right margin of the page. This allows various script readers, including producers, to riffle through the printed pages and find script changes quickly.

    The presence of the asterisk illuminates two notable insights into the process of television (re)writing. First, its normalized presence might tell us something about the ubiquity of Final Draft as a screenwriting software program because it has made possible a specific formatting choice that has since become industry standard. However, I would like to focus instead on what the use of Final Draft means for the television writer, our primary spokesperson for various story documents. Specifically, it suggests that part of the television writer's competence[20] – namely, the ability to format the screenplay correctly – comes in a download that allows writers to activate what they might have been unable to do before. As such, Final Draft can be understood as a plug-in that enhances the competence of a television writer. Following the metaphor of the plug-in, the overall competence of being a television writer does not come in bulk, but in bits and bytes (Latour 2007: 207): in the last chapter, a 'bit' of competence came in the form of experiential knowledge, and in this chapter a 'byte' of competence comes with the use of Final Draft. Plug-ins then lend our human actors the supplementary tools necessary to render a situation interpretable (Latour 2007: 209). In this case, the plug-in of Final Draft renders story revisions visible in a particular way, allowing both writers and producers to collaboratively interpret them as such.

    Second, the asterisk allows for collaborative writing in a way that is different from the writing of bureaucratic documents, which uses other typographic symbols to denote other kinds of textual and human interaction. For example, in the collaborative drafting of a United Nations' document during the Fourth World

Conference of Women, brackets (or parentheses) were used to denote a word in contention among delegates. According to Annelise Riles (2006), the bracket for delegates was both a unit of time and a unit of organizational gridlock. The brackets functioned to stop time in the conference in order for appointed delegates to analyze the contentious word and come to some agreement upon the word's proper definition. In contrast, the asterisk in the production draft(s) ensures that time is not stopped to deal with contentious production issues, especially since 'time is money' once shooting begins (e.g. crew, cast, equipment, transport, and catering need to be paid regardless of whether any work is being done). If there is organizational gridlock in the process of television production, it will be 'solved' in the form of asterisked changes in the next version of the production draft. As such, the asterisk marks time, but continuous time over which the story is updated as various production constraints come into play.

Because bureaucratic documents, such as the UN Global Platform for Action (Riles 2006), emerge as printed, complete documents with a singular, definitive version, they are not formatted to allow for growth or what we have been calling 'ripening.' By contrast, the asterisk is used to mark transformations and consequently, the ripening of an episodic story. The effect of the asterisk is also unlike the non-transformative effect of bullet points used in the genre of university mission statements as part of a university's strategy for 'bullet-proofing' itself against government interference in the language of its auditing assessors (Strathern 2006). Bullet points are non-transformative because one cannot do intellectual operations on them, which removes the possibility of argument, critique or discovery (Strathern 2006). While asterisks are similarly non-transformative in and of themselves, they do, however, open up the production draft(s) for discovery and review, by marking transformations in the story, including transformations in the list of characters and sets.

LISTS

Both the sets and characters lists that are appended to the front of the production draft provide a convenient inventory of who and what will be needed for shooting. They also provide a sense of the episode's scale, and how that scale will affect the episode's production budget. As previously mentioned, over the course of several story documents, the episode has been scaled back: the time scheme for the episode has been condensed into a single day of action, most of which now takes place on location at a restaurant. The restaurant is now described in the full white production draft (16 July 2009: 1) as follows:

ACT ONE

FADE IN:

EXT. MOTEL – RESTAURANT – ESTABLISHING – MORNING *

A motel with a restaurant attached to it in front.*

Our breakfast diner has been further qualified and is now a motel diner. As a shooting location, the motel diner, located at the edge of the city of Toronto, is a different kind of location than the downtown restaurant originally envisioned by writers. Because the motel diner is not located in the heart of the city, it is a more affordable location for producers to acquire and to shoot in. For example, producers can better control noise factors when shooting. There would be no need for paid duty police officers to slow down, stop or detour traffic to reduce traffic noise while shooting, since traffic noise is generally reduced at the periphery of the city. Moreover, given the relatively remote location of the motel, there would also be no need to re-route pedestrian traffic. The motel location also has a parking lot that can double as an exterior shooting location (e.g. scenes during which various characters, such as Frank and the ETF squad, arrive at the restaurant), and as unit and crew parking for the production team's various vehicles (e.g. equipment vehicles, hair/makeup and wardrobe trailers, trailers for the screen performers, etc.). If the producers were shooting at a downtown restaurant, parking permits for unit vehicles need to be acquired, since (the limited downtown) parking spaces would need to be reserved in advance for the production team.

When we examine the list of characters, we also notice that the writers have cut down on the number of guest characters that appear in the episode because budgetary constraints serve to limit the number of guest characters with speaking roles. Most remarkably, the mayor who first appears in the network draft now disappears in the full white production draft due to budgetary constraints on the number of screen performers permitted per episode. With the removal of the mayor, Frank no longer learns that Police Chief Wycoff has been plotting with the Attorney General to relieve him of his post. As a result, the set-up for a serialized narrative about the 'brass wall's' corruption is omitted in this revised story document. Although Wycoff appears at the crime scene to provide an obstacle to Frank's attempt to rescue the injured police hostage, he is an episodic antagonist (as are the increasingly incorrigible civilian criminals). With the omission of the mayor, any inkling of Wycoff's serialized corruption has also been omitted.

We will also note that ETF Sergeant Coombs remains in the story as a function of proper police procedure, since the ETF squad is routinely called in to negotiate with hostage-takers. While the original Bad ETF Sergeant Coombs would 'lock and load' and move in to take down the hostage takers without a second thought (beat sheet 8 June 2009), Good Sergeant Coombs refuses to do so. Because Wycoff has given the order for the ETF squad to stand down (i.e. not enter the restaurant and rescue the injured police hostage), Coombs cannot be persuaded by Frank to disobey that order:

> FRANK: Coombs, you gotta [*sic*] cop hurt bad in there, and you need to go in there, and get him out. The hell with the Chief. *
>
> COOMBS: I got a lawful order, Frank. We disobey that order, and we're done.*

(Full white production draft 16 July 2009: 11)

While 'bad apple' Coombs has no issues with working outside the law, Good Coombs follows lawful orders to the very letter. Bad Coombs lives in a house 'decorated by Soldier of Fortune magazine' (writers' outline 11 June 2009: 13), whereas viewers have no glimpse into the home life of Good Coombs. Instead Good Coombs seems to only exist on the job, although he admits to Frank that it is getting harder to do his job as a result of recent police budget cuts (full white 16 July 2009: 12). As a result, the full white production draft completes the moral transformation of ETF Sergeant Coombs into a character that seems even more lawful and morally upright than the show's protagonist who, in contrast, is willing to skirt the edges of the law to save a police officer. To further cement the disappearance of 'bad apple' Coombs, the writers change the name of the revised character of Good Coombs to Sergeant Travers in the full pink production draft (26 July 2009). With the name change, Coombs disappears from the story altogether, taking with him all traces of his existence as a 'bad apple.'

Coombs' name change might arise from a script clearance report, in which the name of Coombs did not 'clear.' The script clearance report highlights all character names, among other names used in the episode (e.g. restaurant name, locations, product names, etc.), that could potentially expose the producers to legal trouble, particularly to lawsuits claiming defamation. Specifically, the report ensures that all character names used in the script do not correspond to any real-life prominent individuals in society. For example, if there is a real-life Sergeant Coombs, then the character name of Coombs might not 'clear.' Often, the script clearance report will provide alternative names that can be used, or the writers will try to 'clear' alternative character names. Usually, producers do not perform script clearances themselves, but delegate the work to an independent company that specializes in script clearances. The clearance report is designed to help television productions satisfy their Errors and Omissions requirements.

Closing the case

Although this episode's story will undergo a few more revisions, the pattern set by the full white production draft is generally seen through to the final revised shooting script (double pink production draft 9 August 2009) with some minor tinkering of dialogue and scene directions along the way. As we come to the end of our investigation, we need to admit that although this investigation was structured by a forensic metaphor, we are not Sherlock Holmes. We cannot definitively answer the question of 'who' ensured the disappearance of our 'bad apples,' because there is no single guilty party. What we do have is a chain of textual suspects, all of which contribute in small ways to their eventual disappearance. None of our textual suspects is the singular cause of Coombs and Cafferty's respective disappearances, at least not in such a significant way that we could easily pinpoint any one of them as the guilty culprit. Instead, if there must be a culprit, it is the television re-writing process, which is itself a matter of negotiation and collaboration among multiple production and network personnel.

As such, the disappearance of Cafferty and Coombs is, as alluded to at the beginning of our investigation, 'built right into the nature of things.' Specifically, it is the nature of television drama production, which tends to entail a process of scaling back the cost of production while still aspiring to tell a compelling story anchored by a dramatic conflict.

In attempting to tell that compelling story, our textual suspects collectively inform us of an overall narrative movement that facilitates the disappearance of our 'bad apples.' Across our story documents, the overall narrative movement becomes oriented towards increasingly modular storytelling and away from serialized storytelling. Part of the movement towards modular storytelling lies in the broadcaster's desire to sell the series overseas. While there are serialized television series on network television, major Canadian and American broadcasters 'prefer to err on the side of [making] shows that are standalones because they know that they are going to ultimately make more money in their foreign distribution' (DA 22 July 2012).

In adjusting the writing of the episode to the networks' desires, serialized elements in the story, including representations of serialized police corruption (e.g. as originally embodied by the figure of Deputy Chief Cafferty), are eventually all omitted over the course of re-writing the episode. Instead, the episode is rewritten as a story that features 'bad seeds' rather than 'bad apples' of the week, evolving from a story about serialized police corruption to one of episodic civilian (career) criminality. The transformation of story focus from 'bad apple' to 'bad seed' is initially set in motion by re-imagining the space of villainy's sphere of action. In undertaking a structural analysis, Vladimir Propp[21] (1968) was interested in identifying particular functions or spheres of action for various stock characters found in the folktale. Most relevant to us, he designates villainy as a sphere of action (e.g. the villain functions to fight or engage in struggle with the hero). In this episode of *The Bridge*, the beat sheet originally imagined two sets of villains: our two 'bad apples' and our two civilian 'bad seeds' (Thugs 1 and 2). While Propp defines spheres of action *at* certain places in the narration, taking into account the spatial articulation of the text itself, our investigation led us to consider how spheres of action are imagined *as* a particular representation of space, taking into account the articulation of setting. Across our story documents, transformations in the setting of restaurant as crime scene and as a site for villainy also suggest a movement towards increasingly modular storytelling: earlier representations of ethnic restaurants with their attendant storylines of serialized 'brass wall' corruption are eventually replaced by a generic motel breakfast diner with its singular set of civilian villains.

As a result of all of these transformations (see Figure 4.1), the episode's story no longer attempts to reveal the political machinations behind police forces. Instead, it has taken on the more standardized format of a police procedural (e.g. a narrative that features a crime, police investigation and then closure) common to shows currently airing on both of the show's co-producing networks, such as *CSI*. In fact, this particular episode was aired out of order: while it was the 12th

Restaurant setting	The Italian steakhouse	The Mediterranean restaurant	The breakfast diner
Story document	The beat sheet: 'Injured Cop'	The network outline	Network draft to full pink production draft: 'The Unguarded Moment'
Writers' reference for the restaurant setting	Italian steakhouse in Harlem, New York City	Carman's steakhouse, Toronto	The 'False Bay Bistro', Toronto
Representations of police corruption as a function of storytelling format (i.e. serialized vs. modular narrative)	Serialized narrative about systemic police corruption involving Cafferty and Coombs	Increasingly modular narrative featuring 'bad apple' Coombs	Modular narrative focused on civilian crime. The representation of police corruption has disappeared. Cafferty no longer appears in the draft, and Coombs is now represented as a good cop.

Figure 4.1 Summary of story revisions

Source: Photographs taken by author.

episode put into production, it was the fourth episode that aired on CTV.[22] This is made possible by the modular storytelling of the episode, which is itself borne out of the television re-writing process. This revision process involves a whole host of small decisions made by numerous people involved with the show's production, which serve to slowly transform the episode's story until, as in this case, it bears little resemblance to its original conceptualization in the writers' room.

Because the revision and re-writing process serve to destabilize representations, there is a methodological danger in treating the script as though it were a single, stable document – that is, as an intermediary. Instead, the story should be recognized as a fluid set of ideas that is embodied at different moments of formation and transformation by various story documents, including not only the final shooting script, but also the various beat sheets, outlines and drafts leading up to that script. In short, these story documents should be treated as mediators because they mediate the multiple decision-making processes that make up the general process of television drama production, including decisions made as a result of story review by other writers, network executives, S&P executives and producers. Consequently, the process of television writing ensures that the production and circulation of ideas and images about crime and criminality are dynamic, never stable, and constantly open to revision; as writers, producers and network executives continually negotiate the balance between aesthetic and commercial imperatives that specifically drive the show's production and generally drive the television industry.

Law's role in the revision process

As various scholars of news production have argued (e.g. Ericson *et al.* 1987, 1991; Hemmingway 2008), news is better understood as the result of particular practices of news organizations than as faithful reproductions of 'real-life' events. Similarly, fictional crime dramas (and their particular episodes) are better understood as the outcome of practices carried out by a specific assemblage of people, creative ideas, commercial interests and broadcasting network demands. Thus, in this chapter, I have described the conditions necessary for the formulation of particular meanings of crime. In doing so, I have alluded (yet again) to how law provides some of those conditions. As the subject of representation, law's linear narrative is represented as characteristic of police work. Police investigations are premised upon the maintenance of a continuous chain of evidence. Consequently, telling a story about police investigations requires the maintenance of a linear story structure, in which events are sequenced like a chain of evidence.

Law also provides the conditions under which certain things cannot be said or shown on the small screen. Because *The Bridge* was indirectly regulated by FCC regulations, network executives from CBS Standards and Practices review the show's episodes for any potential FCC violations. Routinely, S&P executives remove 'dirty words' and 'dirty acts' from the episode's content, but they also police representations that might be construed as trade libel or as negative stereotypes of ethnic minorities. Additionally flagged by script clearance reports, representations that might be perceived as trade libel are removed in accordance with the show's Errors and Omissions requirements. While E&O requirements funnel legal matters through insurance coverage, S&P requirements are a mixture of legal concerns and broadcaster demands. Each broadcaster has a different list of what may not be said or shown on the small screen, depending on the timeslot in which the program will air.[23] Perceived by *The Bridge* showrunner as the most conservative of the big four American networks, CBS' list of prohibited words and acts is likely longer than that of the other networks (e.g. FOX).

In addition to providing the conditions under which television representations are formulated, law acts as one of the initial audiences tasked with reviewing those representations. Echoing Cantor (1971), I argue that television writers and producers create their shows for an audience composed of network executives, S&P executives, and insurers, as well as for the writers and producers themselves. Instead of examining how the writers and producers of *The Bridge* construct their particular consumer audience,[24] I have studied how an actual production-oriented audience responds to an episode's story documents. In contrast to examining what the consumer audience wants, I describe what human actors in the story–revision–actor–network want and how that affects the representations of crime in a specific episodic narrative.

This is a different theoretical and methodological focus than that of previous television production studies, particularly ones done under cultural studies. Because contemporary cultural studies has focused on studying the notion of active audiences and how they make sense of cultural texts (Seaman 1992), the consumer audience has been a privileged site of much research. Thus, contemporary television production studies tend to include a study of the text's reception by a consumer audience (e.g. Gripsrud 1995; Sodano 2008). They have also examined how active audiences are constructed by industrial television practices. For example, Jane Shattuc (1997) has examined how TV talk shows construct an active female audience through the use of a female-dominated studio audience. The talk show is also formulated in the terms of a melodrama, which has been used as a blueprint for the production of feminine narratives. Ultimately, Shattuc concludes that the concept of a knowable audience of female viewers is a fiction used by producers to support their self-ascribed ability to attract specific audiences. In contrast, on an untried show like *The Bridge*, the consumer audience is an unknowable entity, and the show's creative team did not undertake any attempt to 'know' it, preferring to leave concerns about the audience to network executives. The only active audience during the production of an untried show that can be empirically studied is its production-oriented audience.

A few notes on following the paper trail

In contrast to studies that have analyzed consumer audience response through the use of interviews and ethnography, I have examined the responses of the story–revision actor–network by documenting textual transformations in story documents over the course of a single episode's production. In so doing, I have examined how story documents were 'activated' (Smith 1990) during the production process as a means to mobilize and coordinate the efforts of the show's entire production team. This 'activation' was related to my analysis of the interaction between story documents as they either survived or perished in successive 'trials of strength.' In this analysis, texts were recognized as actants capable of acting on each other and on human actors rather than simply as objects to be acted upon by human analysts.

While this chapter acknowledges that the action of television production is distributed among textual agents, there are certain methodological implications related to treating texts as my primary informants. By following textual actors rather than human actors, the story–revision actor–network highlights a particular actor that is rarely, if ever, discussed in television or film production analyses. For example, I consider the scriptwriting software Final Draft as an actor in this actor-network. The software not only helps to produce the production drafts in a particular format, it also standardizes a typographic symbol, the asterisk, as a sign of revision, which helps writers and producers quickly 'activate' revised texts.

While I was able to highlight an oftentimes missing actor by following the paper trail of story documents, I may also have over-emphasized the role of legal actors in the story-revision actor-network precisely because they tend to produce many written documents (e.g. script clearance reports and S&P guidelines). By focusing primarily on texts, I may have over-emphasized law's role in the revision process and underestimated the role of creative actors. As I have discussed in the last chapter, the creative team of writers primarily communicates through orally told anecdotes. As I was not given access to lurk behind writers as they type at their computers or eavesdrop on all of their conversations, I did not capture all of those anecdotes. Moreover, I was also not privy to phone calls between the creative team and network executives. Because the oral communication between creative actors in the actor-network cannot be captured by examining texts, this chapter might have underplayed the creative negotiation and finessing that occurs at the re-writing stage. While the story documents carry with them the evidentiary traces of ideological assumptions made by network executives and writers about 'bad apples' and villainy, I am cautious about drawing conclusions about the episode's ideological effects without having directly observed conversations between creative personnel. While the textual actors are born out of the give-and-take negotiations between creative human actors, they are not by themselves a substitute for those discussions, especially when it comes to detailing the specific ways in which showrunners and producers are:

> always making the show with the network in mind because they're [*sic*] the ones that can tell you 'we're not airing that episode.' [Any network] can ultimately give you enough of a hard time about what you're doing. So what you try to do when you have story meetings or your note meetings with your network, you always try to find a middle ground. They may say that 'we think that this episode needs this, this and this.' And you may say, 'well, I think you're right about this, but I would argue with you about that. I would say that this does fulfill what you're looking for, but I can tweak it a little bit.' You can't be saying 'absolutely no' because they could be saying 'absolutely no.' So you never want to get to that point with networks.
>
> (DA 22 July 2012)

Notes

1 Here, I am assuming that there is a separation between the consumer audience and the people who work in television production. While it is true that television production personnel are also consumers of fictional television dramas, they might not be consumers of their *own* television series (BO 29 January 2009). Often, they are working on another film or television project when their previous show airs. When they do watch their own shows, they certainly do not watch them in the same way as the consumer audience. For example, the boom operator is attuned to the sound quality of the production (BO 29 January 2009), background extras focus on the work of other background extras (BG 18 February 2009), writers concentrate on the show's story structure, etc.

2 I use the term 'ideology' to broadly refer to the nature and origin of ideas.

3 There is a file cabinet in which hard copies (printed versions) of the story documents can be found in file folders. These physical hard copies are kept by the show's script coordinator whose job is to essentially 'coordinate scripts.' That is, s/he is responsible for archiving all the material documents associated with the show's storytelling for all

of its episodes. This includes keeping track of revised scripts, memos and other relevant documentation to the show's production of an episode. Because I did not have access to this filing cabinet, I can only surmise that it serves as a physical archive for all of the production's story materials, some of which are creative (e.g. scripts) and some of which are legally related (e.g. clearance reports, which I will discuss later in this chapter). While story documents have taken the form of electronic formats for ease of circulation, the actual task of reading and revising these documents still depends on the use of physical texts.

4 Some of *The Bridge*'s human informants (e.g. network executives) were inaccessible. For example, CBS network executives preferred to give their notes to the writers over a telephone call, and were generally at a distance from the actual production and shooting of the show.

5 Binning (2009/2010: 20) notes that the writing on Canadian–American co-productions is made more difficult because there are 'a lot of cooks in the kitchen, and the rules aren't clearly defined.' While Canadian networks are willing to air episodes with controversial content (e.g. abortion), American networks are not willing to take that risk for fear of negative American audience reactions. Writers need to be aware of some of these cultural differences that make themselves known through the reviewing process undertaken by different network executives.

6 To avoid confusion, all quotations attributed to initials are quotations from *The Bridge* writers. When quoting story documents, I will refer to the text itself, such as beat sheet, outline, production draft, etc.

7 During the making of *The Godfather* (1972), the film crew encountered resistance during production in New York City from the Italian-American Civil Rights League because the League felt that the film portrayed a stereotypical and negative representation of all Italians as Mafia related (Lebo 1997). It should be noted that the Italian-American Civil Rights League was an odd organization because it was founded by a New York mobster. As the head of the Colombo crime family, Joseph Colombo founded the League in order to reduce the public's awareness of the Mafia, by publicly censoring its representation in news and entertainment media. Colombo sought a return to 'the omerta of turn-of-the-century Little Italys, where Mafia was a whispered word and bosses were not badgered by grand juries, tax investigators and wiretaps' (Time 12 July 1971).

8 As one of the first scholars to examine the semiotics of food, Barthes (1972) analyzes the bloody steak as a signifier for French national identity and imperialism.

9 I am taking up Richard Sparks' (1996) suggestion that criminologists study the gendered implications of standard film and television characters (e.g. the hero, police officer, villain, etc.), particularly the images of masculinity personified by law enforcement and criminal characters. However, I do so indirectly through an examination of restaurant setting, such that the representation of space/place already pre-configures a kind of man (and masculinity) who will frequent that space/place.

10 Because police officers are generally assumed to routinely enjoy 'meat and potatoes,' police procedurals themselves have been described as '[m]eat and potatoes' (Schneider 20 February 2009) in the menu of television programming.

11 The outline stage can be circumvented, however, if the episode is written by the showrunner (as was the case for the season finale) since it is assumed that both he and the networks will approve of his outline, presuming that its contents are in line with the overall vision of the show.

12 The network outline is more accurately the first opportunity for network review of an episode's entire outline. Typically, by this stage in the writing process, the networks

should have already approved of the overall story arc through their feedback on the beat sheet or story area sheet. The approval is often thought of as a 'handshake deal' between the showrunner, the writer and the network(s) (DA 22 July 2012). The creative team has agreed to do a particular story, and the networks have also conditionally accepted the story so long as certain changes are made to the story.

13 To avoid confusion, I will refer to these characters functionally (as they are conceived functionally by the writers) rather than by name since their names change over the course of story documents. For example, in the beat sheet, they are Jenk (Thug 1) and Chucky (Thug 2). In the outlines, they are Jenko and Lennie. In the network draft (12 July 2009), they become Ben and Nells. Ben is renamed Dex beginning with the full blue production draft (22 July 2009).

14 Implicitly, this is the perspective of Cafferty. The killing of the thugs could be justified by ETF Sergeant Coombs as necessary, and this justification would hold because the raid itself would create enough 'confusion in the restaurant [with] people screaming and diving under tables' (network outline 17 June 2009) that there would be no eyewitnesses to contradict Coombs' version of events. Of course, Frank 'sees clearly' that Coombs murders Thug 1 despite the confusion in the restaurant.

15 While production drafts are read by producers for these kinds of budgetary constraints, the writers think through some of the story's implications for production prior to this point in (re)writing.

16 In the writers' outline (11 June 2009: 3), the restaurant is described as 'getting ready to close. Only one table of customers remain, four people in their twenties.'

17 While Mikhail Bakhtin (1981) coined the term 'chronotope' in relation to the novel, it is reworked for semiotic analyses of criminal spaces by Mariana Valverde (2006: 137–8). Specifically, each space appears to its observer as embedded in a particular temporality.

18 In contrast to the American reality TV show *COPS*, the Canadian version of the program, *To Serve and Protect*, is also notable for shooting in broad daylight as opposed to at night (Valverde 2006: 106). This tendency to shoot during the day allows Canadian producers to save money on extensive night lighting that might otherwise be necessary for night-time shoots.

19 The FCC defines obscene material as lacking serious literary or scientific value, and indecent material as that which depicts or describes sexual or excretory organs or activities.

20 Here, competence is distinctly different from creativity. Competence refers to the ability to do a specific task – in this instance, screenwriting – successfully, and does not necessarily refer to the innovative or creative quality of the product created from such a task.

21 The Proppian narrative is one that conceives of human activity in the form of confrontations, rather than as (contractual) exchanges (Greimas and Courtés 1982: 238). As such, we can certainly see how the conflict-driven television drama is essentially a Proppian narrative. Because the writing of network television dramas needs to conform to the unwritten S&P mandate that 'good triumph over evil,' such storytelling is also in line with Propp's subject of narrative analysis: the fairytale (or what he calls the folktale).

22 It would also have been the fourth episode aired on CBS. However, CBS cancelled the show after three episodes and as such, never had the chance to air 'The Unguarded Moment.'

23 Across all North American broadcasters, television dramas airing at 8 pm have more content restrictions (in terms of limiting the amount of graphic language, and graphic

images of sex, nudity and violence) than those airing at 10 pm. *The Bridge* was scheduled to air in the 10 pm timeslot.
24 The showrunner and executive producer assume that their consumer audience is intelligent and probably male dominated. The latter observation is related to the fact that the series has a male lead protagonist. Otherwise, they make no other speculations about their potential consumer audience.

Chapter 5

Showcasing Hamilton: how place becomes relevant in the making of Canadian crime dramas

Cra$h & Burn follows streetwise [Protected Insurance] adjuster Jimmy Burn as he navigates the gritty streets of Hamilton ('The Hammer'). He's squeezed between the cutthroat corporate culture that is big insurance; the con artists that make a living claim by claim; and the city-wide infiltration of organized crime.

(Showcase 18 November 2009)

Here's the thing [about Canadian–American co-produced police procedurals] *Flashpoint, Rookie Blue* and *The Bridge*].[1] Absent the gorgeous scenery and the occasional glimpse of an Ontario license plate, you would never guess this was a Canadian show. The cops work for a 'big city police force,' with no identifying uniform or cruiser markings.

(Beam 20 July 2010)

In previous chapters, we have discussed the writers' room as a laboratory that creates and fortifies representations over various trials of strength. In contrast, this chapter examines a stage of production prior to the setting up of a writers' room: pilot development and production. In television production, the pilot establishes the concept for a series and is made specifically for review by broadcasters.[2] As such, it becomes the basis on which broadcasters determine which series to develop. However, by studying pilot development and production, we begin our investigation outside the laboratory. In doing so, I address one of the main limitations of laboratory studies. As Latour (1988: 261) notes, these studies 'start out from a place without asking if this place has any relevance at all and without describing how it becomes relevant. In only a very few cases are labs the place to start with if we wish to see' fictional crime stories in the making. Thus, this chapter is interested in examining and describing how place becomes relevant, particularly as the setting of crime television dramas.

The question of place has plagued both the English-Canadian imagination and media scholars writing on Canadian television. As an elegant articulation of the question, Northrop Frye (1971) has stated that the Canadian sensibility is less perplexed by the question of 'who am I?' than by the riddle of 'where is here?'

In other words, the English-Canadian imagination is better understood, not as a question of national identity, but as a question that taps into a peculiarly Canadian sensibility (see Tinic 2009). This Canadian sensibility is thought to be inseparable from the question of geography and place. Celebrated Canadian author Margaret Atwood[3] (1972) similarly suggests that the Canadian imagination is preoccupied with attempting to explore the land because Canada is ultimately an unknown territory for the people who live in it. In contrast to England and the United States, Atwood argues that Canada does not have a single, unifying symbol that unambiguously[4] informs Canadians about themselves. America has The Frontier, which is attached to the sense of constantly conquering new territory (e.g. the West, outer space, or the rest of the world). England is The Island, a self-contained territory ruled by Kings and Queens. In comparison, Canada does not have a single, geographical symbol, perhaps as a result of its vast wilderness. Instead, Atwood contends that the central symbol for Canada is undoubtedly Survival, which is encapsulated not by the image of thriving but of simply staying alive. That is:

> Our central idea is one which generates, not the excitement and sense of adventure or danger[5] which The Frontier holds out, not the smugness and/or sense of security, of everything in its place, which The Island can offer, but an almost intolerable anxiety. Our stories are likely to be tales not of those who made it but of [. . .] [t]he survivor [who] has no triumph or victory but the fact of his survival.
>
> (Atwood 1972: 33)

The story of English-Canadian television as told by Canadian media critics and scholars has also largely been a tale of bare survival, always (forgettably) stuck between The Island and The Frontier. Unlike British television, Canadian television does not embody a sense of security (as continual reviews of the 'life' of the Canadian film and television industry will attest) that will allow it to take provocative risks. Unlike American television, Canadian television does not push the envelope, attempting to conquer new territory. As Steve Blackman (quoted in Hill 2002), co-creator of Canadian lawyer drama series *The Associates* (2001–2002) notes:

> Canadian television is trapped between two places.[6] You've got British television on the one side, which tends to be very smart, really well-written character-driven stuff that really has a market. On the other hand, you have the American flash, $2.8 million per episode *West Wing* where the sky's the limit. We're stuck in between because we don't have the money to make it flashy and no one is willing to take the risk to make it edgy enough to justify why a viewer would watch our show over the American show.

This chapter examines the strategies of contemporary Canadian crime dramas that attempt to pull themselves out of the liminal space of Canadian television, by taking up the symbol of The Frontier as an inspirational symbol under which Canadian writers and producers can find some success. In doing so, we will be exploring what Serra Tinic (2005) has called the 'Canadian media-identity problematic,' a problematic that links discussions of place to media representations and community formations in a global cultural economy. Much of this scholarly debate has examined how Canadian media producers position themselves between the poles of cultural specificity and universality, where the global and the homogeneous have tended to triumph over the local, the regional, and the national (Levine 2009; Matheson 2003).

In this formulation, representations of crime become the basic building blocks for Canadian television dramas poised for American and international export. While American crime dramas (e.g. *Hawaii 5-0*, *Miami Vice*, and the recent slew of place-based crime drama franchises, such as *CSI* and *NCIS*) have been set in a specific American city since the television production of *Dragnet* (1951–1959), Canadian–American co-produced crime procedurals often do not foreground a particular Canadian city as their setting. In doing so, Canadian police dramas have often been accused by Canadian viewers and television critics for being 'too American' (DA 22 July 2012).

In the trio of Canadian–American co-produced police dramas – *Flashpoint*, *Rookie Blue* and *The Bridge* – crime stories take place in 'a non-specific Canadian city that tries to stand in for the United States if [viewers] aren't paying that close of [*sic*] attention' (VanDerWerff 24 June 2010). That is, these stories are played out on the generic streets of a metropolitan city. While the producers of these three dramas do not hide the fact that they are shot in Toronto (e.g. Toronto street names and landmarks can be seen in the background by eagle-eyed local viewers), they also do not go out of their way to explicitly highlight this fact to viewers. For example, according to its lead male performer (quoted in Patch 21 July 2010), *Rookie Blue* is set in 'Generica,' which is a generic big city 'kind of like [the fictional American cities of] Metropolis or Gotham.' Likewise, *The Bridge*'s executive producer explains that his series 'could be in Toronto, it could be anywhere in Canada, it could be any major police service anywhere' (BC quoted in Patch 21 July 2010). In remarking upon the creation of such a generic setting, American television critics have deemed these Canadian co-productions 'not Canadian enough' (Patch 21 July 2010). American critics wanted these procedurals to 'own [their] Canadianness' (Dawn 8 July 2010), by explicitly representing their police as the *Toronto* police. This entailed showing viewers Toronto as Toronto rather than as some generic North American setting. In addition to the shows' non-specific setting, some critics were bothered by how the screen performers spoke 'generic North American,' whereby nary an 'eh?' or 'aboot' pass their lips (Beam 20 July 2010). In this instance, it seems as though the shows were not stereotypically Canadian enough, representing generic police officers clothed in blue uniforms rather than the distinctively Canadian figure of the Mountie (i.e. an officer of the Royal Canadian Mounted Police).

While Canada is the only nation-state with a policeman, the Mountie, as its symbol (Hutcheon 1990), its recent co-produced police dramas veer away from representing this uniquely Canadian law enforcer. This production strategy can be contrasted with the one used by the producers and writers of *Due South* (1994–1996), one of the first Canadian–American co-produced crime dramas. Created by Academy Award-winning writer Paul Haggis, *Due South* uses the figures of the Mountie and the American cop as stereotypical representations of each country. While the Mountie is represented as clean cut, courteous, honourable, friendly and by-the-book, the American detective is described as 'cynical, rough-and-tumble, to-hell-with-procedure minion of the law' (Berkowitz 6 January 1998: 3E). While Chicago, serving as the embodiment of America, is represented as dirty, corrupt and dangerous, Toronto is portrayed as family oriented, clean and civil (Tate and Allen 2004). Although the production strategy of *Due South* entailed accentuating Canadianness, current co-production strategies opt to downplay stereotypically Canadian elements.

In contrast to these recent co-produced procedurals set in a generic city anywhere, this chapter examines how *Cra$h & Burn* is unapologetically set in Hamilton, Ontario, as a condition of pilot development. Initially, the original pilot script had been written for the premium American cable network HBO, and the television drama had been set in New York City. When Canadian specialty channel Showcase became interested in the script, the broadcaster demanded that the showrunner MM translate the American setting of *Cra$h & Burn* into a Canadian one, in order to satisfy broadcasting and funding requirements. In examining the production of the *Cra$h & Burn* pilot, I am interested in examining the processes by which place is made relevant in the production of Canadian crime television dramas through certain key translations.

Translations fuse together interests, and programs of research and representation. Specifically, the strategic meaning of translation defines 'a stronghold established in such a way that, whatever people do and wherever they go, they have to pass through this contender's position, by helping him further his own interests' (Latour 1988: 253). In television production, the broadcaster is such a stronghold, and producers and showrunners translate their projects in such a way as to further the broadcaster's programming interests. The broadcaster assumes this position because a television show that is not broadcast might as well be a falling tree in a forest without any observers. Although the broadcaster assumes the stronghold position in general, different broadcasters have different programming interests, resulting from different market orientations. Since the 1990s, the niche market orientation of premium cable networks, such as HBO, has informed the production of particular kinds of television drama, all of which tend to focus on the journey of a morally ambiguous anti-hero in a specific city. Over time, (North American) television critics have lauded these series as 'quality' television in contrast to the 'popular' fare provided by large broadcasters, which attempt to appeal to the masses through morally clear-cut stories in which good triumphs over evil. (I have previously referred to this kind of programming as 'network television.') Thus, in this chapter, we will pay attention to the ways in which Canadian showrunners and producers translate their series into ways that fit with either 'quality' cable or 'popular' network programming. This in turn has implications for the representation of setting: while cable programming has veered towards the representation of particular, specific settings, commercial broadcasters generally prefer series that take place in more generic urban settings.

Before delineating the road map for this chapter, it should be noted that translations are needed to *make equivalent* two different things (Latour 1988: 253). As Latour (1988: 170) notes, the difference between equivalent and making equivalent is analogous to the difference between driving an automobile and building a freeway. Certainly, more work is needed to build the freeway than to drive the automobile. In the production of television dramas, storytelling in the context of a writers' room is analogous to driving an automobile down the freeway already built and paved by the pilot. Both the writing staff and directors of a television series work under the framework established by the pilot. Sometimes, the framework is explicitly codified in a text called the series bible,[7] and the writing staff simply ensures that their episodic stories are equivalent to the kinds of story found in the bible. By contrast, in developing the pilot, the showrunner, producer and director need to *make* their creative interests equivalent to the particular creative-commercial interests of a specific broadcaster. Thus, this chapter examines the 'freeway' being built during the stage of pilot development and production: what are the implicit rules underlying the construction of this storytelling highway? What kinds of knowledge and aesthetic considerations make it possible? And more importantly, where is this 'freeway' located and how is its location made relevant?

We will address these questions through a case study analysis of the pilot development and production of *Cra$h & Burn*. This analysis will be juxtaposed against the translation strategies of the aforementioned trio of Canadian–American co-produced police dramas. *Cra$h & Burn* is interesting precisely because it reverses the direction of geographic translation(s) made in the production of those Toronto-shot, co-produced dramas: instead of making a Canadian city equivalent to an American one, the success of the *Cra$h & Burn* pilot is contingent on the showrunner, producer and director's combined ability to make a well-known American city analogous to a local, Canadian one. Hamilton, Ontario, becomes a relevant setting in which the series takes place through translations that make 1) American cable programming interests equivalent to those of Canadian specialty channel Showcase; and 2) the pilot's production feasible in terms that are agreeable to both an independent production company and Canadian government funding agencies. Lastly, we will examine the specific knowledge and aesthetic translations that follow from a representational strategy that focuses on immersing viewers in a particular, local setting.

Beginning in New York with HBO: the story of *Lawyers, Guns and Money*

Cra$h & Burn began life under a different title – *Lawyers, Guns and Money* (*LGM*) – and for an American television network. It was initially a project that had been moving forward under the supervision of American premium cable network HBO until it was stopped by the network's (former) president. The show's core concept entailed exploring the world of insurance adjusters, which was something that had not been done before on television. As such, this offered a novel playground for staging the stories that the showrunner MM had heard of Progressive Insurance through one of its founders, particularly about 'these bikers [the company] was insuring, the crazy scams that were going on in the business' (MM 27 October 2009). Inspired by these anecdotal stories about insurance scams, the original script follows insurance adjuster Jimmy Shea as he navigates the tricky terrain towards becoming a legitimate, law-abiding family man while trying to avoid any lapses back into illegitimate, criminal activity. Specifically, he attempts to avoid being sucked into an elaborate insurance scam run by the Russian mob, involving staged car accidents and personal injury fraud.

While the world of insurance would be new territory for a North American television drama, the world of *LGM* was set in the familiar playground of New York City, as the show's idea was originally conceived shortly after September 11, 2001 in New York with help from a New York director. As a result, protagonist Jimmy Shea traveled across a New York represented by various well-known landmarks. In *LGM*, which was set in Brighton Beach, Jimmy lived in a sad high-rise apartment that backed onto the Coney Island Amusement Park. He worked at the Brooklyn branch of Protected Insurance, which was 'sealed off like Fort Apache from the public' (HBO script 2001: 7). The head of Protected Insurance's fraud investigations had a photograph in his office of him posing with the cast members of *Law and Order*. *Law and Order*, of course, is a very successful American crime drama series that has shot for so long in New York that it can probably be considered a New York institution in and of itself. Lastly, as the pilot script was entitled 'Freedom,' characters searched for their own freedom in various ways, all of them eventually converging on a yacht that circled the Statue of Liberty – the most iconic American image of freedom – in the New York Harbor. The Statue was contrasted with New York's 'wounded skyline' (MM 19 June 2008: 55) and the visible absence of the Twin Towers. With the show's conceit revolving around insurance, the script referenced how some American insurance companies had been impacted by the events of 9/11, including their refusal to pay damages on the grounds that the destruction of the Twin Towers was an act of war (MM 19 June 2008: 55). After all, American insurance policies contain clauses that exempt acts of war from coverage.

As a script, *LGM* fits into the mould of television drama series produced by HBO in the late 1990s in several ways. First, it is set in New York, which has also been the setting of many of HBO's other acclaimed television drama series, including *Sex and the City* (1998–2008) and *The Sopranos*[8] (1999–2007). The setting of New York makes sense in light of the fact that HBO itself has its headquarters in New York City.

Second, *LGM* is about the world of insurance, which allows HBO to bring a relatively unexplored world to television. Conceiving itself as The Frontier of television programming, HBO had ventured into exploring worlds that no major American broadcaster would dare to explore, such as prisons (*Oz*), organized crime (*The Sopranos*) and the funeral business (*Six Feet Under*). In seeking to differentiate itself from conventional network fare, HBO's programming formula in the late 1990s had ceded the basic dramatic universes of politics, law, and medicine to the broadcasting networks (see Simon 2004b). After all, HBO's network logic can be summed up at that time by its motto, 'It's not TV. It's HBO.' Primarily operating under the mode of counterprogramming (Banet-Weiser *et al.* 2007), HBO constituted itself as the binary opposite to the broadcasting networks (i.e. TV itself) and as a provider of Quality drama.

Dana Polan (2007) argues that there are two kinds of Quality television drama. One strand of Quality originates in the elegant adaptation of canonic Western literature (e.g. *Masterpiece Theatre*), and has primarily followed a British model of cultural uplift.[9] In contrast, HBO mobilizes an indigenously American Quality, which focuses on a working-class Everyman as he confronts life's quandaries. *LGM*'s protagonist is just such a working-class stiff. The series revolves around Jimmy's struggle and toil to become not a great man, but an ordinary (middle-class) one. As an insurance adjuster, he is actively involved in mediating life's ordinary obstacles, by selling security in an insecure world where one increasingly 'can't do anything in life without insurance' (MM 27 October 2009).

Although *LGM* fits the general outline of HBO's television dramas, the premium cable network ultimately passed on the project. However, the project itself retained its pedigree of HBO 'Quality' as it was presented to other potential networks for production and/or distribution. The showrunner knew that given his vision for the show, it was probably never going to be aired on conventional network television. If it were to air in Canada, it was not going to be a CBC or CTV show. Instead, 'if it's anything, it's [a show for American cable channels] Showtime, FX, that kind of world' (MM 27 October 2009). Even when seeking American distribution after completing 13 episodes, the showrunner and producer are keen on finding a home for the series on 'cable-y networks' rather than broadcasting networks (MM 27 October 2009). Such a strategy underlies how the content and format of television dramas vary in accordance with the market orientation of media organizations. Like newspapers (see Ericson *et al.* 1995), television networks create and pursue distinct markets, and in doing so select new television series that fit well with their own conceptualization of the audience and their own brand identity.

The broadcaster as stronghold: popular vs. quality in the post-network era

We will take a moment to consider the distinction between 'popular' and 'quality' representations in television.[10] In doing so, we will take a scenic detour through discussions of the North American broadcasting landscape in the post-network era, and how 'popular' and 'quality' are defined in relation to the markets of

Canadian television. In doing so, we will consider the *location* of particular broadcasters, where their location is largely determined by their particular regulatory structure and targeted audience. This discussion examines the broadcaster as a 'stronghold' with particular programming interests. The broadcaster's position is made 'strong' in the name of the audience to which it caters (see Gitlin 1983), necessitating that showrunners fit themselves and their shows into the particular programming position held by a specific broadcaster. Places within a television drama (i.e. setting) are informed by where the drama itself fits into the broadcasting landscape.

In considering the notion of markets tailored towards the production of either 'popular' or 'quality' representations, criminologists have primarily focused on the production of newspapers. In their groundbreaking study of the production of newspapers, Ericson *et al.* (1995) distinguish between two kinds of market orientation. Pitched to a broad demographic, 'popular' newspapers seek acceptance through formats that include iconic elements presented in an entertaining and lively manner. These elements include pictures, brief items on simple themes, strongly opinionated columns, colloquial expressions and parochial interests. They produce the effect of being 'close to reality' by playing on readers' hearts. In contrast, 'quality' newspapers seek acceptance through literary and symbolic means. That is, they are formatted to include longer items and continuing stories on complex matters affecting business and political elites on both the national and international scale. Attention to language and details is part and parcel of the 'quality' newspaper's concern with being an accurate and authentic source of record. Unlike the mass appeal of the 'popular' newspaper, the 'quality' newspaper appeals to a richer, more educated niche market. There are also, of course, newspapers that include both 'popular' and 'quality' elements.

Parts of Ericson *et al.*'s (1995) analysis can be applied to television programs. 'Quality' television dramas, like 'quality' newspapers, allow for longer features through continuing, serialized storylines. Because the HBO model of television production is made possible through subscription fees rather than through advertising, its programs contain narratives that are not broken up by commercial breaks. Since writers of television dramas do not aspire to objectivity in the same way that journalists do, however, the distinction between 'popular' and 'quality' dramas cannot be drawn on the criterion of entertainment. Both kinds of television drama are designed to play on the viewer's heart or tastes. The difference might lie instead on representations of moral complexity. While 'popular' television dramas might dramatize simple themes, such as good vs. evil, 'quality' dramas highlight instead moral ambiguity.

While Ericson *et al.* (1995) do not provide a chronology of the 'popular' vs. 'quality' distinction that typifies newspapers, it is possible to delineate one for television in which 'popular' network fare has been increasingly pitted against 'quality' cable fare. To that end, it is instructive to examine how showrunner David Simon argued for the development and production of *The Wire* as a future HBO series. *The Wire* is an American television drama that follows a police investigation into a complex drug-dealing operation, highlighting its impact on not only its youthful participants but also on city politicians, police bureaucrats and news journalists. Despite the critical acclaim that *The Wire* has received since its debut, HBO initially had doubts about the crime drama's fit with the cable network. As a result, David Simon (2004b: 36–7) made the following passionate argument in order to persuade HBO's then President of Original Programming of its compatibility with the cable network's programming interests:

> *The Wire* is, I would argue, the next challenge to the network logic and the next challenge for HBO. It is grounded in the most basic network universe – the cop show – and yet, very shortly, it becomes clear to any viewer that something subversive is being done with that universal. Suddenly, the police bureaucracy is amoral, dysfunctional, and criminality, in the form of drug culture, is just as suddenly a bureaucracy. Scene by scene, viewers find their carefully formed presumptions about cops and robbers undercut by alternative realities. [. . .] Police work is at time marginal or incompetent. Criminals are neither stupid nor cartoonish, and neither are they all sociopathic. [. . .] The argument is this: It is a significant victory for HBO to counterprogram alternative, inaccessible worlds against standard network fare. But it would, I argue, be a more profound victory for HBO to take the essence of network fare and smartly turn it on its head, so that no one who sees HBO's take on the culture of crime and crime fighting can watch anything like *CSI*, or *NYPD Blue*, or *Law & Order* again without knowing that every punch was pulled on those shows [. . .]. The numbers would still be there for *CSI* and such; the relevance would not.

In the US, the television landscape has long been historically dominated by four broadcasting networks – namely, CBS, ABC, NBC and more recently FOX. Because they are over-the-air broadcasters, their programming content is intended to be accessible to everyone, and as such is subject to legal regulation by the Federal Communications Commission (FCC). As discussed in Chapter 4, these broadcasting networks created their own Standards and Practices department as a way to self-regulate in order to avoid much interference from the FCC. However, because of the quasi-legal regulation of programming content, these networks needed to air 'prosocial' content, which encouraged representations of good clearly triumphing over evil. This notion of 'prosocial' content has shaped images of police officers as generally competent crime fighters, which has consequently become a standard representation in the popular cop shows aired by these networks, such as the aforementioned *CSI* and *Law and Order*. As David Simon points out, these 'popular' representations historically preceded the emergence of 'quality' representations, precisely because they formed the standard against which the latter are produced and measured. That is, these popular representations provide the norm against which cable networks can deviate through the production of creative counter-images and alternative realities. These counter-images are also made possible since American cable networks are not subject to the same level of regulation by the FCC, which began de-regulating cable television in 1972. Since 1985, the cable industry has been fully freed from FCC regulation because they are not over-the-air broadcasters (Cantor and Cantor 1992). As cable networks are not accessible to everyone but only to their subscribers, their broadcasting capabilities are not tied to providing 'prosocial' content in 'the public interest.' Because of their particular economic model, cable networks do not need to define success in terms of mass popularity, as measured by numbers. Instead of commercial success, they strive to achieve relevance in their programming, where relevance is geared towards the more educated, urban sophisticates who subscribe to the network (Polan 2007).

With the critical success of cable television dramas[11] and their attendant stamp of 'quality' since the late 1990s, some scholars have heralded the beginning of a new 'post-network era' of television (Lotz 2006, 2009). Television in the network era[12] could be understood as a fairly monolithic entity, where broadcast systems operated in an era of scarcity (Ellis 2000). With few channels and few programs, we could assume that the majority of the population would be watching the same program at the same time, allowing television to bring together a nation. During this era of scarcity, television was understandably fundamental for projects of social and cultural integration. In contrast to the network era, the post-network era suggests that the object of television has been redefined by various cultural and industrial factors. Specifically, the increasing number of cable networks is associated with the increasing fragmentation of audiences. While broadcasting networks still attempt to appeal to the masses,[13] the proliferation of cable networks target particular fragments of the overall audience, whereby a niche market is captured by catering to particular interests and demographics.

Canada's broadcasting landscape

In Canada's three-tiered broadcasting system (i.e. broadcasters, specialty channels; and premium cable networks), there has also been a shift towards the catering of niche markets through the increase in number of specialty channels. Specialty channels were licensed by the Canadian Radio-Television Telecommunications Commission (CRTC) on the condition that they would air content associated only with a specific genre and would not include general interest services, which are seen to be the domain of over-the-air Canadian broadcasters. For example, MuchMusic is licensed to air music-related content, and The Sports Networks (TSN) is licensed to deliver sports-related coverage. While the US experienced a proliferation of premium cable networks, Canada has fewer premium cable networks (HBO Canada and The Movie Network) than it does specialty channels.[14] In contrast to premium cable channels, specialty channels use an economic model where revenue depends not only on subscriptions but also on advertising. As a result, a 'successful' television drama on a specialty channel would not only be relevant to its subscribers, but should also be able to pull in solid ratings on a weekly basis from the channel's niche audience.

Although crime-related series have been developed and aired on various Canadian specialty channels, their content and format vary with how those particular 'narrowcasters' conceive of their audience. For example, crime docudramas are a popular hybrid genre in which true crime stories are told through a combination of documentary storytelling and dramatic enactments. They have been commissioned and developed by the Discovery Channel and Canada's the W network.

For example, Discovery Channel initially bought the rights to distribute *Exhibit A: The Secrets of Forensic Science* in 1997, which examined how real-life forensic scientists solved crimes. According to anecdotal accounts, the docudrama series has influenced the writing of several fictional episodes of *Law and Order* (SB 30 July 2008) and may have possibly inspired the development of the fictional series *CSI* (LB 22 August 2008). Initially, the Discovery Channel was interested in *Exhibit A* because it fit the network's attempt to re-position non-fiction as 'edu-tainment' (i.e. educational *and* entertaining) in the television industry (see Chris 2007). This network mandate encompassed 'repatriat[ing] science and technology' to a general public lacking in knowledge of these subjects (Tedesco 18 June 1990: 22). As such, *Exhibit A* was sold as science programming (LB 22 August 2008) that included an entertainment factor through its inclusion of dramatic re-enactments. Although the network was initially hesitant to pick up the series because of its innovative format, the program's success eventually led the network to privately commission its own crime docudrama series, *Forensic Factor*. Given the network's experience with crime docudramas, stemming from its initial involvement with *Exhibit A*, *Forensic Factor* targets a particular niche audience that has been aggregated into the figure of 'Discovery Dan'[15] (KS 17 November 2008). Specifically, *Forensic Factor* targets male viewers between the ages of 25 and 40 years old through its subject matter (crime), genre (docudrama), and the procedural storytelling approach[16] (KS 17 November 2008).

In contrast, the W network (formerly known as the Women Network) targets female viewers with its crime docudramas. Unlike *Exhibit A* and *Forensic Factor*, where science is used to solve crimes, the W network commissions paranormal crime docudramas in which psychics solve crimes. It is not clear why the paranormal premise was selected as particularly appealing to women; however, it is clear that the network imagines the busy housewife as its target audience. This has influenced the content of the series: the W network issued a ban on true crime stories involving children as victims, believing that this would upset female viewers (SN 8 August 2008). Moreover, the imagined 'busy housewife' viewer has also influenced the show's formatting. Specifically, the network required that writers include a constant repetition of minimal information in the simplest language possible. This was to ensure that the show would be understandable to a viewer 'who is [also] watching two kids right now, got something in the microwave [. . .], the dog is running around [. . .]; she missed the first five minutes of the show; she missed the first minute back after the commercial break' (SN 8 August 2008). Thus, the general repetition and 'dumbing down' of language (SN 8 August 2008) is particular to the series' production and distribution on the W network, and not to the genre of crime docudrama.

While Canada has been quite successfully producing and exporting crime docudramas over the past two decades, docudramas are rarely considered by television critics or Canadian academics because they have been peripheral to the discussion of Canadian popular culture. By and large, they would probably be considered 'popular' television fare that does not venture near the territory of 'quality.' In contrast, the fictional, one-hour television drama has been considered the cornerstone of Canadian television and Canadian culture (see Writers Guild of Canada 2003), where 'quality' might be produced. Because Canadian television writers and producers watch American television, they have been affected by the 'popular' network vs. 'quality' cable distinction that has played out in the US. As *Flashpoint*'s executive producer remarks, in Canada, 'there's a snobbery about commercial shows [such as her own show] here, among writers particularly. Everyone dreams of doing a dark *HBO* [or cable] series' (Anne Marie La Traverse quoted in Onstad 7 June 2009). The popular–quality distinction has also been playing out in the case of Canadian private, commercial broadcasters, such as CTV and Canwest Global. To set themselves apart from Canada's public broadcaster CBC, these private, commercial broadcasters and their specialty channel subdivisions have historically proceeded under a programming strategy that focused on producing Canadian television dramas that were just as popular and competitive as the American television programs that were being aired in Canada (Gittins 1998). In pursuing this strategy, these commercial broadcasters tended to emulate American television programs.

While American discussions of 'popular' vs. 'quality' television series have largely been mapped onto their network origins (i.e. over-the-air broadcaster vs. premium cable network), the Canadian discussion is complicated by 1) the existence of specialty channels that are neither premium cable nor general broadcaster, and 2) the desire to define 'quality' as particularly Canadian. As a result, Canadian cultural critics tend to subscribe to an additional binary division (see Matheson 2003). For them, 'popular' television fare is American like, in which Canadian cities are disguised as generic, possibly American ones.[17] It is Canadian industrial television made in the mould of American television dramas. By contrast, a 'quality' Canadian television show is capable of signifying the local and social particularities of living in specific Canadian locales, and reflects 'Canadian attitudes, opinions, ideas, values and artistic creativity' (Government of Canada 1991).

For the rest of this chapter, we will be interested in exploring how the producers and showrunner of *LGM* translate a script originally written for HBO into a viable pilot for Canadian specialty channel Showcase. That is, how does the showrunner translate HBO Quality into 'quality' Canadian television programming? By translation, we will be interested in the convergences and homologies (see Gherardi and Nicolini 2000) that the showrunner and producers of *LGM* make, in order to make a 'quality' Canadian television drama. Now back to the main story.

Playing with Showcase

As a specialty channel that specifically airs only fictional dramatic programming, Showcase received its first license from the CRTC in 1994. It is owned by Canadian private, commercial broadcaster Canwest Global, and was originally licensed under the following conditions: 95 per cent of the aired content must be dramatic programming, and 95 per cent of this content must be produced outside the US (CRTC 6 June 1994). These conditions went hand in hand with the specialty channel's own mandate: the channel aimed to redress the lack of viewing opportunities for Canadian drama, by creating a service that is predominantly and distinctively Canadian. This focus on Canadian content was translated into prime-time slots on the programming schedule. Showcase would broadcast only Canadian programming during prime time or peak viewing hours of 7 pm to 10 pm. Initially, Showcase provided this Canadian content in the form of independent movies and second window[18] broadcasts of classic CBC drama productions (e.g. *Wojeck, Street Legal,* and *King of Kensington*). However, the specialty channel shifted from simply re-broadcasting Canadian content to creating original Canadian television series. This move resulted in half-hour television series, such as the soap opera *Paradise Falls* (2001–8), the documentary series *KinK* (2001–6) and the mockumentary series *Trailer Park Boys* (2001–8). With their relatively risqué and 'adult' content (e.g. frank discussions and depictions of sexuality), these 'Showcase Originals' were deemed successful and the channel continued to search for programs with an 'edgy' bent.

In 2008, Showcase was looking to commission a one-hour, fictional television drama series (MM 27 October 2009), which would be new programming and production territory for the specialty channel. Specifically, the channel wanted something in the vein of American television drama *Rescue Me* (2004–2011), which had been well received by the channel's audience. *Rescue Me* is a series that focuses on the personal and professional lives of a group of New York City firefighters. As it originally aired on FX, an American network that has built its brand on the provision of edgy, original cable programming, the main protagonist is a male anti-hero: he is a self-destructive, hypocritical, manipulative, ill-tempered alcoholic on the mend. As such, Showcase was interested in a gritty drama interspersed with black comedy. Thus, *LGM*'s showrunner pitched his show as *The Sopranos* (a television drama) meets *The Office* (a situation comedy),[19] although it veers more towards the gritty than the funny. What is important in this articulation is that *LGM* is also simultaneously imagined as the child begotten by a premium cable series and a network series, placing it into the intermediate market orientation of a Canadian specialty channel.

In seeking a gritty dramatic series, the specialty channel was distinguishing itself from the kind of drama sought by CBC, Canada's public broadcaster. Unlike

Showcase, CBC network executives were looking for 'ongoing, multiyear, thirteen-episode, 9 pm adult dramas that will run for many, many years' (Tom Hastings, head of CBC drama, quoted in Parker 2010: 35), but were not looking for dramas that were particularly dark in tone. They preferred dramas that were lighter in tone, and that could reach a broad audience rather than a niche one (Parker 2010).

Because the tone of a dramatic series is pre-set by the broadcaster that commissions it, television writers and producers need to have some understanding of the kind of tone desired by a particular network. This knowledge is quite important, particularly since writers and producers need to be able to find a receptive network that will hear their series pitch. Because Showcase was interested in an edgy drama series, they responded well to the initial HBO script for *Lawyers, Guns and Money* with its trappings of 'quality' cable programming. However, the network executives wanted the showrunner to produce a pilot episode of *LGM* for review.

Pilots

Often, the pilot becomes the first episode of a television series.[20] In Canada, making a pilot is a recent step in the evolution of making a television series, and has become more common in the mid-2000s (Montagu 2009). Canada's public broadcaster shifted towards pilot development and testing in 2006 (Smith 2006), and its commercial broadcasters, such as CTV, began venturing into pilot production in 2007 (Andreeva and Vlessing 1–3 February 2008). Previously, Canadian broadcasters would order series directly from scripts by known writers and producers, in which case the making of a pilot was a rare occurrence. As Canadian broadcasters are increasingly flirting with American ways of creating new entertainment television content, they have turned towards creating pilots for potential television series. Unlike their American counterparts, Canadian broadcasters cannot afford to shoot more than a handful of pilots per year (see Figure 5.1).

However, they do use the pilot as a way to test a series' core concept. Thus, the pilot is written and produced as proof of concept. In this sense, the pilot is analogous to what Latour (1988: 85) has described as the 'theatre of the proof.' Latour argues that Louis Pasteur's genius lay in his invention of demonstrative and dramatic experiments that would convince his spectators of a particular phenomenon. Pasteur's ideas did not emerge fully formed from the laboratory, and spread outwards through society. Instead, he gave them a lot of help by visually 'forcing' others to 'share' his point of view. In convincing an educated lay public about the existence of anthrax, Pasteur did not require the public to sift through difficult statistical data that could explain what an epidemic was. He displayed the effects of anthrax to a crowd by visually demonstrating the differential death that struck a group of chickens in the laboratory, which was something that could be seen 'in broad daylight' (Latour 1993: 85). So, too, the purpose of the pilot is to convince a particular broadcaster that a creative concept is worth pursuing

	American					Canadian		
Broadcaster	ABC	CBS	FOX	NBC	CW	GLOBAL	CBC	CTV
Pilot	25	22	14	12	6	5	10	3
Series pick-up (Season 1)	11	6	6	5	4	4	3	3
Season 2 pick-up	4	2	3	2	2	2	2	2

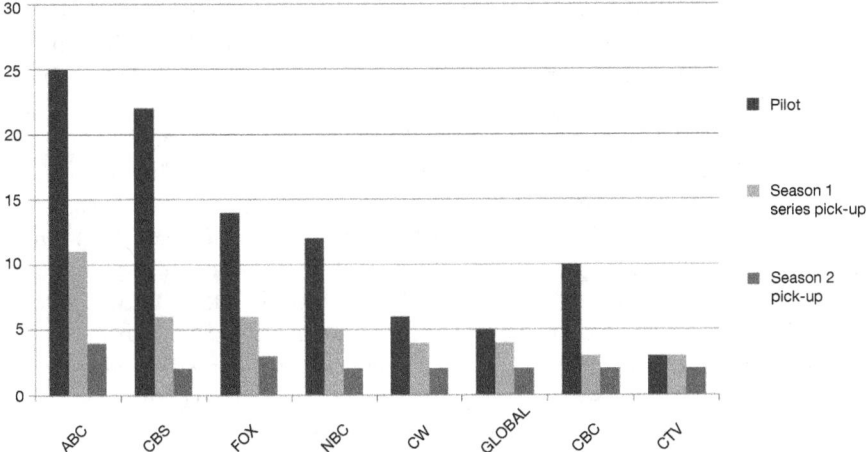

Figure 5.1 The number of scripted pilots commissioned and aired by major North American broadcasters between fall 2009 and spring 2010

Sources: Data on scripted American pilots are based on information from *The Hollywood Reporter's* (2010) pilot log. Data on scripted Canadian pilots are based on information compiled by Archer (2009–2010), Andreeva and Vlessing (1–3 February 2008), and Vlessing (27 October 2008). The pilots commissioned by CanWest Global include those that air on its specialty channels (e.g. Showcase). Series pick-ups were counted if they were immediately announced within a year of the pilot's commission. As a result, these data do not reflect the number of pilots that were eventually picked up as a series after fall 2010.

through visual demonstration. Thus, when Canadian broadcasters shifted away from producing and distributing series based solely on scripts, they were edging away from a model of production that lacked a visual proof of concept and moving towards a 'theatre of the proof.'

As such, we can also conceptualize the pilot as yet another experimental trial where the conceptual ingredients for a series are first assembled for review by broadcasters. The pilot is proof that the following three basic elements can come together in a compelling way: 1) the creation of main characters, 2) the establishment of the series' tone, and 3) the creation of the main settings or the world in which the series takes place (Lucas 2009). In the case of *LGM*, the showrunner needed specifically to prove that the New York setting of the initial HBO script could be translated to an analogous Canadian setting. Here, the Canadian setting is conceptualized as especially important because 1) it will become necessary for Canadian funding purposes, and 2) it is expected to creatively inform both the construction of the main characters and the series' tone.

Moving to Hamilton, Ontario

At this point, the showrunner of *LGM* is tasked with making a pilot, and in order to do so needs to partner with an independent Canadian film and television production company. He also needs to partner quickly because his is not the only drama pilot being made for Showcase. Indeed, his pilot is one of four pilots commissioned by Showcase's parent company, Canwest Global (Vlessing 27 October 2008). The competing pilots include the following: 1) *Shattered* is premised on an ex-cop who solves crimes with his multiple personality disorder, enabling him to simultaneously be both good cop and bad cop; 2) *Clean* is about an addiction counsellor who is close to checking himself into rehabilitation; and 3) *Lost Girl* is a paranormal drama about a woman with supernatural powers.[21] These competing pilots would all go into production around the same time, and Showcase was likely to pick up the first season of whichever pilot was completed first. Thus, there was a need to move 'very quickly because [*LGM*] wanted to be first in line, to be [Showcase's] first one-hour show' (MM 27 October 2009). In this race to the finish line of pilot completion, *LGM*'s showrunner quickly partners with Toronto-based Whizbang Films, since they had recently worked together on an original television drama series *ZOS: Zone of Separation* for Canadian premium cable channel The Movie Network (TMN).

Whizbang Films

Whizbang Films is founded by award-winning Canadian screen performer Paul Gross and producer FS. Of the founding pair, Gross is most well known for playing Canadian Mountie Benton Fraser in *Due South*, and Geoffrey Tennant in the critically acclaimed Canadian mini-series *Slings & Arrows* (2003–6). Within the Canadian television industry, Gross has been described as the 'bankable 800 lb. Gorilla of Canadian production' (McGrath 12 June 2009). That is, he is one of the few Canadian performers-producers known for making television series that are both commercial and critically acclaimed. As such, his involvement in the production of a series endows the project with a certain amount of heft. The heavy lifting in producing *LGM*, however, was primarily done by Gross' producing partner FS. As a result of FS' input into the production process of the pilot, Hamilton was selected as the specific setting for the world of *LGM*.

Before examining the aesthetic implications of this decision, I will first discuss the practical ramifications of choosing Hamilton, Ontario, as the pilot's setting. Practically, the choice of Hamilton is related to FS' experience in making television series and films in that particular city, which includes knowledge of who needs to be on scene in order to film a specific stunt. For example, in *LGM*, viewers are first introduced to protagonist Jimmy when he arrives on the scene of a traffic accident. The victim of the car crash is being pulled out by a hydraulic rescue tool known as the 'Jaws of Life.' Because of safety regulations, firefighters need to be on set in order to operate the 'Jaws of Life.' However, the Hamilton

Professional Firefighters Association was at that time in a contract dispute, and refused to engage in any paid duty work. This did not deter FS who was aware that Dofasco, a major steel company, had its own private fire department, which could be persuaded to help the production crew operate the 'Jaws of Life' (personal production notes 9 October 2009). Moreover, during the time in which *LGM* is slotted to film, FS was also scheduled to (line) produce[22] and supervise the production of the made-for-television movie *The Good Witch II* in Hamilton. Shooting two projects within close physical and geographic proximity would allow FS to oversee both productions.

Because permanent sets are not built for pilots, *LGM* needed to be shot entirely on location. As a shooting location, Hamilton is more pleasant and affordable than Toronto. While neighbourhood and traffic disruptions that occur as a result of filming tend to elicit grumbling and much complaining in Toronto, Hamilton residents are simply excited that filming is happening in their city (Barnard 7 February 2010). Consequently, location managers perceive Hamilton as an easy shooting location (Barnard 7 February 2010). In addition, it is also cheaper to shoot in this particular city because both parking and overnight hotel stays are less expensive. The city also offers film and television productions an additional 10 per cent tax credit for shooting outside the Greater Toronto Area. The additional percentage of tax credit is an important incentive for Canadian television producers who are attempting to multiply and enhance a production's funding sources.

Funding

Canadian television productions, such as *LGM*, need to access as many funding sources as possible[23] (MM 27 October 2009). As we have just seen, funding is often attached to filming in particular Canadian locations through tax incentives. Additionally, a television drama could qualify for financial support from the Canadian Television Fund (CTF)[24] and Telefilm Canada, two different sources of federal government money intended to increase both the quantity and quality of Canadian programming for Canadian viewers. In order to be eligible for this funding, the project needs to fulfill the following requirements: 1) it is shot and set primarily in Canada; 2) key creative personnel are Canadian citizens;[25] 3) the project's underlying (intellectual property) rights are owned, and significantly and meaningfully developed by Canadians; and 4) the project speaks to Canadians about, and reflects Canadian themes and subject matters (Ministry of Cultural Heritage 2009). These sources of funding arise out of cultural and broadcasting policies that aim to preserve Canadian national identity, and to protect the uniqueness of this identity from American dominance[26] (Beaty and Sullivan 2006). However, there is nothing in the cultural and broadcasting policies themselves that spell out what 'Canadian' content actually entails. As such, showrunners make a choice about how 'Canadian' their production ought to be. Ultimately, this is a choice borne out of balancing commercial and creative demands, and has implications for how showrunners represent the city in which a crime series takes place.

Representational strategies: translating the city

In balancing creative and commercial imperatives, showrunners endeavour to make these imperatives align with each other. As a result of this balancing, this leads to two different strategies for representing the city in crime procedurals, stemming from differences in the network's market orientation. The first strategy represents the city in a generic manner, and is employed by the showrunners of Canadian–American co-produced police procedurals destined for over-the-air broadcast and export. In contrast to conventional and 'popular' network fare, the showrunner of *LGM* represents the city in a very specific way, highlighting its local particularities. This is in line with how original cable programs, particularly 'quality' HBO dramas, have represented the city.

The generic city: Toronto as a 'world-class' city

Richard Sparks (1992) notes that the vast majority of police television shows have been set in great cities as a means to represent the metropolitan experience. Supported by the history of American literature and cinema, American cities have long provided archetypal settings for crime stories (Knight 1980). In line with this understanding, Canadian television producers have attempted to translate a Canadian city into an implicitly American setting in their co-produced police dramas.

For example, despite being shot in Toronto and inspired by real-life Toronto cases of police corruption, *The Bridge* is set in the archetypal big, urban Generic City, patrolled by black-and-white police cars without any explicit affiliation to a specific city. If translations fundamentally entail making one thing equivalent to another (Latour 1988), then *The Bridge*'s showrunner translates the Toronto setting in a particular way: he makes Toronto equivalent to any other large, urban city through the concept of the 'world-class' city.[27] For the trio of Toronto-shot, Canadian–American co-produced police dramas – *The Bridge*, *Flashpoint* and *Rookie Blue* – the translation move of Toronto as a 'world-class' city is commercially significant because it places Toronto on a different scale of measurement. As a world-class city, Toronto measures up to other cities in the world, and hence it is no longer about measuring the city's Canadian-ness on a national scale.

The notion of Toronto as a world-class city became a popular catchphrase for the city in the 1980s. This phrase was connected to a top-down approach to seeing the city, emphasizing Toronto's place within the global flow of capital through images of skyscrapers and corporate towers (Matheson 2003). It is this image of Toronto as 'glamorous [and] expensive-looking' (head-writer of Flashpoint and showrunner of *Rookie Blue*, Tassie Cameron quoted in Onstad 7 June 2009) that is captured and sold by *Flashpoint*. As *Flashpoint* co-creator Mark Ellis (quoted in Barr 15 July 2010) notes:

> Well I think Toronto is a big city and we often label ourselves here as being a 'world class city' and I don't think New York or Chicago or LA go around labeling themselves as a 'world class city' but it's something we Canadians feel like we need to do. But I think Toronto is a great looking, big, diverse city and [. . .] why not film it there?

With an additional American co-producing broadcaster, these police dramas have higher production values than the average television drama made solely through Canadian funding. Cross-border co-productions typically have budgets of over $1.8 million per episode, compared to the $1.2 million on a purely Canadian-produced series (Binning 2009/2010).[28] As a result, the series' 'expensive-looking' aesthetic ensures that 'it doesn't look Canadian,' which is paradoxically the highest compliment in Canadian television (Onstad 7 June 2009). That is, the series measures up in appearance to the more expensive American television dramas that air on Canadian television networks, and avoids the distinctive Canadian low-budget aesthetic of jerky pacing, sparse sets and fuzzy film stock.

While these showrunners make use of the concept of the 'world-class city,' it is more precise to note that their reference point for such a city is an American one. Although *The Bridge* has been described as being set in 'Anytown, U.S.A.' by its lead performer (quoted in Onstad 7 June 2009), it is not the case that these showrunners are imagining just *any* American city. They are not imagining Podunk, USA,[29] but instead are imagining two 'world-class' American cities in particular: Los Angeles or New York City. This is not surprising given how New York City and Los Angeles, both being major film and television production centres in the US, have established themselves in the cinematic imagination.

Because the city is more than just a backdrop to the action in television police dramas, it also implicitly informs the kind of policing model that the show represents. Writers for these Canadian–American co-produced police dramas do not conceptualize policing models as wholly abstract, placeless entities, and instead situate them within 'world-class' cities. In doing so, they tend to ensure that a particular Toronto policing style is comparable to policing done in an American 'world-class' city. For example, *Flashpoint*'s Strategic Response Unit is modelled on Toronto's Emergency Task Force (ETF), but the show's executive producer Bill Mustos also takes pain to highlight how this ETF policing model is quite comparable to that of New York's SWAT team (Bernstein 12 August 2010). Both operate on a policing model that emphasizes negotiation[30] over the aggressive action favoured by the LA SWAT team.

Conceptualized as the anti-*Flashpoint* in order to gain its own distinction, *The Bridge*'s policing world implicitly takes cues from the LA policing world in two specific ways. First, while President of the Toronto Police Association, *The Bridge*'s technical consultant BC went to California to learn the policing model adopted by his LA union counterpart, including aggressive take-down measures (Fulton 2003). Second, *The Bridge* showrunner's own historical reference point for a corrupt police department revolves around the LA police department:

> [in] the [19]40s, the Los Angeles police department was extremely corrupt, but it was a common thing. You'd have to start back at the turn of the century. Police departments were contracted by the city. In fact, New Orleans in the 1890s had three or four departments that were all operating, all running their own prostitution houses, all taking payoffs from having battles in the street. This isn't to say that they weren't protecting people, but that they had their side businesses. Now why did they do this? Because they were paid shit. So it was very common for a cop to take a perk, and I'm not just talking about money. If you wanted to get a sandwich from a guy, you could go into a bar and get a sandwich and a beer and continue around. And the guy at the bar knows that that cop is his friend, and is going to take better care of him. And he also knows that that cop has got a family to support. This created an element of, however, larger corruption. When [eventual police chief] William H. Parker came into the Los Angeles police department, he kind of structured things in a very militaristic style. This kind of pseudo-militaristic style had existed previously. And it was set up . . . you'd like to think of it as an old boys' network.
>
> (DA 20 March 2009)

In the above excerpt, the showrunner clearly explains why the city is imagined as inextricably intertwined with policing models, particularly in North America. Public police departments are contracted by cities to protect and serve its inhabitants, and given the character of the city different policing models might develop, such as a para-militaristic style of policing anchored to an old boys' network. When speaking about police corruption, the showrunner ties it back to police salaries. Corruption is fostered in cities that pay their public police officers low wages. What is interesting, however, is the implicit translation move that the showrunner makes in conceptualizing *The Bridge*'s policing world: the contemporary Toronto policing world (from which *The Bridge* derives its stories) is made analogous to the LA policing world of the 1940s and 1950s, where the latter has been popularized in American film noir as a corrupt institution (Davis 1992). He makes this move on the assumption that certain policing issues, such as corruption, are universal (i.e. not confined to particular times and places), and could be recognizable to audiences outside of the production's point of North American origin and reference. In doing so, the showrunner is anticipating the series' distribution on the international market.

Research on the global media industries has shown that any television product that too fully embraces local specificity has less of a chance of success in the international market. Instead, it will suffer a 'cultural discount' that fundamentally devalues it (Havens 2006; Hoskins and Mirus 1988), since foreign audiences lack the cultural background and knowledge that are presumably needed for full appreciation of the product (Lee 2006). While specificity of place is favoured by North American television critics[31] and is related to the tradition of 'quality,' it is not the best commercial strategy for producers with an eye on the international market. Instead, an emphasis on universality and generic setting literally pays off when it comes to international sales of a television drama series. For example, *The Bridge* has since been sold for broadcast in Australia and South Africa. *Flashpoint* has been sold to 50 countries outside North America, including New Zealand, Spain, Sweden, France, Germany, etc. (Vlessing 24 July 2008). *Rookie Blue* has been sold to 21 countries outside of North America, including the Czech Republic, the Republic of Korea and Japan among others.

The specific city: Hamilton and its particularities

In contrast to the aforementioned trio of Canadian–American co-produced police dramas, the production of *LGM* lacked an American co-producer despite attempts to procure one during the pilot stage. As a result, the production needed to rely entirely on Canadian funding sources, which translates to a strategy of representing a Canadian city in all its local and specific glory rather than representing it in generic terms.[32] Thus, *LGM*'s showrunner and producer do the reverse translation: they do not translate Hamilton into a 'world-class' American city, but instead make an American city (New York City) analogous to a Canadian one, particularly one that is on the economic decline. In doing so, *LGM* fulfills its HBO pedigree[33] by following in the footsteps of how David Simon represented Baltimore in *The Wire*. Indeed, *The Wire* alumnus and *LGM*'s second male lead performer Clark Johnson describes the world of *LGM* as 'Baltimore Light' (quoted in Patriquin 3 December 2009).

In describing *The Wire* as primarily about The City, David Simon (2004a: 10; author's emphasis added) writes that the drama's 'stories are rooted in the logic and ethos of a second-tier city, of a forgotten *rust*-belt America.' Baltimore is neither characterized nor represented as a 'world-class' city, because *The Wire* is not a 'television show written and produced [. . .] from Hollywood [or] even from New York' (Simon 2004a: 10). Similarly, in selecting Hamilton, 'a *rusty* can sitting [in] the middle of a bed of flowers' (KG[34] 2009; author's emphasis added), it is aesthetically significant precisely because it is neither Toronto nor Vancouver (i.e. the Canadian equivalent to LA in the sense of being a major West coast production centre). Instead, in *LGM*, Toronto figures into the pilot as Hamilton's rich 'Other,' as 'the distant emerald city' (*LGM* script 11 August 2008: 18) that beckons working class Hamiltonians from across the waters of Lake Ontario. In focusing on Hamilton, the showrunner is able to develop and explore the particular world of a second-tier city often obscured by more conventional television images of 'world-class' metropolitan cities. For the remainder of this chapter, we will examine how the showrunner, producer and director translate *LGM*'s original setting of Brighton Beach, New York, into Hamilton, Ontario. In making this geographical translation, they need to also translate 1) the insurance-crime-legal world from New York to Hamilton through research; 2) the signs of New York City into the signs of Canadian content for funding and broadcasting purposes; and 3) the city of Hamilton into visual images in particular thematic ways.

Translating the world of insurance: laws, scams and crimes

LGM's success as a pilot largely hinged on the extent to which the showrunner could make equivalent the quasi-legal world of New York state insurance with that of Ontario insurance regulation. Insurance is regulated by each individual state in the US, and by each individual province in Canada. In exploring whether these legal worlds could be made analogous, the showrunner needs to also ensure that the criminal underbelly of the insurance world – its 'dark figures' of scams, frauds and organized criminal activity – was also plausibly analogous. These are intertwined and inseparable translations, not only because crime and its legal response are mutually constitutive (Valverde 2006) but also because the entire series' conceit revolved around the insurance investigation of a medical mill run by a Russian crime organization. 'Medical mill' is an American term for an actual or imaginary private medical clinic that processes fraudulent personal injury claims for financial benefit. Canadian insurance fraud investigators favour the term 'rehabilitation clinic,' because the Ontario Health Insurance Plan (OHIP) covers medically necessary expenses but does not always cover expenses required for rehabilitation, such as physiotherapy. OHIP certainly does not cover the 'aromatherapy' referenced in the *LGM* script (full white draft 30 September 2008: 34), nor any of the 'treatments' listed on the door of the fictional rehabilitation centre featured in the *LGM* pilot (see Figure 5.2).

In order to make these cross-border insurance translations, the showrunner and producer needed research on the Canadian insurance industry. As a criminologist, I was hired by Whizbang Films to do this research, which was primarily distilled to the showrunner in the form of a short précis. While knowledge and research inform the process of making fictional television dramas and also true crime docudramas, the researcher is expected to wade through mountains of data and succinctly summarize all that she has learned in one or two pages (GK 3 July 2008). Very few, if any, television writers want to read more than the researcher's summary. Unlike academia, the dissemination of knowledge in television production does not take the form of (peer-reviewed) articles or books. Instead, knowledge dissemination takes the form of a research binder. In the case of *LGM*, the binder includes brief outlines about the Ontario insurance industry and personal injury scams prevalent in the province, and a series of news clippings about Canadian insurance scams that might inspire the showrunner. Conceptually, the summaries provide the showrunner with the factual 'bare bones' of the way insurance and insurance scams work in Ontario, and the newspaper clippings 'flesh' out some of the ways in which actual Ontarians have attempted to scam the insurance system.

Showcasing Hamilton 155

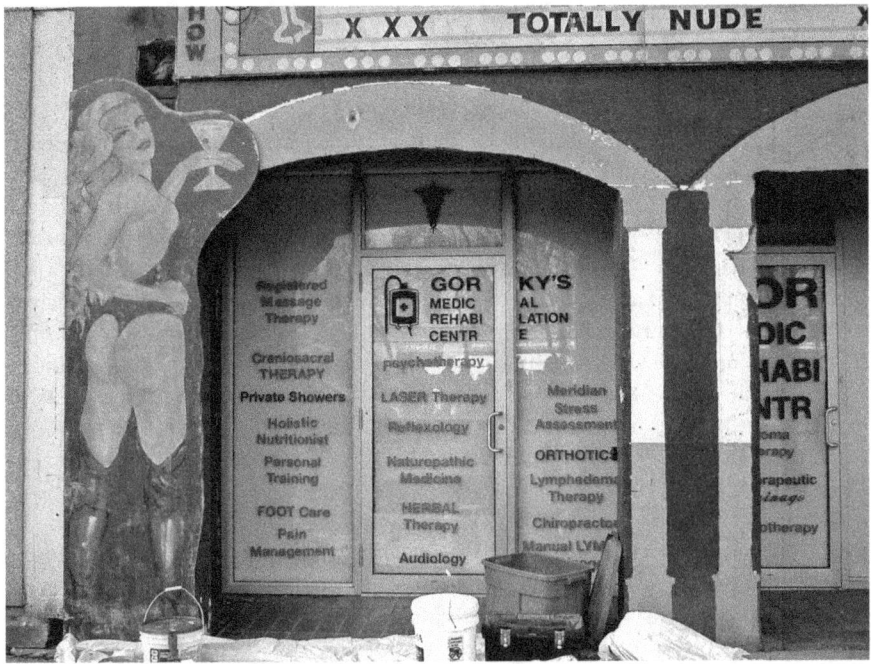

Figure 5.2 Gorky's Medical Rehabilitation Centre (formerly known as Porky's Strip Bar)
Source: Photograph taken by author.

In doing this research, I tapped various heterogeneous knowledge sources, including 1) online research published by the New York state and Ontario insurance industries, 2) Ontario newspapers, 3) academic books on the insurance industry (e.g. Ericson and Doyle 2004; Ericson, Doyle, and Barry 2003) and 4) technical consultants.[35] From textual sources, it was clear that Ontario operated under a similar automobile insurance regime to that of the state of New York: both proceeded under a no-fault insurance scheme. Broadly speaking, in a no-fault automobile insurance scheme, the insurance company reimburses its policyholder (and her passengers) for any medical expenses in the case of personal injury in an automobile accident. This reimbursement is provided without proof of fault (i.e. regardless of who caused the car accident in the first place). Both New York state and Ontario have a verbal threshold no-fault scheme. That is, the injured party needs to meet a particular verbal threshold in order to sue the other party for damages (e.g. pain and suffering) in civil court. The verbal threshold is related to a description of severely debilitating injuries incurred as a result of the car accident. Consequently, the criterion of verbal threshold limits the amount of civil lawsuits, by preventing individuals with minor, non-debilitating injuries from litigating. However, the no-fault insurance regime does lend itself to particular insurance scams.

Because Ontario and New York insurance companies will reimburse personal injury claims regardless of fault, organized criminals have taken advantage of this insurance scheme through the creation of staged car accident rings and medical mills. In fact, the core plot of the *LGM* pilot was originally inspired by a large-scale insurance scam that originated in Brighton Beach, New York, known as BORIS (Big Organized Russian Insurance Scam). It involved Russian émigrés in a complex and coordinated automobile and medical fraud ring (Stein and Burke 8 December 2003). The scam involved the staging of a car accident, causing passengers to suffer 'personal injuries.' These 'injured' passengers would then proceed to a medical mill for various kinds of 'treatment,' which would be covered by insurance companies. However, the passengers, later called 'crash dummies' by police detectives, were only injured on paper (i.e. in documents that diagnose 'injury' from medical mills) and not in fact. Nevertheless, Operation BORIS managed to bilk the insurance industry out of $500 million over the course of more than 1,000 staged car accidents in the New York area (Stein and Burke 8 December 2003).

However, the paper trail of newspaper clippings, articles from the insurance industry, and academic texts did not provide any clues about how such an extensive fraud could play out in Ontario. Well-done insurance frauds are kept secret by the insurance industry to prevent copycats, and are consequently not publicized in news articles. In order to know about elaborately executed insurance frauds, I needed to enlist a technical consultant into the *LGM* pilot production process through what Michel Callon (1986) calls 'interressement,' whereby a technical consultant is enlisted in a project by appealing to her own explicit interests (Latour 1987: 108–9). Because the Canadian insurance industry is interested in changing people's perceptions about the severity of insurance fraud and a television drama could serve as such a perception-changing vehicle, the industry agreed to provide *LGM* with a technical consultant: a practicing Ontario-based insurance fraud investigator. The showrunner (27 October 2009) has since dubbed him 'the Canadian fraud guy' (the CFG).

From speaking with the CFG, it became clear how Operation BORIS could easily be translated into the Ontario setting. Like *LGM*'s showrunner, the principal players of BORIS have actually moved their project from New York to Ontario. Since the bust in New York, they have set up fraudulent rehabilitation clinics and paralegal law firms in the Greater Toronto Area and in Hamilton. In contrast to the organized staged car accident rings in New York, those in Hamilton are not only connected to Eastern European (Russian) crime syndicates, but to law firms. These facts are fictionalized in the *LGM* script in the following exchange between Walker Hearn, head of Protected Insurance's Special Fraud Investigations Unit, and the company's supervisor, Dick Dimaio:

Original HBO script (2001: 46–7)	Revised script for Showcase (30 September 2008: 50)
INT. WALKER HEARN'S OFFICE – DAY A gloomy looking [Dick] Dimaio [Protected Insurance's Eastern states supervisor] sits watching the VIDEO of the Russian medical mills that Walker filmed. They seem endless. One after another all along Ocean Ave. WALKER: We got maybe half of Brighton Beach. DIMAIO: How many of these you figure are tied to the Russian mafia? WALKER: No way of telling . . . (grins) Look at this one now. He FREEZE FRAMES at Gorky's. The ex-strip club. WALKER (cont'd): Gorky's Medical Center. A month ago this was a peeler bar. Want to guess what it was called? (off his look) Porky's. The assholes change a letter. Roll some MRI crap in. And boom. They're in the medical mill business. DIMAIO: I've seen enough.	INT. WALKER HEARN'S OFFICE – DAY [Protected Insurance's Senior VP Dick] Dimaio scans Walker's REPORT on the dodgy rehab clinics. [In house lawyer] Angela is there with them. WALKER: There's at least three we red-flagged on Barton. Three more on Main. Lots more if we had the time to dig. ANGELA: All Russian owned? WALKER (shakes head): Law firms, paralegals, East Asians; the whole gamut.

According to *LGM*'s technical consultants, there is a trend in which American ideas about the commission of fraud have been brought to the Greater Toronto Area for experimentation. These ideas and fraudulent practices are perfected in Ontario before being implemented in the US. By and large, this is related to the fact that Canada does not prosecute frauds as energetically or aggressively as the US does. As a result, accident frauds in Canada are seen as extremely lucrative enterprises because they are high profit–low risk activities. Offenders are punished with sanctions that are described as 'slaps on the wrist' (e.g. fines, withdrawn charges, and conditional sentences). Because Canada has been viewed as a safe haven for fraud, it has become a testing ground for scams that need to be refined before the fraudsters set up shop in American cities, in which fraud is deemed a higher profit–higher risk activity.

Thus, the legal-criminal-insurance world of New York was easily translated into that of Hamilton due to the serendipitous alignment of facts and circumstances: New York and Ontario have analogous no-fault insurance regimes that make possible the same kind of automobile and medical scams, which are committed by the same organized crime group. It is not clear what would have happened had Ontario differed significantly from New York in terms of insurance regime and fraudulent activity. Certainly, the showrunner would have had to engage in a more complex translation process in order to analogize divergent legal-criminal-insurance worlds.

Translating the signs of New York into signs of 'Canadian content'

Jimmy Shea:

[The Protected Insurance dispatcher has] got me up in The Sinai. The Gulag. Brownsville for christsakes [sic]. And then back down to Ocean Park. [. . .] [T]ake my Pakitown.

—Original HBO script (2001: 7)

Jimmy Burn:[36]

[The Protected Insurance dispatcher has] got me up The Mountain. To Borelington. East fucking Flamborough. Down to Tony Creek for christsakes [sic]. [. . .] [T]ake my Tony Creek.

—Full blue script (24 October 2008: 8–9)

As I have previously mentioned, *LGM* needs to demonstrate 'Canadian content' in order to satisfy both broadcasting requirements and governmental funding requirements. For Showcase, the development of a one-hour, original Canadian television drama falls under its licensing condition of providing 'Canadian content'[37] to Canadian viewers. According to its broadcasting license, the specialty channel had promised to air a certain amount of Canadian television drama in prime time, and *LGM* is developed to fulfill this promise to the CRTC. Additionally, *LGM* needs to demonstrate 'Canadian content' in order to qualify for funding from Telefilm Canada and the Canadian Television Fund. That is, the project needs to reflect and speak to Canadians about Canadian themes and subject matters (Ministry of Cultural Heritage 2009).

Because *LGM*'s appeal to Showcase was premised on its veneer of HBO 'Quality,' the showrunner capitalized on the image of The Frontier in creating the series pitch to the Canadian specialty channel. The image of The Frontier reminds Showcase network executives not only of how cutting-edge the series will be, but of the showrunner's previous employment as a television writer for HBO's Western drama *Deadwood* (2004–2006). Thus, *LGM* (series synopsis 16 October 2008; author's emphasis added) was pitched in the following way:

> Our hero, Jimmy Shea, is a cocky young insurance adjuster squeezed between the faceless corporation that employs him and the tough Hamilton turf he has to cover – overrun with con artists. He's new to *the Wild West World of insurance scams*. So he has to learn quickly how to maneuver in the *No Man's Land* between big business on the one hand and the criminal business on the other.

However, as *LGM* was revised under the mentorship of Showcase network executives, the image of The Frontier was completely removed in later synopses of the series. While the image of The Frontier anchored the initial conceptualization of the *LGM* pilot, it was slowly removed through successive Canadianizing script revisions. In revising the pilot script for Showcase, *LGM*'s showrunner translates signs initially associated with New York to signs that evoke the new Canadian setting.

For example, references to the Federal Bureau of Investigation (FBI) have been revised to references about the 'Mounties,' Canada's federal police force. When updating references to sports teams, the New York Knicks have been replaced by the local Hamilton Tiger Cats and the Mississauga Ice Dogs. The (fictional) Red Hook Housing Project in Brooklyn has been translated into the (fictional) Tombit Park Public Housing[38] in Hamilton. In describing this public housing project, also known as the 'Tombs,' the revised script (21 July 2008: 19) notes that a graffiti artist had changed the sign for Tombit Park to read 'Timbit Park,' referencing the brand name of bite-sized, donut balls sold at Tim Hortons franchise restaurants in Canada. Most well known for its coffee and donuts, Tim Hortons was founded in Hamilton in 1964 by Canadian hockey player Tim Horton, and has since become Canada's largest (and ubiquitous) fast-food service. As another nod to the Hamilton setting, local Hamiltonian viewers would also recognize local radio personality Dan Duran who was cast in the role of the Protected Insurance Man. In this role, Duran becomes the public face of Protected Insurance, starring in various commercials for the insurance company. However, we could categorize these revisions as relatively superficial script changes to incorporate 'Canadian content.'

At a deeper level of script revision, the *LGM* showrunner translates the BORIS scam in a manner that invokes multiculturalism, which has been recognized as both a distinctly Canadian social ideal and demographic reality. In representing multiculturalism, the *LGM* pilot takes a distinctly Canadian turn, particularly since it is deemed the one element that needed to be toned down if the production was to find an American co-producer (FS 8 October 2008). Nevertheless, the representation of multiculturalism in *LGM* was not only a matter of casting (i.e. casting ethnoculturally diverse background extras), but impinged on the representation of insurance fraud and organized crime. According to the 'Canadian fraud guy,' what made BORIS' Canadian manifestation distinctive was multicultural cooperation among different ethnocultural groups to commit large-scale insurance fraud. For instance, the CFG tells the anecdotal story of a real-life staged accident ring run in the Toronto region by Somalis. While these Somalis belonged to different tribes and would not interact with one another in Somalia, they were clearly working together in order to run this particular criminal ring in Canada (CFG 10 July 2008). While most insurance frauds tend to occur within ethnocultural groups (technical consultant 5 July 2008), an enterprising member of a law firm connected different ethnic groups together in the mid-1990s in order to commit automobile and personal injury fraud. As a result, since the mid-1990s, organized crime in cases of Ontario insurance fraud had become multicultural in terms of personnel. *LGM*'s showrunner represents this fact, by dramatizing the criminally creative side of multiculturalism as part of the pilot's 'Canadian content.' Although the Canadian Multiculturalism Act (1985/1988: 3(1)(g)) aims to 'promote the understanding and creativity that arise from the interaction between individuals and communities of different origins,' it is not clear that policymakers intended to encourage criminal creativity resulting from the interaction and cooperation between various ethnocultural groups. Nevertheless, *LGM*'s showrunner is inspired by this take on multiculturalism, resulting in the following script change:

Original HBO script (2001: 19)	Revised script (21 July 2008: 13)
LIONEL, Protected Insurance's Eastern States supervisor (scanning and then reading): 'Coalition Building Needed to Repeal New York State's No Fault Law?'	LIONEL, Protected Insurance's Senior VP Operations: 'Coalition Building Needed to Amend Ontario's No Fault Insurance Law?'
ANGELA, in-house lawyer (V.O.): That's it. The No Fault's bleeding us to death Lionel. The Russian mills bill us fifty thou per accident victim and there's not a damn thing we can do about it. Unless we get all the insurance providers to play ball.	ANGELA (V.O.): That's it. We know that the worst of the Russian and East Europe conmen who were pushed out of New York by the BORIS bust have set up show in the GTA and the Niagara region.
[...]	LIONEL: Who the hell's Boris?
LIONEL: What's the SIU [Special Investigations Unit] response?	CUT TO:
WALKER, Head of the Brooklyn office's SIU: About all I can do is document the problem. The cops don't give a shit. The FBI was keen on the Russian angle. But as you may have read they've been a little busy lately.	WALKER (answers flatly): Big Russian Organized Insurance Scam.
	ANGELA: They're here and they and many others have already made the Horseshoe the car theft capital of North America. But it's the No Fault Law that's bleeding us to death, Lionel. The phony rehab centers bill us up to a hundred grand per phony accident victim and there's not a damn thing we can do about it. Unless we can convince all the insurance providers to lobby together.
	LIONEL (V.O.): Uh-huh. What's our Fraud Squad response?
	WALKER: All I can do is document it. The local cops don't give a shit. I'm trying to interest the FBI and the RCMP in the Russian/Balkans angle.
	LIONEL (V.O.): You mean the Mounties? (chuckles) Oh Christ.
	WALKER: We're also seeing close cooperation between the Slavic gangs and

other ethnic groups – East Indian, Asian, what have you. Unheard of in New York but the new deal here. Some kind of Multi-culturalism I guess.

Thematic and visual translations: visualizing the hammer

Because HBO had only asked the showrunner for scripts and outlines, it is hard to reconstruct how *LGM* would have visually appeared because it was not developed as a pilot. Showcase, however, required the showrunner to make a pilot, needing further persuasion that the series could be a viable undertaking. In requesting a visual 'theatre of the proof,' the narrowcaster needed some sense of how the showrunner and director KG would translate the city of Hamilton into screen images. That is, how do they imagine the city as a particular character – namely 'The Hammer' – and visualize it?

Cities can be translated into characters in fictional television dramas in one of two inter-related ways: either as a character that reflects the main protagonist, or as an additional character in the series. For example, Dick Wolf calls New York City 'the seventh character' of *Law and Order* (quoted in Wolf and Burstein 2003: 30). It is now relatively common within North American television procedurals to conceptualize the city as an unspoken character, particularly in a cop show. The city is thought to shape the streets being patrolled by the police officers, the people (e.g. both criminals and victims) living on them, and the back-story for each crime (Dawn 21 June 2010). In this instance, the city's character is most strikingly represented through exterior establishing shots in the television drama, where a sense of the city comes from filming on location rather than on a sound stage.

In the case of *LGM*, Hamilton is a reflection of protagonist Jimmy Burn, both of which are conceptualized as dichotomies premised on the difference between their past and future selves:

> That's important because both Jimmy and the city he lives in are struggling to redefine themselves. Jimmy is leaving his past behind, pining for greener pastures and picket fences. Hamilton is leaving its past, the recession may kill it unless it can rewrite itself.
>
> (KG 2009)

As a reflection of the same general type of character, both the city and Jimmy are, however, stand-ins for the Everyman (*LGM* synopsis 16 October 2008). While the Everyman has been considered an element that makes HBO television dramas appealing to urban sophisticates (Polan 2007), the Everyman is a construct that implicitly has both a gender and class. While the Everyman represented by Jimmy is clearly a working-class male, Hamilton takes on the same gender and class through its official nickname: the masculine epithet of 'The Hammer' (Wilson 6

December 2006). While previous nicknames for the city had included Steeltown or Steel City in the early 1980s when the city's steel industry was well underway and in its prime, 'The Hammer' is a more recent epithet following the decline and closing of various steel plants (Wilson 6 December 2006). It became the symbol of a city that lacks pretence (or perhaps pretentiousness), struggling through the tough economic time that has come its way as the blue-collar work that shaped its workforce is no longer in great supply. Characterized as 'The Hammer,' a 'hard-edged, post-industrial playground' (full white script 30 September 2008: 1), Hamilton is tough, hard and gritty, much like Jimmy Burn himself, and surrounded by what it would like to be (KG 2009).

Both city and protagonist struggle to 'hold onto a piece of the Canadian dream' (*LGM* synopsis 16 October 2008), which is later clarified as 'a piece of the middle-class dream: Home. Family. Security' (Showcase 18 November 2009). In this struggle, one can easily turn towards crime and/or insurance fraud as a quick way to obtain some financial security. In this sense, the Canadian middle-class dream is not so different from the American dream, which has also been primarily defined by economic success. Because the key to financial success in Hamilton is envisioned by *LGM*'s director as an individual's ability to 'play the angle,' be that the insurance angle, the criminal angle or the law-abiding angle, Hamilton is visualized as a place full of lines and angles (KG 2009). Directors are thus encouraged to find the lines and angles in Hamilton's various natural and manufactured landscapes, by focusing the camera on steel 'I' beams, the lines supporting the Burlington Skyway, and the shoreline of Lake Ontario (KG 2009). Unlike 'world-class' cities that have distinctive landmarks made familiar to global audiences through frequent media exposure (e.g. Toronto's CN Tower, New York's Statue of Liberty, the Las Vegas Strip, etc.), Hamilton is most well known for its industrial smokestacks, which breathe 'rusting metal and fire' (KG 2009) across the city. These polluting smokestacks, along with the Burlington Skyway Bridge,[39] are featured in *LGM*'s animated opening credit sequence in a singular image that is meant to evoke the very essence of the city (see Figure 5.3).

By now, it should be no surprise that the Canadian, middle-class dream is wrapped up in and geographically represented by the image of the 'world-class' city, which appears in *LGM*'s background shots like a mirage in the distance. While the showrunner originally represented Brooklynites aspiring to live the American dream in Manhattan (HBO script 2001: 14), the same yearning sentiment is translated into Hamiltonians' desire to live the Canadian dream in Toronto (MM 21 July 2008: 18), or in the affluent district of Hamilton Mountain:

> [On 'The Mountain,'] above the proletariat, gazing down from the top of the escarpment, is the money. Palatial mansions dot the hillside. The money from [formerly successful steel companies] Dofasco, INCO and Foster Wheeler, built these places.
>
> (KG 2009)

Figure 5.3 Screenshot of Hamilton as illustrated in *Lawyers, Guns and Money*'s opening title sequence
Source: Whizbang Films (www.whizbangfilms.com)

Although factually speaking, Hamilton Mountain also includes economically disadvantaged neighbourhoods, the showrunner and director are more interested in the semiotic implications of 'The Mountain,' which primarily stem from the relation of top/bottom embedded in the Western imagination of the balcony. In the nineteenth century, the balcony became a significant architectural entity and consequently an important image in Western literature and painting (Stallybrass and White 1986). Due to fears of the 'great, unwashed masses' and their contaminating touch, the upper class would only enjoy the sights and sounds of the street from the safe space of their own balcony, where they would be above the fray of the lower classes (Stallybrass and White 1986). Following this particular semiotic logic, the Hamilton Mountain is represented as a balcony that provides the Hamilton upper class with a view of the city and its streets. As Hamilton's balcony, 'The Mountain' becomes emblematic of the Canadian dream and its fulfillment. Although in the past the cultural dream could be purchased through hard work in the steel industry, Hamilton is currently a 'one industry town in decline' (KG 2009) with skyrocketing unemployment rates. Now more than ever, the cultural dream seems impossible to attain, at least through legitimate means.

In developing the strain theory of deviance, Robert K. Merton (1938) notes a discrepancy between a shared cultural goal that defines what constitutes success in life – e.g. the goal of the American/Canadian dream – and a culture's norms about the appropriate means to achieve that goal. People vary in the extent to which they have legitimate access or means to achieve a particular cultural goal. Although Merton's analysis is primarily based on statistical aggregates and not aimed at the individual, it is useful to note that his analysis acknowledges that 'crime pays'[40] for a particular group of individuals. In the world of *LGM*, Hamiltonians know that both crime and insurance fraud are viable means to the Canadian dream. Unemployed Hamiltonians make use of 'one of the most deeply entrenched chronic care infrastructures in the country' (KG 2009): they unabashedly take advantage of their insurance coverage, even if it means putting in fraudulent claims in order to buy 'wheel-scooters' and boost their pharmaceutical allotment. Members of the Russian Mafia that have infiltrated the city finance their monster homes through a version of the BORIS insurance scam. As a reformed criminal, Hamilton-born Jimmy knows that insurance scams and crime can be lucrative. He can spot the scams because he is a scammer at heart. However, in attempting to build a future through legitimate means (i.e. working as an insurance adjuster), he tries to ignore that knowledge over the course of the series, but still manages to become embroiled in an analogous BORIS scam.

Conclusion

This chapter has examined how place becomes relevant in the making of crime dramas, paying particular attention to the stage of pilot development and production. The strategy of representing place (or setting) in a fictional crime drama is informed by the place of the commissioning broadcaster in the broadcasting landscape of the post-network television era. A broadcaster's place is located at the intersection of a quasi-legal broadcasting regulatory structure and a particular market orientation. Working in the tradition of 'quality' television, North American premium cable networks cater to their niche market by providing crime dramas that are set in specific cities. By contrast, major commercial broadcasting networks cater to their mass audience by creating co-productions that generically set their series in a large, urban city. Using case studies, we examined how recent Canadian–American co-produced police dramas tended to proceed through a process that translates Toronto into a 'world-class city' analogous to any metropolitan (North American) city. In contrast, we examined how the showrunner of *Lawyers, Guns and Money* geographically relocated his series from New York City to Hamilton, Ontario, as the script moved from American premium cable network HBO to Canadian specialty channel Showcase. Additionally, we analyzed how he translated Showcase's particular Canadian network and funding demands into the specific representation of Hamilton with its particular legal-crime-insurance world. These cultural translations can be considered successful because Showcase picked up the first season of the series.

These case studies reveal that showrunners form and translate their particular crime television dramas in ways that fit within a particular broadcaster's 'stronghold' position and programming interests. However, it should be noted that this position is not set in stone. Broadcasters may have changing programming interests over time, especially when there are significant changes in personnel. For example, although CTV had initially picked up *The Bridge* for a second season and scripts were developed towards that end (DA personal communication with author), the series was cancelled following significant personnel changes at the network, including the departure of the head of Dramatic Programming (Krashinsky and Marlow 8 February 2011). CBC also had a recent shakeup as executive vice president Richard Stursberg, most well-known for his 'ratings-driven, populist, pop-culture-obsessed [. . .] lightweight' programming strategy, left the public broadcaster (Doyle 14 August 2010). During Stursberg's reign, the CBC turned away from gritty, urban crime dramas (e.g. *Intelligence*, and *Da Vinci's Inquest*) and towards more comedic series set in small towns (e.g. *Republic of Doyle*). While Canada's public broadcaster turned towards frothier concoctions, Canadian television critic John Doyle (2 March 2010) noted that the private, commercial broadcasters were churning out 'more intractable, tough-minded material' in the vein of American cable programming. Doyle's examples of such gritty material were *The Bridge* and *Cra$h & Burn* (formerly *LGM*). Overall, this suggests that programming *and* counter-programming strategies shift over time in relatively unpredictable ways. A broadcaster's stronghold position is constantly made and remade, and showrunners need to scramble to translate their ideas into a broadcaster's changing terms and interests.

Notes

1 Of these three shows, *The Bridge* has been touted as the best of the bunch by American TV critics, and generally as a 'very good' show. However, unlike *Rookie Blue* and *Flashpoint*, it was not picked up for a second season by its American co-producing broadcaster.
2 Because Canadian pilots are at least partially funded through government money, all pilots are legally required to air within a fiscal year. Consequently, pilots can be viewed by the general public even if they are not further developed into a series by their broadcaster. In contrast, American television pilots that do not receive a series pickup are usually not aired at all.
3 Will Straw (2002) categorizes Atwood's argument as being characteristic of an 'essentialist' position when it comes to defining national cultural traditions in English Canada. The essentialist position aims to find common thematic traits among various works of Canadian culture. In doing so, this position argues that Canadian culture possesses a distinctive essence. In contrast to the essentialist position, the 'compensatory' position argues that no such distinctive essence exists. Instead, Canadian culture emerges out of a need to compensate for the gaps left open by the cultural products produced in more successful cultural industries elsewhere, such as the US, the UK and France. Strategically, Canadian culture fills those gaps by identifying open and under-served markets. For example, Canadian television programs are often not as flashy as those made in the US because Canada increasingly depends on sales to overseas market (e.g. Europe) where flashiness is not so highly valued. To receive funding from the Canadian government, Canadian producers and showrunners make an essentialist argument by highlighting all of the Canadian elements in their production, while simultaneously acknowledging (e.g. the novel elements in the production) that their production will be profitable because it compensates for gaps in the television market.
4 Linda Hutcheon (1990) has argued that the English-Canadian imagination traffics in postmodern irony, and consequently every statement is made ambivalent by the

166 Making Crime Television

doubled, forked tongue of irony. The same ambivalence towards Canadian television can be found in interviews with Canadian television writers and producers (see Levine 2009).

5 As Atwood (1972) notes, in contrast to the US, Canada's history is known for its failed revolutions. For the most part, Canadians whole-heartedly believe in 'peace, order and good government.' While this might be valuable for legislative purposes, it is arguably not wonderful inspirational fodder for making exciting television dramas.

6 Trapped between two extremes, Canadian television can also be described as one of middleness (Beaty and Sullivan 2006: 19). On the one hand, Canadian television cannot be highbrow like British television, because those pretensions might alienate mass audiences. On the other hand, Canadian television cannot be lowbrow either because 'that is the position we have ceded to the Americans, and the occupation of this position would fail to sufficiently distinguish Canada from the culture of the US' (Beaty and Sullivan 2006: 19).

7 Depending on the showrunner and the show itself, not all series strictly adhere to a bible. Some shows have bibles specifically for the writing staff and for directors.

8 Although *The Sopranos* is primarily set in New Jersey, Tony Soprano travels quite often to New York City.

9 On the Canadian front, public broadcaster CBC initially took this route in contrast to the private, commercial broadcasters CTV and Global.

10 The 'popular' vs. 'quality' distinction corresponds well with Nicole Rafter's (2000) 'conventional' vs. 'critical' crime film distinction. However, this chapter goes beyond Rafter's content analysis of cultural products to analyze how those products are made within a particular regulatory and (television) production regime.

11 This also includes television dramas from AMC (*Mad Men*), FX (*The Shield*), Showtime (*Dexter*), etc.

12 See Todd Gitlin's (1983) seminal work for a description of how American broadcasters operated during the network era.

13 The increasing fragmentation of the audience has impacted broadcasting networks through their declining advertising revenue. Because advertising revenue has generally gone towards the production of television dramas, which have been increasing in production budget over the past decade, this has spurred more attempts at television drama co-productions as networks attempt to find cheaper ways in which to produce content.

14 HBO's success in the US in the 1970s is what spurred the creation of specialty channels in Canada (Killingsworth 2005).

15 Although Discovery Dan is the target, the show's producers and network executives have a sense of who watches, but not why they watch or are drawn to the show.

16 It is assumed by the show's executive producer that men gravitate towards procedural storytelling (KS 17 November 2008).

17 To be fair, 'popular' American television dramas set in generic cities have made Canadian cities, particularly Toronto and Vancouver, 'pass' for American ones.

18 The first window broadcast is often done by the producing network, or the network given distribution rights by the independent production company. The second window opens up once that network has finished its first broadcast of a film or an entire series. As such, it refers to the second opportunity for broadcast or distribution.

19 In pitching series, showrunners and producers tend to describe it in recombinant terms (Gitlin 1983). That is, new television drama X is just like Y meets Z, where Y and Z are well-known, popular and/or critically acclaimed television dramas.

20 This is not always the case. The pilot of *Cra$h & Burn* later became its third episode.

21 Showcase did end up picking up the first seasons of *Shattered* and *Lost Girl*. *Lost Girl* has since been picked up for a second season.
22 Line producers not only take care of the project's budget, but also oversee the day-to-day physical aspects of the project's production. As such, they are often on location and on set.
23 This discussion does not include provincial funding sources. Tax credits are available at the federal, provincial, and municipal level. Often, a film or television production will make use of all three levels of tax credit.
24 The CTF can be administered either directly to the production company or through Broadcaster Performance Envelopes (BPEs). In the case of BPEs, each Canadian broadcaster would then be responsible for administering the fund to both the pilots it develops and to the production of on-going television series. Part of the broadcaster's stronghold position is economically anchored through the administration of the BPE.
25 This requirement is quantified in the following way: the project has achieved 10 out of 10 points on the Canadian Audio-Visual Certification Office (CAVCO) scale. Through the Canadian Film or Television Production tax credit, CAVCO works to ensure that the project is primarily under the creative control of Canadian citizens. For each Canadian citizen in the following key creative functions, the production is awarded various points (Office of the Auditor General of Canada November 2005): director (2 points), screenwriter (2 points), lead performer (1 point), second lead performer (1 point), director of photography (1 point), art director (1 point), music composer (1 point), and picture editor (1 point).
26 Richard Collins (1990) has argued that Canadian political sovereignty does not depend as much on Canadian content in television drama as supposed by Canadian broadcasting and cultural policies. Like Atwood (1972), Collins concludes that Canada has no national symbolic culture. However, he notes that the country has held together as a political unit for far more than a century without one, and consequently having such a symbolic culture is not necessary for political sovereignty.
27 The notion of the 'world-class' city is not unique to Canadian television writers and producers. Some scholars (e.g. Kompare 2010) have argued that *CSI*'s success is partially a result of its notable 'world-class' setting in Las Vegas. With the show's success, *CSI* became a place-based franchise, setting its spin-offs in other 'world-class' cities – namely, Miami and New York. These cities are 'world class' in the sense that they are internationally well-known tourist destinations that appear glamorous and expensive.
28 Despite the higher budget per episode, these co-productions have lower budgets than purely American television series. For example, *The Bridge* was shot for $2 million per episode. If CBS were footing the entire bill, the show would have had a $3 to $3.5 million per episode budget (Binning 2009/2010).
29 Although *The Bridge*'s showrunner does not translate Toronto into Podunk, USA, he is aware that CBS does test screenings of the series with audience members composed of tourists visiting Las Vegas from 'Podunk, Arkansas' (DA 2 June 2009). According to Tinic (2009), American networks tend to buy their television dramas on the basis of conformity to a Heartland formula. This formula acknowledges that American network series are homogenized in order to be well received by the Mid-West (i.e. the audience in rural Indiana or Ohio). Interestingly enough, although both American crime television dramas and exported Canadian crime dramas to the US need to play well to America's Heartland, they do not tend to imagine or represent the Midwest.
30 As an additional rationalization for representing a less aggressive style of policing, showrunner Mark Ellis (10 May 2011) has explained that the emphasis on negotiation

and compromise can be read as a uniquely Canadian trait, especially since Canada celebrates itself as a nation of peacekeepers.
31 E.g. see Randee Dawn's (21 June 2010) review of *Rookie Blue*.
32 Although the producers of *LGM* later partnered with BBC Worldwide for international distribution (Canwest Global 19 February 2010), it is not clear whether or not the series has actually been sold for broadcast in a foreign country. Given how much the showrunner and director emphasized the particularities of the show's Canadian setting, it is quite possible that the series did come with a large 'cultural discount,' which hampered its international sales.
33 *LGM*'s HBO pedigree stems not only from its original script, but from the various HBO alumni it has assembled as key players in the pilot's production. The showrunner has written for HBO's *Deadwood*. The lead male performer cast to play Jimmy has starred in HBO's short-lived television drama *Tell Me You Love Me*. The second male lead performer has starred in and directed various episodes of *The Wire*.
34 As shorthand for this chapter, all references to KG are references to the director primer that he wrote.
35 Although I do not discuss all the technical consultants that played a part in making the *LGM* pilot, they included a journalist from the *Hamilton Spectator* and a Toronto defence lawyer specializing in fraud cases.
36 Jimmy undergoes a change in surname because 'Jimmy Shea' did not clear. A person of prominence named 'Jimmy Shea' could be found in Hamilton, and consequently the name could not be used. Instead, Jimmy's new surname 'Burn' is referenced in *LGM*'s new title *Cra$h & Burn*.
37 Because co-productions require a negotiation of divergent audience expectations, Paul Attalah (in Matheson 2003: 247) has argued that these compromises lead to equivocation with regard to specifically or uniquely Canadian content.
38 Although *The Bridge* also did not shy away from representing a public housing project, it did so without explicitly naming the area or the housing project itself, which is in keeping with its overall strategy of representing a generic city. The generic city also includes a generic bridge that connects Toronto's richer neighbourhoods to its lower-income neighbourhoods. The actual referent for the titular bridge is the Prince Edward Viaduct, which is patrolled by police officers from the 51st Division. The show's technical consultant had been part of this Division prior to retiring from active police duty. Consequently, upon thinking more deeply about the bridge, the technical consultant applied it as a metaphor for law enforcement in general. That is, 'there was also a bridge between the rich and the poor, the good guy and the bad guy, the rank-and-file and the brass. So we use the title as a metaphor for many different opposing elements' (BC quoted in CTV media release 11 February 2010). These opposing categories are articulated in such generic terms – such as rich/poor and good guy/bad guy – that any viewer, regardless of location, could relate to them.
39 The official logo of the City of Hamilton takes the form of a stylized image of a bridge. It refers to both the High Level Bridge on York Boulevard (which evokes Hamilton's past) and the Burlington Skyway Bridge (which evokes Hamilton's present and future).
40 In Merton's (1938) typology, he delineates modes of adaptation to the lack of fit between a culture's goals and means. He calls those who use criminal means to achieve the cultural goal of success 'innovators.'

Conclusion

We have come to the end of our journey where we can now conclude that any television representation of crime is the result of a particular assemblage of logics, people, creative ideas, commercial interests, legal requirements, and programming strategies during a program's production. In travelling along the local roads of television production, we have encountered how the collaborative assembly of television representations – these unique aesthetic-legal-commercial hybrids – is not self-evident, because it cannot be predicted at the outset neither can it be accurately inferred by only watching the television program in its final form. The formation of television representations of crime cannot be retraced after the fact. Instead, we must patiently document the ways in which knowledge and representation come together through actor-networks found within and beyond the television writers' room. By tracing these actor-networks, the primary task of this book has been to document the making of popular criminology – specifically, the way in which entertainment television fictions are assembled through the knowledge and storytelling practices implicated in the production of North American crime dramas. If popular criminology is an influential way of knowing about crime and criminality, how does it know?

Key findings

Let us first review some of the key findings across the chapters in this book before I end with a few reflections about possible avenues for future research into the television production process. Here, it should be noted that my empirical findings are not easily separable from my case studies, and more importantly, from the method used to document them. Social science methods do not simply describe the world as it is, but also help make social realities, particularly those observed by the researcher (Law and Urry 2005). In this book, I have used actor–network theory as a methodological alternative in my exploration of the making of television fictions. In applying ANT, a theory primarily about how *not* to study things, I have highlighted how we should not always take the final products – or the so-called black boxes – of pop culture as our starting point for analysis. When we do examine pop cultural products, we should not assume that they are homogeneous and stable entities. When we break pop cultural products down to their actor-networks and accompanying component parts, we realize that multiple and heterogeneous kinds of 'stuff' – such as anecdotal experiences, writers' imagination, newspaper representations, rival fictional television representations, commercial imperatives, among others – have been combined and ordered in a specific configuration to bring about the existence of a representation. The processes of combining, aligning, and negotiating are not easily gleaned from afar because they do not lead to predictable outcomes. They can as easily lead to failed translations as they can successful ones. As a result, the making of a successful crime television drama is considered quite a feat, especially during the post-network era of television.

I have mostly studied the production of crime dramas made in the shadow of *CSI*'s success, and in doing so have analyzed the post-network era of television production. One of the implications of doing research on the post-network era of television, with its hundreds of television channels and increasing audience fragmentation, entails being far more careful about the kinds of conclusion we make when speaking about a series' ideological effect (Lotz 2009). It is not only the case that universalizing models about media effect, such as Horkheimer and Adorno's hypodermic needle theory, are quite out of touch with the post-network television era, but that different series will have different ideological effects depending on the size and kind of audience they draw. Consequently, there is no 'one-size-fits-all' conclusion about a series' ideological effect or even about its popularity. With its massive domestic and international success, *CSI* redefined what counts as a successful television series in the post-network era. As the exemplar of popular network television fare, *CSI* also helped define what currently counts as successful translations and representational strategies for crime dramas seeking domestic popularity and international export. While researchers have written about the *CSI* effect(s) on potential audiences, it would not be amiss to also discuss a *CSI* effect on the production of crime dramas in North America. Successful translations sought by network executives of major commercial broadcasters tend to mimic the storytelling strategies found within *CSI*.

As we encountered in *The Bridge*'s writing workshop, television writers are encouraged by network executives to write episodic, modular stories about crime rather than serialized narratives about on-going criminal activities. Using a five-act structure, writers tell stories that begin with a crime (in Act One) that is investigated (in Acts Two to Four) and eventually solved (in Act Five). Favoured by network executives, the modular format is thought to maximize potential viewers by attracting casual domestic viewers as well as international viewers. Foreign network executives prefer self-contained episodes because they can be easily slotted into a programming schedule in any order, unlike serialized episodes that require a schedule be re-arranged to fit a particular order of airing (Horan 2007). In order to maximize potential export opportunities and minimize potential litigation from local viewers, *The Bridge*'s success as a Canadian–American co-production was also dependent on its ability to translate the local into the universal: writers and producers translated not only specific and local knowledge sources into universal representations of crime and policing, but also the specific Toronto setting into the universal, placeless setting of the 'world-class city' located in the territory of Anywhere. The representation of generic setting in 'popular' Canadian–American crime dramas can be contrasted to the representational strategy used by 'quality' cable crime dramas. This contrast between 'popular' and 'quality' television dramas plays out in the distinction between making 'another *CSI*' and making a series with relevance and distinction (e.g. *The Wire*). The representational strategy of making a 'quality' crime drama lies in the specificity of its urban setting, often a forgotten working-class city in which the tensions between classes can be more explicitly examined. However, a television drama that embraces local specificity in its representation of setting and crime runs the risk of suffering a cultural discount on the international market. Such a cultural discount devalues the television drama because it assumes that foreign audiences lack the cultural background and knowledge to fully appreciate the program.

Let us now address the research questions that I had initially set out in the introduction.

How do television writers and producers know about crime?

Through their corrective criticism, academic criminologists have tended to treat pop cultural representations as first and foremost inaccurate representations about crime or as questionable matters of fact. In doing so, academic criminologists have assumed that matters of fact are also the primary matters of concern to television producers and writers as they are for academic scholars and social scientists. However, the storytelling process of popular criminology does not centrally concern itself over matters of fact (Chapter 3). Matters of fact are only of interest to writers and producers insofar as they can be usefully mapped onto their matters of concern – namely, the making of 'better' entertainment by providing a greater sense of drama. Here, matters of fact need to provide 'added value' to entertainment, by adding authenticity and plausibility to the dramatic story being told as a means to aid audiences' suspension of disbelief. Or matters of fact are useful to writers and producers because they provide a proactive means to avoid or navigate negative criticism from both network executives and lay viewers.

By entering the television writers' laboratory of fiction-making – namely, the writers' room – we have noted that television writers and producers know about crime through local and heterogeneous knowledge sources, mixing fact with fiction. Factual knowledge sources include newspaper reports, while fictional sources include other popular crime fictions (e.g. crime films, crime television programs, or crime novels). For the most part, television writers of fictional crime procedurals rely on their technical consultants. Police consultants offer writers various kinds of information, ranging from technical information about police procedure to anecdotal stories about their experiences as a police officer. Often, writers do not privilege their consultants' factual information so much as their anecdotal stories about policing. Their consultants' anecdotal stories become fuel for the writers' imagination, and ultimately provide the starting point for writing a fictional episode.

Much of this book has been interested in documenting a relationship between method (how we know about our social reality) and epistemology (what counts as valid knowledge about our social reality). As the social science methods used by academic criminologists and sociolegal scholars have structured what they know about pop cultural representations (Chapter 1), we can make a similar point about how the methods used by television writers and producers shape what they know about crime. Broadly speaking, how we know informs what we know. When the technical consultant is treated by writers as a method for researching criminological reality, it becomes imperative for us to understand how the identity of the consultant plays a large role in determining the writers' knowledge about crime and policing. When local police forces cooperate with the production of crime programs by 'loaning' the production a police consultant, it is not surprising that the consultant does not spontaneously provide writers with knowledge about problematic police practices or cases about 'dirty' police officers. When asked to relay their experiences, most consultants often speak about their most memorable cases, where this memorability is tied to the extraordinariness (and statistical non-representativeness) of the incident. Consequently, what television writers know about crime is already formatted as a remarkable case and is told to them as an anecdotal exemplar about the experiential reality of policing. As writers write what they know, their representations of crime dramatize extraordinary criminal cases, while generally representing police officers in a positive light.

How do writers transform their knowledge about crime into fictional representations that fit within the format of the television drama?

Many criminological and sociolegal scholars have assumed that all mass media use the same format irrespective of the particularities of a specific medium. For example, this presumption has allowed scholars to lump analyses of television programs with scholarship on crime films or law films. In contrast, my research has highlighted the specific (writing) format used to make television dramas. The television writers' knowledge needs to fit into the format of television writing (e.g. beats arranged around commercial breaks), which is not the same format as that used to write films, novels, or newspaper articles. The content and format of a television drama also varies by broadcaster (see Chapter 5). By taking into account a production's format, this book has diverged from academic studies of crime and media that have only considered the informational content of television productions. It also sidelines scholars' critique of mass media transmissions as merely 'misinformation' about crime. As an ANT study, my research has understood information as necessarily entailing transformation, which in turn is not understood as distortion with all of its negative connotations. Consequently,

I have proceeded by examining the meaning-making processes and practices that are used to transform television writers' knowledge about crime into certain representations. Meaning-making in television production takes a specific form, which is the result of both aesthetic and commercial considerations. By considering television as an aesthetic-commercial or material-semiotic hybrid, my analysis has not only examined the aesthetic aspects of representations, but also considered how format translations were related to the market position of a private, commercial broadcaster.

In Chapters 3 and 4, I have followed the representation of a 'bad apple' (specifically, a corrupt Emergency Task Force sergeant) as an actor by documenting its 'life' and 'death,' beginning with its conception as a germ of an idea in the writers' room to its final textual form. By examining the 'growth' of a pop cultural representation, I have documented the making of popular culture by returning to the earliest usage of the term 'culture.' As a noun of process, 'culture' initially referred to cultivation or 'the tending of natural growth' (Williams 1976: 87). Here, 'culture' entails growth through a process of transformations and translations. Following ANT's focus on translations, I have traced how the police consultant's anecdotal representation of a real-life 'bad apple' needed to be translated into a generalized fictional stock character. The translation made through the usage of a 'fiction filter' was necessitated by Errors and Omissions insurance requirements. As *The Bridge* had a limited episodic budget, the level of police corruption embodied by the fictional 'bad apple' was eventually scaled back as characters needed to be financially translated into guest screen performers. Ultimately, the representation of a 'bad apple' disappeared, following suggestions from not only network executives' notes but also the broadcaster's Standards and Practices department. What this particular case study illustrates is the instability of a representation: a representation is always poised on the brink of failure as it is 'attacked' by various inspectors across the multiple trials built into the storytelling process.

In tracing translations from knowledge to representation, I have also highlighted the multiple and heterogeneous human and non-human actors that make up the storytelling actor-network in television production. For example, in Chapter 4, I treat texts themselves (e.g. story documents) as actors rather than as static, textual products on which humans act. When we conceive of story documents as actors, we can trace their intertextuality – specifically, how these texts influence and act on each other, as well as how they transport and transform the content of an episodic story. When these texts circulate, they not only demonstrate their own movement across space (e.g. from the writers' room in Toronto to the offices of network executives in Los Angeles) but also across actors. Prior to having any effect on a consumer audience, these story documents have affected human actors, such as producers, writers, network executives and insurers, in ways that compelled their revision. They have also been themselves affected by a non-human, technological actor: screenwriting software. That is, story documents are subjected to translations made through the use of Final Draft when they are transformed from the format of a beat sheet into the proper format of a script.

Lastly, I have highlighted the ways in which law acts on television representations through the storytelling actor-network. Errors and Omissions insurance and a broadcaster's Standards and Practices are examples of the law in action; albeit law that governs the more mundane, everyday concerns that animate television production and its eventual distribution. In the actor-networks documented in this book, the legal concerns embodied by Errors and Omissions and Standards and Practices have certainly had an effect on the way writers and producers approach the way they tell their fictional crime stories. However, these particular legal concerns have not been recognized by most scholarship on media and popular culture. Media scholars, particularly Canadian communication scholars, have focused on the more visible forms of state broadcasting law, such as the American Federal Communications Commission (FCC) regulations or the various public policies that have governed the operation of the Canadian Radio-Television and Telecommunications Commission (CRTC). However, neither Errors and Omissions nor Standards and Practices can be seen from the macro perspective of state broadcasting law. Instead, they are practices that are tied to a specific television production (Errors and Omissions) or to a specific broadcaster (Standards and Practices). By inspecting representations prior to their distribution, both forms of legal regulation are pre-emptive attempts aimed at preventing viewers' litigation against the production company or the broadcaster.

Future research

Using different case studies

The conclusions drawn in this book are based on an analysis of specific case studies. While ANT is not interested in creating general typologies, it should be noted that different case studies might provide a different picture of television production in the following ways.

American television productions

American case studies might diverge from the Canadian[1] ones provided in this book in important ways. In contrast to Canadian television production, American television production does not have any American content requirements, in the sense of producing and protecting a distinctly American sense of national culture. The Americans have never viewed Canadian television as a cultural threat. As a result, the American broadcaster has a different stance on a series' concept than the Canadian broadcaster, often focusing on how that television drama might be 'the next great creative idea' rather than attending to how 'Canadian' it is. As *The Bridge* showrunner (20 March 2009) notes:

> Canada's the only country in the world that defines itself in the negative, by what it isn't. We are not the United States. They don't ever actually define

themselves by – if you ask a Canadian, 'what is Canadian?' They don't quite know, and it's the only country founded by a department store. This is not to put it down. I'm just saying that the mentality creating television here is a little different. [. . .] So the people who create television here are basically using – even though there is some ad revenue, it's very small compared to the United States. So there's a kind of mentality with that, a kind of bureaucracy that goes with that control, but they [networks] act like it's their money, oddly enough. So it's a little different. This isn't to say that you can't create great television. Well, we can and [we] do. [. . .] In the States, the mentality is 'the next guy who walks in that door is going to make *my* career and make me a million dollars. So I'm going to listen to that guy. If I like that idea, I'm going for it.' It's a little bit more of a gamble.

As we have previously discussed, the American broadcaster's orientation towards risk-taking manifests itself in the relatively large number of pilots made per television season (see Figure 5.1). In contrast, Canadian broadcasters develop a relatively small number of pilots. However, Canadian pilots are much more likely than American ones to be picked up for broadcast. This difference in sheer quantity of production might impact research, particularly research access. The number of research opportunities in Canada is constrained by the relatively small number of original television dramas made in Canada. In contrast, there might be more research opportunities in the US, especially if a researcher were interested in examining pilot production.

In addition to having a different mentality when it comes to making television, the actors involved in American television production might also have different roles than the ones described in this book. Canadian independent production companies take on the role of the American studios during the Canadian television production process. However, they do not provide the creative feedback during the story revision phase that an American studio would provide. As a result, the story–revision actor–network for an American television drama might include additional actors from the studio.

'Well-tried' shows

This book has focused on untried television dramas – that is, a first season of a television drama that is in production, but has yet to air on a broadcasting network. The first season of a television drama is often conceived as experimental, as producers, writers and showrunners figure out what (narratively, aesthetically and commercially) works for their particular series. By the second season, they have often created a workable 'formula'[2] for how to write and direct their television series. As a result of my focus on untried shows, I have been able to highlight the dynamic, transformative nature of the series' concept and its representations. This focus is in line with ANT's theoretical orientation, and also allows for an easy analogy to the experimental work done in laboratories. It is quite plausible that a later season (e.g. second season) of a television drama might be less experimental than the first season, especially if it is produced according to a 'formula.' More importantly, a later season would give the researcher a glimpse of how audience response feeds back into the production process. In the case of my 'untried' shows, the consumer audience did not figure into any of the creative considerations made by the showrunner, because the show had yet to air and had yet to be consumed by a lay audience.

Further research on the production of popular (televisual) criminology

As Carrabine notes (2008: 187), we need further academic research on the texts, audiences and industries implicated in the making of popular criminology. More importantly, our theoretically informed analyses of popular criminology need to be grounded by concrete analyses of case studies. Theory – either centred on popular culture, representations or the media – by itself is not a substitute for empirical research. Towards that end, I propose two different sites of future research on the making of popular criminology. Following my insistence that we take medium specificity into account in our empirical research, future research might continue to examine the television production process in the following ways.

Other laboratories of fiction-making within the television production process

For researchers interested in further examining the transformative meanings of representations during television production, they might consider ethnographically studying the work that is undertaken in the editing suite. Conceptually, editing is the audiovisual version of the textual process of story revision, and can be considered another laboratory within television production. While textual revisions tinker with the sequence of narrative events and the wording of dialogue, editing can re-conceive a sequence of events by changing the juxtaposition of audiovisual frames. It also presents an opportunity for the showrunner to re-assert his or her creative vision against a director's creative conceptualization of an episode. For example, the showrunner of *Cra$h & Burn* re-cut an entire episode to fit his creative vision in the editing suite because he was displeased with a director's efforts. Because directors for television dramas are hired on an episode-by-episode basis, they may put their own aesthetic flourishes on the directing episode. However, these may not always be in line with the showrunner's vision for the series.

The editing process would also illuminate the different cuts required for international distribution. In documenting these various cuts, the different legal and commercial concerns of international distributors can be brought to light. For example, the length of an episode varies depending on the distributor or foreign broadcaster. To account for differing amounts of commercial breaks, an episode of *Forensic Factor*, for instance, is cut three times: the Canadian version is 46 minutes long; the British version is 44 minutes long; and the international version is 48 minutes in length. This in turn impacts the number of acts per episode: the story for the Canadian version is broken down into six acts, whereas the international version has only four acts. The number of acts becomes both a commercial and aesthetic matter.

Legal concerns, such as different Errors and Omissions, might also come to the fore when editing content for particular versions of an episode. For example, *The Bridge* has been sold for broadcast in South Africa through Sony Entertainment Television. While I have discussed how Errors and Omissions has shaped the necessity to downplay the show's setting as Toronto in the North American version of the series, the South African version highlights the series' Toronto setting. In the re-cut opening title sequence, the South African version emphasizes that the series is about 'Toronto's frontline' of policing. Thus, it seems that foreign distributors do not necessarily work under the same set of domestic Errors and Omissions requirements.

Extending the actor-networks of television production to examine distribution

In making popular criminology, work in the editing suite already acknowledges the diversity of domestic and foreign broadcasters as well as potential audiences. By treating a completed television drama as an actor, we can follow it as it travels to new contexts of reception. In doing so, we can begin to document the circulation of popular criminology by extending the production actor-network to include actor-networks of distribution. By tracing a television program's distribution deals, we can examine the potential international flows of television programming, and consequently better theorize how popular culture itself flows (Ferrell, Hayward, and Young 2008). For example, future research can investigate the continued 'life' of television dramas as they are bought for distribution and broadcast outside their place of production. As we have previously discussed, contemporary Canadian television programs have been produced with the expectation that they will be good television exports. Future research might analyze how foreign distributors understand cultural discounts and apply them to their purchase of television dramas. Such research will be valuable for explaining why crime dramas – or in the case of Canada, police dramas – are so easy to export, and what that might mean for the rule of law.

This research would be an empirical step in the direction of Machura and Ulbrich's (2001) previous research on the globalizing of particular genres of law film. Machura and Ulbrich examine why courtroom films made in continental Europe follow the Hollywood formula. Following a content analysis of the aspects of American courtroom dramas, they conclude that the American adversarial criminal justice system is more suitable to storytelling in movies because it provides far more intense drama. Machura and Ulbrich base their conclusion on their own reading of American courtroom dramas compared to the (less dramatic) reality of the continental criminal justice system. Thus, future empirical research might examine whether this conclusion is warranted through interviews with foreign distributors, or through ethnographic research done at industry events in which foreign distributors gather to buy films and television programs.

The book itself is an actor

While future research projects on distribution might examine the continued 'life' of a television program outside of the context of its production, I will end by discussing the continued 'life' of an ANT-inspired book. The work presented here is not meant to be static because its meaning is not set for all time. Scholarship done under the process-centric ANT approach tends to be an incomplete account because it is understood as a work in progress rather than as some definitive final product. Thus, the meaning of this book will be altered by future research. The act of doing more research is not merely about accumulating more knowledge or information about the television production process. Instead, it entails adding more actors to the actor-networks described in this book, thereby expanding them. The addition of new actors might also change some of the dynamics of the documented actor-networks. With those changing dynamics, the meaning and function of this book will also change. The end of this book brings forth the beginning of its journey as an actor in the world, deferring the final word on its meaning and function to the future actor-networks in which it might participate.

Notes

1 This book examined television dramas made in Toronto. It is quite possible that other Canadian production centers might have a different production culture than that of Toronto. Because there has been no comparative research done on regional production cultures in Canada, it is not immediately clear to me what these differences might be. As a gross generalization, Toronto's status as a major Canadian production centre has helped attract highly experienced and professional production personnel to work in the city. I assume that the same can be said for Vancouver and Montreal. In contrast, the quality and quantity of production personnel in regions not as well known for film and television production (e.g. the Prairies, the Territories and the Maritimes) might vary from that of Toronto. Consequently, writers and producers from those regions might espouse different perspectives from the ones quoted in this book. Because I have focused on English-language Canadian television productions, I also cannot comment on the kinds of aesthetic, cultural and commercial concerns that inform the production of Francophone television programs.
2 I use the term 'formula' for lack of a better term. Unlike mathematical formulas, this formula is not fixed. While most episodes will be written in ways that conform to the formula (e.g. number of beats per act, the content of certain beats, etc.), certain episodes will deviate from it.

Bibliography

Adalian, J. (12 July 2010) 'ABC picks up a second season of *Rookie Blue*', *New York Magazine*. Online. Available HTTP: <http://nymag.com/daily/entertainment/2010/07/abc_picks_up_a_second_season_o.html> (accessed 8 September 2010).
Adalian, J. (28 January 2008) 'CBS teams with Canada's CTV', *Variety*. Online. Available HTTP: <http://www.variety.com/article/VR1117979785> (accessed 28 February 2011).
Adams, C.J. (2000) *The Sexual Politics of Meat: a feminist-vegetarian critical theory*, New York: Continuum International Publishing Group.
Altheide, D. and Snow, R. (1979) *Media Logic*, Beverly Hills: Sage.
Andreeva, N. and Vlessing, E. (1–3 February 2008) 'Nets pluck Canucks for primetime', *The Hollywood Reporter*, 403: 1, 105.
Anonymous (15 March 1954) 'Jack, be nimble!', *Time Magazine*. Online. Available HTTP: <http://www.badge714.org/dragtime.htm> (accessed 24 July 2012).
Archer, C. (2009–2010) 'CBC pilot burn-off time', *URBMN*. Online. Available HTTP: <http://www.sweetposer.tk/urbmn/index.php/tag/cbc-pilot-burn-off-time/> (accessed 24 July 2012).
Ascherson, N. (28 November 2002) 'Hitler's teeth: Review of Berlin: The Downfall, 1945 by Antony Beever', *London Review of Books*: 15–16.
Attalah, P. (2009) 'Reading television', *Canadian Journal of Communication*, 34: 163–70.
Atwood, M. (1972) *Survival: A thematic guide to Canadian literature*, Toronto: Anansi.
Babe, R.E. (1990) *Telecommunications in Canada: technology, industry, and government*, Toronto: University of Toronto Press.
Baker, W.E. and Faulkner, R.R. (1991) 'Role as resource in the Hollywood film industry', *American Journal of Sociology*, 97: 279–309.
Bakhtin, M. (1981) *The Dialogic Imagination*, Austin: University of Texas Press.
Banet-Weiser, S., Chris, C., and Freitas A. (eds) (2007) *Cable Visions: television beyond broadcasting*, New York: New York University Press.
Barak, G. (1994) 'Newsmaking criminology: Reflections on the media, intellectuals, and crime', in G. Barak (ed.) *Media, Process, and the Social Construction of Crime: studies in newsmaking criminology*, New York: Garland Publishing, Inc.
Barken, A. (17 August 2010) 'TV Eh? Podcast interview with Adam Barken', *TV, eh?* Online. Available HTTP: <http://www.tv-eh.com/2010/08/17/tv-eh-podcast-episode-7-a-rats%E2%80%99-nest-of-ego-bickering-backstabbing-rumour-and-sour-dislike/> (accessed 28 October 2010).

Barnard, L. (7 February 2010) 'Grit (and tax credits) draw film crews to Hamilton', *Toronto Star*. Online. Available HTTP: <http://www.thestar.com/entertainment/movies/article/761386—hammerwood-dirty-old-town-but-busy> (accessed 12 February 2011).

Barr, M. (15 July 2010) 'Interview: the creators of *Flashpoint*', *Film School Rejects*. Online. Available HTTP: <http://www.filmschoolrejects.com/features/interview-the-creators-of-%E2%80%98flashpoint%E2%80%99.php> (accessed 15 February 2011).

Barthes, R. (1972) *Mythologies*, New York: Noonday.

Basch, P. (2006) 'Report from the Tech Guy #5: how to track changes & collaborate', *Sandler Ink*. Online. Available HTTP: <http://www.sandlerink.com/tech/report5.htm> (accessed 16 July 2010).

BC. (10 May 2007) 'BC', *Toronto Star*: R08.

Beam, A. (20 July 2010) 'Copping out in Canada', *Boston Globe*. Online. Available HTTP: <http://www.boston.com/lifestyle/articles/2010/07/20/copping_out_in_canada/> (accessed 8 September 2010).

Beaty, B. and Sullivan, R. (2006) *Canadian Television Today*, Calgary: University of Calgary Press.

Becker, H.S. (1982) *Art Worlds*, Berkeley: University of California Press.

Benjamin, W. (2002) *The Arcades Project*, Cambridge, MA: Belknap Press of Harvard University Press.

Bennett, D. (24 March 2010) 'This will be on the midterm. You feel me? Why so many colleges are teaching *The Wire*', *Slate*. Online. Available HTTP: <http://www.slate.com/id/2245788/> (accessed 18 April 2011).

Berenson, A. (2 April 2010) 'The writers' room at "24"', *New York Times*. Online. Available HTTP: <http://www.nytimes.com/2010/04/04/weekinreview/04berenson.html> (accessed 8 April 2010).

Berger, P.L. and Luckmann, T. (1966) *The Social Construction of Reality: a treatise in the sociology of knowledge*, New York: Anchor Books.

Bergman, P. and Asimow, M. (2006) *Reel Justice: the courtroom goes to the movies*, Kansas City: Andrews and McMeel.

Berkowitz, R. (6 January 1998) 'Setting a new course: Midway through its third season, the syndicated comedy-drama *Due South* is clearly headed for laughter', *Sun-Sentinel*: 3E.

Bernstein, A. (12 August 2010) 'Executive producer Bill Mustos gets to the "Flashpoint" on his show', *iF magazine*. Online. Available HTTP: <http://www.ifmagazine.com/feature.asp?article=3928> (accessed 12 August 2010).

Biber, K. (2007) *Captive Images: race, crime, photography*, London: GlassHouse Books.

Bielby, D.D. and Bielby, W.T. (1994) '"All hits are flukes": Institutionalized decision making and the rhetoric of prime-time network program development', *American Journal of Sociology*, 99: 1287–313.

—— (2002) 'Hollywood dreams, harsh realities: Writing for film and television', *Contexts*, 1: 21–7.

Binning, C. (2009/2010) 'The colour of money: Pro$ and con$ of the U.S. network deal', *Canadian Screenwriter Magazine*, 12: 18–21.

Black, D. (1999) *Law in Film: resonance and representation*: Board of Trustees of the University of Illinois.

Bordwell, D. (1985) *Narration in the Fiction Film*, London: Routledge.

—— and Thompson, K. (2004) *Film Art: an introduction*, 7th edn, Boston: McGraw-Hill.

Bourdieu, P. (1984) *Distinction: a social critique of the judgement of taste*, trans. R. Nice, Cambridge, MA: Harvard University Press.

—— (1989) *In Other Words: essays towards a reflexive sociology*, Stanford: Stanford University Press.
Brogden, M. (1987) 'The emergence of the police – The colonial dimension', *British Journal of Criminology*, 27: 4–14.
Brown, S. (2003) *Crime and Law in Media Culture*, Buckingham: Open University Press.
Byers, M. and Johnson, V.M. (2009) '*CSI* as neoliberalism: An introduction', in M. Byers and V.M. Johnson (eds) *The CSI Effect: television, crime and governance*, Lanham: Lexington Books.
Caldwell, J.T. (1995) *Televisuality: style, crisis, and authority in American television*: Rutgers University Press.
—— (2006) 'Cultural studies and media production: Critical industrial practices', in M. White and J. Schwoch (eds) *Questions of Method in Cultural Studies*, Malden: Blackwell Publishing.
—— (2008) *Production Culture: industrial reflexivity and critical practice in film and television*, Durham: Duke University Press.
—— (2009) '"Both sides of the fence": Blurred distinctions in scholarship and production (a portfolio of interviews)', in V. Mayer, M.J. Banks, and J.T. Caldwell (eds) *Production Studies: cultural studies of media industries*, New York: Routledge.
Callon, M. (1986) 'Some elements of a sociology of translation: Domestication of the scallops and the fishermen of St Brieuc Bay', in J. Law (ed.) *Power, Action and Belief: a new sociology of knowledge*, London: Routledge & Kegan Paul.
Cantor, M.G. (1971) *The Hollywood TV Producer: his work and his audience*, New York: Basic Books.
—— and Cantor, J.M. (1992) *Prime-time Television: content and control*, 2nd edn, London: Sage.
Canwest Global. (19 February 2010) *Media release*. Online. Available HTTP: <http://www.tv-eh.com/2010/02/19/crah-burn-partners-with-bbc-worldwide/> (accessed 12 February 2011).
Capers, I.B. (2011) 'Crime, legitimacy, our criminal network, and *The Wire*', *Ohio State Journal of Criminal Law* 8: 459–71.
Carrabine, E. (2008) *Crime, Culture and the Media*, Cambridge: Polity.
Cavender, G. and Deutsch, S.K. (2007) '*CSI* and moral authority: The police and science', *Crime, Media, Culture*, 3: 67–81.
CBC News. (24 January 2003) 'Homeless man claims victory in suit against Toronto police officers', *CBC*. Online. Available HTTP: <http://www.cbc.ca/news/canada/story/2003/01/24/thomaskerr030124.html> (accessed 1 March 2011).
—— (10 January 2010) '*Flashpoint, Bridge* missing from CBS lineup', *CBC News*. Online. Available HTTP: <http://www.cbc.ca/arts/tv/story/2010/01/10/cbs-canadian-shows.html> (accessed 8 January 2010).
CBS/Broadcast Group. (1988) 'Program standards for the CBS Television Network', in S. Oskamp (ed.) *Television as a Social Issue*, New York: Sage.
CBS Program Practices. (20 July 2009) *The Bridge – Episode #112*, Los Angeles: CBS Television Network.
Chancer, L. and McLaughlin, E. (2007) 'Public criminologies: Diverse perspectives on academia and policy', *Theoretical Criminology*, 11: 155–73.
Chase, A. (1986) 'Toward a legal theory of popular culture', *Wisconsin Law Review*: 527–68.
Chatto, J. (1998) *The Man who Ate Toronto: memoirs of a restaurant lover*, Toronto: MacFarlane, Walter and Ross.

Chris, C. (2007) 'Discovery's wild discovery: The growth and globalization of TV's animal genres', in S. Banet-Weiser, C. Chris, and A. Freitas (eds) *Cable Visions: television beyond broadcasting*, New York: New York University Press.

Clover, C. (1998) 'Law and the order of popular culture', in A. Sarat and T. Kearns (eds) *Law in the Domains of Culture*, Ann Arbor: University of Michigan Press.

Cohen, S. (1972) *Folk Devils and Moral Panics*, London: MacGibbon and Kee.

—— and Young. J. (eds) (1973) *The Manufacture of News: social problems, deviance and the mass media*, London: Constable.

Cole, S. and Dioso-Villa, R. (2007) '*CSI* and its effects: Media, juries and the burden of proof', *New England Law Review*, 41: 435–70.

—— (2009) 'Investigating the "*CSI* effect" effect: Media and litigation crisis in criminal law', *Stanford Law Review*, 61: 1335–74.

Coleridge, S.T. (1817) *Biographia Literaria*, New York: Kirk and Mercein.

Collins, R. (1990) *Culture, Communication and National Identity: the case of Canadian television*, Toronto: University of Toronto Press.

Cornea, C. (2009) 'Showrunning *The Doctor Who* franchise: A response to Denise Mann', in V. Mayer, M.J. Banks, and J.T. Caldwell (eds) *Production Studies: cultural studies of media industries*, New York: Routledge.

Couldry, N. (2004) 'Actor–network theory and media: Do they connect and on what terms?' Online. Available HTTP: http://www.andredeak.com.br/pdf/Couldry_ActorNetworkTheoryMedia.pdf (accessed 8 September 2010).

CRTC. (6 June 1994) 'Decision 94-280', *Canadian Radio-Television and Telecommunications Commission*. Online. Available HTTP: <http://crtc.gc.ca/eng/archive/1994%5CDB94-280.htm> (accessed 10 February 2011).

CTV. (2010a) '*The Bridge*: About the show', *CTV*. Online. Available HTTP: <http://shows.ctv.ca/TheBridge/About.aspx> (accessed 8 April 2010).

—— (2010b) '*Flashpoint*: About the show', *CTV*. Online. Available HTTP: <http://shows.ctv.ca/FlashPoint/About-(1).aspx> (accessed 8 April 2010).

—— (11 February 2010) '*The Bridge* premieres on CTV March 5', *TV, eh?* Online. Available HTTP: <http://www.tv-eh.com/2010/02/11/the-bridge-premieres-on-ctv-march-5/> (accessed 18 February 2011).

Currie, E. (2007) 'Against marginality: Arguments for a public criminology', *Theoretical Criminology*, 11: 175–90.

D'Acci, J. (1994) *Defining Women: television and the case of Cagney and Lacey*, Chapel Hill: University of North Carolina Press.

Davis, M. (1992) *City of Quartz: excavating the future in Los Angeles*, New York: Vintage Books.

Dawn, R. (21 June 2010) '*Rookie Blue* – TV review', *The Hollywood Reporter*. Online. Available HTTP: <http://www1.hollywoodreporter.com/hr/tv-reviews/rookie-blue-tv-review-1004099491.story> (accessed 21 February 2011).

—— (8 July 2010) '*The Bridge* – TV review', *The Hollywood Reporter*. Online. Available HTTP: <http://thebridgetv.com/2010/07/08/the-bridge-hollywood-reporter-review/> (accessed 16 April 2011).

deMint, J. (4 March 2011) 'Public broadcasting should go private', *Wall Street Journal*. Online. Available HTTP: < http://benton.org/node/51975> (accessed 4 March 2011).

Denvir, J. (ed.) (1996) *Legal Reelism: movies as legal texts*, Urbana: University of Illinois Press.

Djankov, S., McLiesh, C., Nenova, T. and Shleifer, A. (2001) *Who Owns the Media?* Online. Available HTTP: <http://citeseerx.ist.psu.edu/viewdoc/download?doi=10.1.1.17.6161&rep=rep1&type=pdf> (accessed 11 April 2011).

Donaldson, M.C. (1996) *Clearance and Copyright: everything the independent filmmaker needs to know*, Los Angeles: Silman-James Press.
Dornfeld, B. (1998) *Producing Public Television, Producing Public Culture*, Princeton: Princeton University Press.
Douglas, P. (2005) *Writing the Television Drama Series*, Studio City: Michael Wiese Productions.
Douzinas, C., Warrington, R. and McVeigh, S. (1991) *Postmodern Jurisprudence: the law of text in the texts of law*, London: Routledge.
Dowler, K., Fleming, T., and Muzzatti, S.L. (2006) 'Constructing crime: Media, crime, and popular culture', *Canadian Journal of Criminology and Criminal Justice*, 48: 837–50.
Doyle, A. (1998) 'COPS: Television policing as policing reality', in M. Fishman and G. Cavender (eds) *Entertaining Crime: television reality programs*, New York: Aldine de Gruyter.
—— (2003) *Arresting Images: crime and policing in front of the television camera*, Toronto: University of Toronto Press.
—— (2006) 'How not to think about crime in the media', *Canadian Journal of Criminology and Criminal Justice*, 48: 867–85.
Doyle, J. (2 March 2010) 'So what if CBC goes for light entertainment?', *Globe and Mail*. Online. Available HTTP: <http://www.theglobeandmail.com/subscribe.jsp?art=1487196> (accessed 27 March 2010).
—— (14 August 2010) 'The post-Stursberg CBC: Tilt goes the tightrope', *Globe and Mail*. Online. Available HTTP: <http://www.theglobeandmail.com/news/arts/television/john-doyle/the-post-stursberg-cbc-tilt-goes-the-tightrope/article1671986/> (accessed 27 February 2011).
Druick, Z. and Kotsopoulos, A. (eds) (2008) *Programming Reality: perspectives on English-Canadian television*, Waterloo: Wilfred Laurier University Press.
du Gay, P. (ed.) (1997) *Production of Culture: cultures of production*, London: Sage.
Duncanson, J. (4 February 2000) '"Bullying" police union blasted by Lastman', *Toronto Star*: A1.
Durkheim, E. (1965) *The Division of Labor in Society*, trans. G. Simpson, New York: Free Press.
Egner, J. (5 April 2012) 'The game never ends: David Simon on wearying *Wire* love and the surprising usefulness of Twitter', *The New York Times*. Online. Available HTTP: <http://artsbeat.blogs.nytimes.com/2012/04/05/the-game-never-ends-david-simon-on-wearying-wire-love-and-the-surprising-usefulness-of-twitter/?src=tp> (accessed 1 October 2012).
Elkins, J.R. (2006–2007) 'Popular culture, legal films, and legal film critics', *Loyola of Los Angeles Law Review*, 40: 745–91.
Ellis, J. (1982) *Visible Fictions: cinema, television, video*, London: Routledge.
—— (2000) *Seeing Things: television in the age of uncertainty*, London: I.B. Tauris.
—— (2004) 'Television production', in R.C. Allen and A. Hill (eds) *The Television Studies Reader*, New York: Routledge.
Ellis, M. (10 May 2011) '*Flashpoint* – Mark Ellis, Stephanie Morgenstern', *Writers Talking TV*. Online. Available HTTP: <http://itunes.apple.com/ca/podcast/writers-talking-tv/id335802768> (accessed 24 July 2012).
Ericson, R.V. (1981) *Making Crime: a study of detective work*, Toronto: Butterworth.
—— (1989) 'Patrolling the facts: Secrecy and publicity in police work', *British Journal of Sociology*, 40: 205–26.

—— (1991) 'Mass media, crime, law, and justice: An institutional approach', *British Journal of Criminology*, 31: 219–49.
—— (1995) 'Introduction', in R.V. Ericson (ed.) *Crime and the Media*, Aldershot: Dartmouth.
——, Baranek, P.M., and Chan, J.B.L. (1991) *Representing Order: crime, law and justice in the news media*, Toronto: University of Toronto Press.
——, Chan, J.B.L., and Baranek, P.M. (1987) *Visualizing Deviance: a study of news organization*, Toronto: University of Toronto Press.
—— and Doyle, A. (2004) *Uncertain Business: risk, insurance and the limits of knowledge*, Toronto: University of Toronto Press.
——, Doyle, A., and Barry, D. (2003) *Insurance as Governance*, Toronto: University of Toronto Press.
Ettema, J.S., Whitney, D.C., and Wackman, D.B. (1997) 'Professional mass communicators', in D.A. Berkowitz (ed.) *Social Meaning of News: a text reader*, Thousand Oaks: Sage.
Ewick, P. and Silbey, S.S. (1998) *The Common Place of Law: stories from everyday life*, Chicago: University of Chicago Press.
Eyerman R. and Ring, M. (1998) 'Towards a new sociology of art worlds: Bringing meaning back in', *Acta Sociologica*, 41: 277–83.
Feilzer, M. (2009) 'The importance of telling a good story: An experiment in public criminology', *Howard Journal*, 48: 472–84.
Ferrell, J. and Sanders, C. (eds) (1995) *Cultural Criminology*, Boston: Northeastern University Press.
——, Hayward, K., Morrison, W., and Presdee, M. (eds) (2004) *Cultural Criminology Unleashed*, London: GlassHouse Press.
——, Hayward, K., and Young, J. (2008) *Cultural Criminology: an invitation*, Los Angeles: Sage.
Fine, G.A. (1992) 'The culture of production: Aesthetic choices and constraints in culinary work', *American Journal of Sociology*, 97: 1268–94.
Fine, S. (15 February 1999) 'He's out to re-arm a force under fire', *Globe and Mail*: A1.
Fiske, J. (1989) *Television Culture*, London: Routledge.
Fixmer, A. (9 March 2009) 'CBS, NBC buy Canadian TV programs to save on cost (Update 2)', *Bloomberg*. Online. Available HTTP: <http://www.bloomberg.com/apps/news?sid=afYDvToAWJks&pid=newsarchive> (accessed 8 September 2010).
Foucault, M. (1977) *Discipline and Punish: the birth of the prison*, trans. A. Sheridan, New York: Vintage Books.
Frank, S. (2003) 'Reel reality: Science consultants in Hollywood', *Science as Culture*, 12: 427–69.
Freeman, M. (ed.) (2005) *Law and Popular Culture*, Oxford: Oxford University Press.
Friedman, L.M. (1988–1989) 'Law, lawyers, and popular culture', *Yale Law Journal*, 98: 1579–606.
Friend, T. (19 November 2001) 'You can't say that: The networks play word games', *The New Yorker*. Online. Available HTTP: <http://www.uvm.edu/~jhaig/tv/Youcantsaythat.pdf> (accessed 16 July 2010).
Frye, N. (1971) *The Bush Garden: essays on the Canadian imagination*, Toronto: Anansi.
Fulton, R.G. (2003) 'How to beat the cops', *Eye Magazine*. Online. Available HTTP: <http://injusticebusters.com/2003/Thomas_Kerr.htm> (accessed 11 April 2011).
Gamson, J. (1998) *Freaks Talk Back: tabloid talk shows and sexual nonconformity*, Chicago: University of Chicago Press.

Garland, D. (2001) *The Culture of Control: crime and social order in contemporary society*, Oxford: Oxford University Press.
—— (2006) 'Concepts of culture in the sociology of punishment', *Theoretical Criminology*, 10(4): 419–47.
—— and Sparks, R. (2000) 'Criminology, social theory and the challenge of our times', *British Journal of Criminology*, 40: 189–204.
Geertz, C. (1973) *The Interpretation of Culture*, New York: Basic Books.
Gerbner, G., Gross, L., Morgan, M., and Signorielli, N. (1980) 'The "mainstreaming" of America: Violence profile no. 11', *Journal of Communication*, 30: 10–29.
Gherardi, S. and Nicolini, D. (2000) 'To transfer is to transform: The circulation of safety knowledge', *Organization*, 7: 329–48.
Gillers, S. (1988–1989) 'Taking *L.A. Law* more seriously', *Yale Law Journal*, 98: 1607–23.
Gitlin, T. (1983) *Inside Prime Time*, New York: Pantheon Books.
Gittins, S. (1998) *CTV: the television wars*, Toronto: Stoddart Publishing Co., Ltd.
Golick, J. (2008) 'Joss and four acts', *Running with my Eyes Closed*. Online. Available HTTP: <http://www.jillgolick.com/2008/04/joss-and-four-acts/> (accessed 8 April 2010).
Goodman, D.J. (2006) 'Approaches to law and popular culture', *Law and Social Inquiry*, 31: 757–84.
Goodrich, P. (2005) 'Slow reading', in P. Goodrich and M. Valverde (eds) *Nietzsche and Legal Theory: half-written laws*, New York: Routledge.
Gottdiener, M. (1985) 'Hegemony and mass culture: A semiotic approach', *American Journal of Sociology*, 90: 979–1001.
Government of Canada. (1985/1988) *Canadian Multiculturalism Act*, Ottawa: Author.
—— (1991) *Canadian Broadcasting Act*. Online. Available HTTP: <http://laws.justice.gc.ca/en/B-9.01/> (accessed 21 February 2011).
Gray, H. (1995) *Watching Race: television and the struggle for "blackness"*, Minneapolis: University of Minnesota Press.
Greenfield, S., Osborn, G., and Robson, P. (2001) *Film and the Law*, London: Routledge.
Greer, C. (2007) 'News media, victims and crime', in P. Davies, P. Francis, and C. Greer (eds) *Victims, Crime and Society*, London: Sage.
—— (ed.) (2010) *Crime and Media: a reader*, London: Routledge.
Greimas, A.J. and Courtés, J. (1982) *Semiotics and Language: an analytical dictionary*, Bloomington: Indiana University Press.
Grindstaff, L. (2002) *The Money Shot: trash, class, and the making of TV talk shows*, Chicago: University of Chicago Press.
Gripsrud, J. (1995) *The Dynasty Years: Hollywood television and critical media studies*, New York: Routledge.
Griswold, W. (1981) 'American character and the American novel: An expansion of reflection theory in the sociology of literature', *American Journal of Sociology*, 86: 740–65.
Haggerty, K.D. (2001) *Making Crime Count*, Toronto: University of Toronto Press.
Hall, S., Critcher, C., Jefferson, T., Clarke, J.N., and Roberts, B. (1978) *Policing the Crisis: mugging, the state, and law and order*, London: Macmillan Press.
Haltom, W. and McCann, M.J. (2004) *Distorting the Law: politics, media, and the litigation crisis*, Chicago: University of Chicago Press.
Harari, J.V. and Bell, D.F. (eds) (1982) *Hermes: literature, science, philosophy*, Baltimore: Johns Hopkins University Press.
Hartley, J. (2006) '"Read thy self": Text, audience, and method in cultural studies', in M. White and J. Schwoch (eds) *Questions of Method in Cultural Studies*, Malden: Blackwell Publishing.

—— (2008) *Television Truths*, Malden, MA: Blackwell Publishing.
Havens, T. (2006) *Global Television Marketplace*, London: British Film Institute.
——, Lotz, A.D., and Tinic, S. (2009) 'Critical media industry studies: A research approach', *Communication, Culture and Critique*, 2: 234–53.
Hayward, K. and Young, J. (2004) 'Cultural criminology: Some notes on the script', *Theoretical Criminology*, 8: 259–73.
—— (2007) 'Cultural criminology', in M. Maguire, R. Morgan, and R. Reiner (eds) *The Oxford Handbook of Criminology*, 4th edn, Oxford: Oxford University Press.
Hemmingway, E. (2008) *Into the Newsroom: exploring the digital production of regional television news*, London: Routledge.
Henderson, A.M. and Doktori, H. (1988) 'How the networks monitor program content', in S. Oskamp (ed.) *Television as a Social Issue*, New York: Sage.
Herman, E.S. and Chomsky, N. (1988) *Manufacturing Consent: the political economy of the mass media*, New York: Pantheon Books.
—— and Waterman McChesney, R. (1997) *The Global Media: the new missionaries of global capitalism*, London and Washington: Cassell.
Hesmondhalgh, D. (2006) 'Bourdieu, the media and cultural production', *Media, Culture and Society*, 28: 211–32.
—— (2007) *The Cultural Industries*, London: Sage.
Hill, K. (2002) 'Drama goes down the tubes', *Canadian Screenwriter Magazine*, 4: 12–15.
Hirsch, P.M. (1980) 'The "scary world" of the nonviewer and other anomalies: A reanalysis of Gerbner et al.'s findings on the cultivation analysis, part I', *Communication Research*, 7: 403–56.
—— (1981) 'On not learning from one's mistakes: A reanalysis of Gerbner et al.'s findings on the cultivation analysis, part II', *Communication Research*, 8: 3–37.
Hollywood Reporter, The. (2010) 'Pilot log: 2009–2010 development season', *The Hollywood Reporter*. Online. Available HTTP: <http://reporter.blogs.com/pilotseason/200910-development-season.html> (accessed 24 July 2012).
Horan, D. (2007) 'RTE and the *CSI* franchise', in M. Allen (ed.) *Reading CSI: Crime TV under the microscope*, New York: I.B. Tauris.
Horkheimer, M. and Adorno, T. (1972) *Dialectic of Enlightenment*, New York: Herder & Herder.
Hoskins, C. and Mirus, R. (1988) 'Reasons for the U.S. dominance of the international trade in television programmes', *Media, Culture and Society*, 10: 499–515.
Hughes, M. (1980) 'The fruits of the cultivation analysis: A reexamination of some effects of television viewing', *Public Opinion Quarterly*, 44: 287–302.
Hutcheon, L. (1990) *As Canadian as Possible . . . Under the Circumstances!* Toronto: York University and ECW Press.
Hutchings, P.J. (2001) *The Criminal Spectre in Law, Literature and Aesthetics: incriminating subjects*, London: Routledge.
Jenkins, H. (1992) *Textual Poachers: television fans and participatory culture*, New York: Routledge.
—— (2006a) *Convergence Culture: where old and new media collide*, New York: New York University Press.
—— (2006b) *Fans, Bloggers, and Gamers: exploring participatory culture*, New York: New York University Press.
—— (4 September 2006) 'Picking favorites: The Flow television poll', *Confessions of an Aca-Fan*. Online. Available HTTP: <http://www.henryjenkins.org/2006/09/picking_favorites_the_flow_tel.html> (accessed 28 October 2010).

Jewkes, Y. (2004) *Media and Crime*, London: Sage.
—— (ed.) (2009a) *Crime and Media, Volume I*, London: Sage.
—— (ed.) (2009b) *Crime and Media, Volume II*, London: Sage.
—— (ed.) (2009c) *Crime and Media, Volume III*, London: Sage.
Johnson, R. (1986/1987) 'What is cultural studies anyway?', *Social Text*, 16: 38–80.
Johnson, R. and Buchanan, R. (2001) 'Getting the insider's story out: What popular film can tell us about legal method's dirty secrets', *Windsor Yearbook of Access to Justice*, 20: 87–110.
Kalifa, D. (2004) 'Crime scenes: Criminal topography and social imaginary in nineteenth-century Paris', *French Historical Studies*, 27: 175–94.
Kamir, O. (2005) 'Why "law-and-film" and what does it actually mean? A perspective', *Continuum: Journal of Media and Cultural Studies*, 19: 255–78.
—— (2006) *Framed: women in law and film*, Durham: Duke University Press.
Katz, J. (1988) *Seductions of Crime: moral and sensual attractions in doing evil*, New York: Basic Books.
KG. (2009) *Director Primer for Cra$h & Burn*.
Killingsworth, J. (2005) 'License and poetic license: A critical examination of the complicated relationship between the CRTC and the specialty channels', *Canadian Journal of Communication*, 30: 211–32.
Kirby, D.A. (2003) 'Science consultants, fictional films, and scientific practice', *Social Studies of Science*, 33: 231–68.
—— (2011) *Lab Coats in Hollywood: science, scientists, and cinema*, Cambridge: MIT Press.
Knight, S. (1980) *Form and Ideology in Crime Fiction*, Bloomington: Indiana University.
Knorr-Cetina, K. (1999) *Epistemic Cultures: how the sciences make knowledge*, Cambridge, MA: President and Fellows of Harvard College.
Kompare, D. (2010) *CSI*, Malden: Wiley-Blackwell.
Krashinsky, S. and Marlow, I. (8 February 2011) 'CTV's shakeup sets stage for BCE's digital push', *Globe and Mail*. Online. Available HTTP: <http://m.theglobeandmail.com/globe-investor/bce-cleans-house-at-ctv/article1898812/?service=mobile> (accessed 24 February 2011).
Lam, A. (2012) 'Making "bad apples" on *The Bridge*: A production study of the making of a police drama', in P. Robson and J. Silbey (eds), *Law and Justice on the Small Screen*, Oxford: Hart Publishing.
Lasswell, H.D. (1927) *Propaganda Technique in the World War*, London: K Paul, Trench, Trubner.
—— (1948) 'The structure and function of communication in society', in L. Bryson (ed.) *The Communication of Ideas: a series of addresses*, New York: Harper.
Latour, B. (1987) *Science in Action: how to follow scientists and engineers through society*, Milton Keynes: Open University Press.
—— (1988) *The Pasteurization of France*, Cambridge, MA: Harvard University Press.
—— (1996) *Aramis, or, The Love of Technology*, Cambridge, MA: Harvard University Press.
—— (2004) 'Why has critique run out of steam? From matters of fact to matters of concern', *Critical Inquiry*, 30: 225–47.
—— (2007) *Reassembling the Social: an introduction to actor–network theory*, New York: Oxford University Press.
—— (2010) *The Making of Law: an ethnography of the Conseil d'Etat*, Cambridge: Polity Press.
—— and Woolgar, S. (1979) *Laboratory Life: the social construction of scientific facts*, Beverly Hills: Sage.

Law, J. (1992) *Notes on the Theory of the Actor–Network: ordering, strategy and heterogeneity*. Online. Available HTTP: <http://www.lancs.ac.uk/fass/sociology/papers/law-notes-on-ant.pdf> (accessed 8 September 2010).

—— (2007) *Actor Network Theory and Material Semiotics*. Online. Available HTTP: <http://www.heterogeneities.net/publications/Law2007ANTandMaterialSemiotics.pdf> (accessed 11 March 2011).

—— (2008) 'On sociology and STS', *Sociological Review*, 56: 624–49.

—— and Urry, J. (2005) *Enacting the Social, Economy and Society* 33(3): 390–410.

Lazarsfeld, P.F., Berelson, B., and Gaudet, H. (1968) *The People's Choice: how the voter makes up his mind in a presidential campaign*, 3rd edn, New York: Columbia University Press.

Lebo, H. (1997) *The Godfather Legacy: the untold story of the making of the classic 'Godfather' trilogy featuring never before-seen production stills*, New York: Simon & Schuster.

Lee, F.L.F. (2006) 'Cultural discount and cross-culture predictability: Examining the box office performances of American movies in Hong Kong', *Journal of Media Economics*, 19: 259–78.

Lenz, T. (2003) *Changing Images of Law in Film and Television Stories*, New York: P. Lang.

Levine, E. (2001) 'Toward a paradigm for media production research: Behind the scenes at *General Hospital*', *Critical Studies in Media Communication*, 18: 66–82.

—— (2009) 'National television, global market: Canada's *Degrassi: The Next Generation*', *Media, Culture and Society*, 31: 515–31.

Levinson, S. (1982) 'Law as literature', *Texas Law Review*, 60: 373–403.

Liu, K. (19 November 2009) 'Carman's Dining Club steak house finally put out of its misery', *Toronto Life*. Online. Available HTTP: <http://www.torontolife.com/daily/daily-dish/deathwatch/2009/11/19/carman's-dining-club-steak-house-finally-put-out-of-its-misery/> (accessed 8 July 2010).

Livingstone, S. (1996) 'On the continuing problem of media effects', in J. Curran and M. Gurevitch (eds) *Mass Media and Society*, 2nd edn, London: Arnold.

Loader, I. and Sparks, R. (2010) 'What is to be done with public criminology?' *Criminology and Public Policy*, 9: 771–81.

—— (2011) *Public criminology?* Abingdon: Routledge.

Lotz, A.D. (2006) *Redesigning Women: television after the network era*, Urbana: University of Illinois Press.

—— (2009) *Beyond Prime Time: television in the post-network era*, New York: Routledge.

Lucas, S. (2009) 'Bible study: A roundtable conversation moderated by Steve Lucas', *Canadian Screenwriter Magazine*, 11: 18–22.

Lyons, J. (2010) *Miami Vice*, Malden: Wiley-Blackwell.

Macaulay, S. (1988–1989) 'Symposium: Popular legal culture', *Yale Law Journal*, 98: 1545–58.

Macdonald, I.W. (2010) '"... So it's not surprising I'm neurotic": The screenwriter and the screen idea work group', *Journal of Screenwriting*, 1: 45–58.

McGrath, D. (12 June 2009) 'Paul Gross says what you can't', *Dead Things on Sticks*. Online. Available HTTP: <http://heywriterboy.blogspot.com/2009/06/paul-gross-says-what-you-cant.html> (accessed 12 February 2011).

—— (13 August 2009) 'TV series scripting: Part four: The second draft', *Dead Things on Sticks*. Online. Available HTTP: <http://heywriterboy.blogspot.com/2009/08/tv-series-scripting-part-four-second.html> (accessed 13 July 2010).

Machura, S. and Robson, P. (2001) 'Law and film: Introduction', *Journal of Law and Society*, 28: 1–8.

—— and Ulbrich, S. (2001) 'Law in film: Globalizing the Hollywood courtroom drama', *Journal of Law and Society*, 28: 117–32.

McKee, R. (1997) *Story: substance, style, and the principles of screenwriting*, New York: Regan Books.
McLuhan, M. (1964) *Understanding Media: the extensions of man*, New York: McGraw-Hill.
MacNeil, W.P. (2007) *Lex Populi: the jurisprudence of popular culture*, Stanford: Stanford University Press.
McShane, M. and Williams, F. (1994) 'Series foreword', in G. Barak (ed.) *Media, Process, and the Social Construction of Crime: studies in newsmaking criminology*, New York: Garland Publishing, Inc.
Mamet, D. (23 March 2010) 'Memo to the writers of The Unit', *Slashfilm*. Online. Available HTTP: <http://www.slashfilm.com/2010/03/23/a-letter-from-david-mamet-to-the-writers-of-the-unit/> (accessed 8 April 2010).
Mann, D. (2009) 'It's not TV, it's Brand Management TV: The collective author(s) of the *Lost* franchise', in V. Mayer, M.J. Banks, and J.T. Caldwell (eds) *Production Studies: cultural studies of media industries*, New York: Routledge.
Maras, S. (2009) *Screenwriting: history, theory and practice*, London: Wallflower Press.
Marenin, O. (1996) 'Policing change, changing police: Some thematic questions', in O. Marenin (ed.) *Policing Change, Changing Police: international perspectives*, New York: Taylor & Francis.
Marshall, L. (2004) 'The effects of piracy upon the music industry: A case study of bootlegging', *Media, Culture and Society*, 26: 163–81.
Mason, P. (2003) 'Introduction: Visions of crime and justice', in P. Mason (ed.) *Criminal Visions: media representations of crime and justice*, Oregon: Willan Publishing.
Matheson, S.A. (2003) 'Televising Toronto from Hogtown to Megacity', unpublished thesis, University of Southern California.
Mawby, R.I. (1990) *Comparative Policing Issues: the British and American system in international perspective*, London: Unwin Hyman Ltd.
Mayer, V., Banks, M.J., and Caldwell, J.T. (eds) (2009) *Production Studies: cultural studies of media industries*, New York: Routledge.
Meehan, E. (1992) 'Conceptualizing culture as commodity: The problem of television', in H. Newcomb (ed.) *Television: The Critical View*, New York: Oxford University Press.
Merton, R.K. (1938) 'Social structure and anomie', *American Sociological Review*, 3: 672–82.
Meyers, L. (2010) *Inside the Writers' Room: practical advice for succeeding in television*, Syracuse: Syracuse University Press.
Miller, M.J. (1987) *Turn Up the Contrast: CBC television drama since 1952*, Vancouver: University of British Columbia Press.
Miller, W.I. (1998) 'Clint Eastwood and equity: Popular culture's theory of revenge', in A. Sarat and T. Kearns (eds) *Law in the Domains of Culture*, Ann Arbor: University of Michigan Press.
Ministry of Cultural Heritage. (2009) 'Canadian television fund', *Canadian Heritage*. Online. Available HTTP: <http://www.pch.gc.ca/pgm/flm-vid/publctn/2009-04/103-eng.cfm> (accessed 15 February 2011).
MJ (21 July 2010) 'Change of plans', *Do Some Damage: an inside look at crime fiction*. Online. Available HTTP: <http://dosomedamage.blogspot.com/2010/07/change-of-plans.html> (accessed 11 April 2011).
MM (27 October 2009) 'Interview with Jill Golick', *Writers Talking TV Podcast*. Online. Available HTTP: <http://www.wgc.ca/nolevel/wgcpodcasts.html> (accessed 15 February 2011).

Mnookin, J.L. (2005) 'Reproducing a trial: Evidence and its assessment in *Paradise Lost*', in A. Sarat, L. Douglas, and M.M. Umphrey (eds) *Law on the Screen*, Stanford: Stanford University Press.

Mol, A. (2002) *The Body Multiple: the ontology in medical practice*, Durham: Duke University Press.

—— and Law, J. (eds) (2002) *Complexities: social studies of knowledge practices*, Durham: Duke University Press.

Montagu, K. (2009) 'Test pilots: The how and why of TV pilots in Canada', *Canadian Screenwriter Magazine*, 11: 12–15.

Mopas, M. (2007) 'Examining the "CSI effect" through an ANT lens', *Crime, Media, Culture*, 3:110–17.

Moscovitch, P. (2008) '*Flashpoint*: Authentic SWAT team drama', *Canadian Screenwriter Magazine*, 10: 8–15.

Mould, O. (2009) 'Lights, camera, but where's the action? Actor–network theory and the production of Robert Connolly's *Three Dollars*', in V. Mayer, M.J. Banks, and J.T. Caldwell (eds) *Production Studies: cultural studies of media industries*, New York: Routledge.

Muller-Doohm, S. (2005) *Adorno: a biography*, Cambridge: Polity Press.

Mulvey, L. (1975) 'Visual pleasure and narrative cinema', *Screen*, 16: 6–18.

Muraskin, R. and Feuer Domash, S. (2007) *Crime and the Media: headlines versus reality*: Pearson.

Murdock, G. and Golding, P. (1973) 'For a political economy of mass communications', *Socialist Register*, 10: 205–34.

—— (2005) 'Culture, communications and political economy', in J. Curran and M. Gurevitch (eds) *Mass Media and Society*, 4th edn, London: Arnold.

Newcomb, H. and Alley, R.S. (eds) (1983) *The Producer's Medium: conversations with creators of American TV*, New York: Oxford University Press.

Newman, M.Z. (2006) 'From beats to arcs: Towards a poetics of television narrative', *Velvet Light Trap*, 58: 16–28.

Nichols, B. (2001) *Introduction to Documentary*, Bloomington: Indiana University Press.

O'Brien, M., Tzanelli, R., Yar, M., and Penna, S. (2005) '"The spectacle of fearsome acts": Crime in the melting p(l)ot in *Gangs of New York*', *Critical Criminology*, 13: 17–35.

O'Connor, A. (ed.) (1989) *Raymond Williams on Television: selected writings*, Toronto: Between the Lines.

Office of the Auditor General of Canada. (November 2005) 'Key creative functions points system for a Canadian audio-visual production', *Report of the Auditor General of Canada*. Online. Available HTTP: <http://www.oag-bvg.gc.ca/internet/English/att_2005 1105xe04_e_14061.html> (accessed 21 February 2011).

Ohmann, R. (ed.) (1996a) *Making and Selling Culture*, Hanover: Wesleyan University Press.

—— (1996b) 'Knowing/creating wants', in R. Ohmann (ed.) *Making and Selling Culture*, Hanover: Wesleyan University Press.

Onstad, K. (7 June 2009) 'Funny, you don't look Canadian', *New York Times*. Online. Available HTTP: <http://www.nytimes.com/2009/06/07/arts/television/07onst. html> (accessed 22 February 2011).

Oswald, B. (22 July 2010) 'Don't let U.S. summer gig go to Canuck producers' heads', *Winnipeg Free Press*. Online. Available HTTP: <http://www.winnipegfreepress.com/ entertainment/TV/dont-let-us-summer-tv-gig-go-to-canuck-producers-heads-98998334.html> (accessed 8 September 2010).

Parker, M. (2010) 'On the other side of the fence', *Canadian Screenwriter Magazine*, 12: 35.

Patch, N. (21 July 2010) 'Canuck cop shows called not Canadian enough', *The Canadian Press*. Online. Available HTTP: <http://entertainment.ca.msn.com/tv/article.aspx?cp-documentid=24948080> (accessed 22 February 2011).

Patriquin, M. (3 December 2009) 'In this show, the hero really sweats: Gangsters, insurance money, and two Canuck alums of HBO's *Deadwood* and *The Wire*', *Macleans*. Online. Available HTTP: <http://www2.macleans.ca/2009/12/03/in-this-show-the-hero-really-sweats/> (accessed 28 January 2011).

Peelo, M. (2006) 'Framing homicide narratives in newspapers: Mediated witness and the construction of virtual victimhood', *Crime, Media, Culture*, 2: 159–75.

Peterson, R.A. and Anand, N. (2004) 'The production of culture perspective', *Annual Review of Sociology*, 30: 311–34.

Podias, K. (2007) 'The "*CSI*" effect" and other forensic fictions', *Loyola of Los Angeles Entertainment Law Review*, 27: 87–126.

Podolny, J.M. (2001) 'Networks as the pipes and prisms of the market', *American Journal of Sociology*, 107: 33–60.

Polan, D. (2007) 'Cable watching: HBO, *The Sopranos*, and Discourses of Distinction', in S. Banet-Weiser, C. Chris, and A. Freitas (eds) *Cable Visions: television beyond broadcasting*, New York: New York University Press.

Poovey, M. (1998) *A History of the Modern Fact: problems of knowledge in the sciences of wealth and society*, Chicago: University of Chicago Press.

Posner, R.A. (1988) *Law and Literature: a misunderstood relation*, Cambridge, MA: Harvard University Press.

Presdee, M. (2000) *Cultural Criminology and the Carnival of Crime*, London: Routledge.

Propp, V. (1968) *Morphology of the Folktale*, 2nd edn, Austin: University of Texas Press.

Raboy, M. (1990) *Missed Opportunities: the story of Canada's broadcasting policy*, Montreal: McGill-Queen's University Press.

Rafter, N. (2006) *Shots in the Mirror: crime films and society*, 2nd edn, New York: Oxford University Press.

—— (2007) 'Crime, film and criminology: Recent sex-crime movies', *Theoretical Criminology*, 11: 403–20

—— and Brown, M. (2011) *Criminology Goes to the Movies: crime theory and popular culture*, New York: New York University.

Rapping, E. (2003) *Law and Justice as seen on TV*, New York: New York University Press.

Ravage, J. (1978) *Television: the director's viewpoint*, Boulder: Westview Press.

Rawlings, P. (1998) 'True crime', *British Society of Criminology Conferences, Volume 1: emerging themes in criminology*. Online. Available HTTP: <http://www.britsoccrim.org/volume1/010.pdf> (accessed 11 April 2011).

Reiner, R. (2007) 'Media made criminality: The representations of crime in the mass media', in M. Maguire, R. Morgan, and R. Reiner (eds) *The Oxford Handbook of Criminology*, 4th edn, Oxford: Oxford University Press.

Rice, L. (2 May 2007) 'The Q&A: No sh—! TV execs, uncensored', *Entertainment Weekly*. Online. Available HTTP: <http://www.ew.com/ew/article/0,,20037552,00.html> (accessed 14 July 2010).

Riles, A. (2006) '[Deadlines]: Removing the brackets on politics and bureaucratic and anthropological analysis', in A. Riles (ed.) *Documents: artifacts of modern knowledge*: University of Michigan Press.

Robson, P. and Silbey, J. (2012) 'Introduction', in P. Robson and J. Silbey (eds) *Law and Justice on the Small Screen*, Oxford: Hart Publishing.

Rosenberg, C.B. (1989) 'An LA Lawyer Replies', *The Yale Law Journal*, 98: 1625–9.
Rosenthal, A. (2007) *Writing, Directing, and Producing Documentary Films and Videos*, 4th edn: Southern Illinois University Press.
Rosten, L. (1970) *Hollywood: the movie colony, the movie makers*, New York: Arno Press.
Sacco, V.F. (1995) 'Media constructions of crime', *Annals of the American Academy of Political and Social Science*, 539: 141–54.
Sandeen, C.A. and Compesi, R.J. (1990) 'Television production as collective action', in R.J. Thompson and G. Burns (eds) *Making Television: authorship and the production process*, New York: Praeger.
Sarat, A. (1985) 'Legal effectiveness and social studies of law: On the unfortunate persistence of a research tradition', *Legal Studies Forum*, 9: 23–32.
—— (2000) 'Imagining the law of the father: Loss, dread, and mourning in *The Sweet Hereafter*', *Law and Society Review*, 34: 3–46.
——, Douglas, L. and Umphrey, M.M. (eds) (2005) *Law on the Screen*, Stanford: Stanford University Press.
—— and Silbey, S. (1988) 'The pull of the policy audience', *Law and Policy*, 10: 97–166.
Scafidi, S. (2005) *Who Owns Culture? Appropriation and authenticity in American law*: Rutgers University Press.
Schiller, H.I. (1989) *Culture, Inc.: the corporate takeover of public expression*, New York: Oxford University Press.
Schneider, M. (20 February 2009) 'In tough times, pilots go broad: New shows follow familiar trends', *Variety*. Online. Available HTTP: <http://www.variety.com/article/VR1118000408.html?categoryId=1300&cs=1> (accessed 14 July 2010).
Schramm, W., Lyle, J., and Parker, E.B. (1961) *Television in the Lives of our Children*, Stanford, Stanford University Press.
Schudson, M. (1989) 'The sociology of news production', *Media, Culture and Society*, 2: 263–82.
—— (2000) 'The sociology of news production revisited (again)', in J. Curran and M. Gurevitch (eds) *Mass Media and Society*, New York: Oxford University Press.
Seaman, W.R. (1992) 'Active audiences theory: Pointless populism', *Media, Culture and Society*, 14: 301–11.
Seglins, D. (28 April 2008) 'CBC News investigation: The report that led to charges and the Crown's problems', *CBC News*. Online. Available HTTP: <http://www.cbc.ca/news/background/torontopolice/> (accessed 4 March 2011).
Serres, M. (1980) *Hermes V: le passage du Nord-Ouest*, Paris: Les Editions de Minuit.
—— (2007) *Parasite*, Minneapolis: University of Minnesota Press.
Shattuc, J.M. (1997) *The Talking Cure: TV talk shows and women*, New York: Routledge.
Sherwin, R.K. (2000) *When Law goes Pop: the vanishing line between law and popular culture*, Chicago: University of Chicago Press.
Showcase. (18 November 2009) '*Cra$h & Burn* schedule', *Showcase.ca*. Online. Available HTTP: <http://www.showcase.ca/ontv/titledetails.aspx?Root_Title_Id=248746> (accessed 21 February 2011).
Silbey, S.S. (2005) 'After legal consciousness', *Annual Review of Law and Social Science*, 1: 323–68.
Simon, D. (2004a) 'Introduction', in R. Alvarez (ed.) *The Wire: truth be told*, New York: Pocket Books.
—(2004b) 'Letter to HBO', in R. Alvarez (ed.) *The Wire: truth be told*, New York: Pocket Books.
Smith, D.E. (1990) *Texts, Facts, and Femininity: exploring the relations of ruling*, London: Routledge.

Smith, V. (2006) 'Is the CBC on target to develop great dramatic programming?' *Writers Guild of Canada*. Online. Available HTTP: <http://www.wgc.ca/magazine/articles/summer06/cbcdrama.html> (accessed 24 July 2012).

Smoodin, E. (2005) '"Everyone went wild over it": Film audiences, political cinema, and *Mr. Smith Goes to Washington*', in A. Sarat, L. Douglas, and M.M. Umphrey (eds), *Law on the Screen*, Stanford: Stanford University Press.

Smythe, D.W. (1981) *Dependency Road: communications, capitalism, consciousness and Canada*, Norwood: Ablex.

Sodano, T. (2008) 'All the pieces matter: A critical analysis of HBO's The Wire', unpublished thesis, Syracuse University.

Soothill, K. and Walby, S. (1991) *Sex Crimes in the News*, London: Routledge.

Sparks, R. (1992) *Television and the Drama of Crime: moral tales and the place of crime in public life*, Buckingham: Open University Press.

—— (1996) 'Masculinity and heroism in the Hollywood "blockbuster": The culture industry and contemporary images of crime and law enforcement', *British Journal of Criminology*, 36: 348–60.

Staiger, J. (2005) *Media Reception Studies*, New York: New York University Press.

Stallybrass, P. and White, A. (1986) *The Politics and Poetics of Transgression*, London: Methuen.

Stam, R. (2000) *Film Theory: an introduction*, Malden: Blackwell.

Stark, S. (1987–1988) 'Perry Mason meets Sonny Crockett: The history of lawyers and the police as television heroes', *University of Miami Law Review*, 42: 229–83.

Stein, N. and Burke, D. (8 December 2003) 'Inside Operation Boris', *Fortune*. Online. Available HTTP: <http://money.cnn.com/magazines/fortune/fortune_archive/2003/12/08/355094/index.htm> (accessed 11 February 2011).

Steinert, H. (2003) *Culture Industry*, trans. S. Spencer, Cambridge: Polity Press.

Stelter, B. (29 January 2008) 'O Canada, where the writers aren't on strike', *New York Times*. Online. Available HTTP: <http://mediadecoder.blogs.nytimes.com/2008/01/29/o-canada-where-the-writers-arent-on-strike/> (accessed 28 February 2011).

—— (19 July 2010) 'It's a Canadian summer for U.S. television', *New York Times*. Online. Available HTTP: http://www.nytimes.com/2010/07/20/business/media/20rookie.html (accessed 9 September 2010).

Stepakoff, J. (2007) *Billion-dollar Kiss: the kiss that saved "Dawson's Creek" and other adventures in TV writing*, New York: Penguin.

Stevens, D.J. (2011) *Media and Criminal Justice: the CSI effect*, Sudbury: Jones and Bartlett.

Story, A. (7 April 1990) 'Morality officer ran sex-for-pay service', *Toronto Star*: A1.

Strange, C. (2011) 'Stanley Kubrick's *A Clockwork Orange* as art against torture', *Crime, Media, Culture*, 2: 267–84.

Strathern, M. (2006) 'Bullet-proofing: A tale from the United Kingdom', in A. Riles (ed.) *Documents: artifacts of modern knowledge*, USA: University of Michigan Press.

Straw, W. (2002) 'Dilemmas of definition', in J. Nix and J. Sloniowski (eds) *Slippery Pastimes: reading the popular in Canadian culture*, Waterloo: Wilfred Laurier University Press.

Street, J. (2008) '"Meat and potatoes" cops', *Blue Line Forum: the voice of law enforcement on the Internet*. Online. Available HTTP: <http://forums.blueline.ca/viewtopic.php?f=1&t=16864#p343812> (accessed 8 July 2010).

Surette, R. (2009) 'The entertainment media and the social construction of crime and justice', in Y. Jewkes (ed.) *Crime and Media, Volume II*, London: Sage.

Tate, M.A. and Allen, V. (2003) 'Integrating distinctively Canadian elements into television drama: A formula for success or failure? The *Due South* experience', *Canadian Journal of Communication*, 28: 67–83.

—— (2004) '*Due South* and the Canadian image: Three perspectives'. Online. Available HTTP: <http://mtateresearch.com/DSARCSppr.pdf> (accessed 24 July 2012).
Tedesco, R. (18 June 1990) 'Discovery looks to build a programming empire', *Cablevision*: 22.
Thomas, R.R. (1999) *Detective Fiction and the Rise of Forensic Science*, New York: Cambridge University Press.
Thompson, J.B. (1990) *Ideology and Modern Culture: Critical social theory in the era of mass communication*, Stanford: Stanford University Press.
Thompson, K. (1999) *Storytelling in the New Hollywood*, Cambridge, MA: Harvard University Press.
Thompson, R.J. and Burns, G. (eds) (1990) *Making Television: authorship and the production process*, New York: Praeger.
Time. (12 July 1971) 'The Mafia: Back to the bad old days?', *Time Magazine*. Online. Available HTTP: <http://www.time.com/time/magazine/article/0,9171,902997-1,00.html> (accessed 10 April 2011).
Tinic, S. (2005) *On Location: Canada's television industry in a global market*, Toronto: University of Toronto Press.
—— (2009) 'Borders of production research: A response to Elana Levine', in V. Mayer, M.J. Banks, and J.T. Caldwell (eds) *Production Studies: cultural studies of media industries*, New York: Routledge.
Turow, J. (1997) 'James Dean in a surgical gown: Making TV's medical formula', in L. Spiegel and M. Curtin (eds) *The Revolution wasn't Televised: sixties television and societal conflict*, New York: Routledge.
Tzanelli, R., Yar, M., and O'Brien, M. (2005) '"Con me if you can": Exploring crime in the American cinematic imagination', *Theoretical Criminology*, 9: 97–117.
Ugger, C. and Inderbitzin, M. (2010) 'Public criminologies', *Criminology and Public Policy*, 9: 725–49.
Vaidhyanathan, S. (2002) 'The copyright as cudgel', *Chronicle of Higher Education*, 48. Online. Available HTTP: <http://rfrost.people.si.umich.edu//courses/SI110/readings/IntellecProp/Copyright%20as%20Cudgel.pdf> (accessed 11 April 2011).
Valier, C. (2004) *Crime and Punishment in Contemporary Culture*, London: Routledge.
Valverde, M. (2006) *Law and Order: images, meanings, myths*, Abingdon: Routledge-Cavendish.
—— (2007) 'Theoretical and methodological issues in the study of legal knowledge practices', in A. Sarat, L. Douglas, and M.M. Umphrey (eds) *How Law Knows*, Stanford: Stanford University Press.
VanDerWerff, T. (24 June 2010) '*Rookie Blue* – "Fresh Paint"', *The A.V. Club*. Online. Available HTTP: <http://www.avclub.com/articles/rookie-blue-fresh-paint,42347/> (accessed 25 February 2011).
VanLaerhoven, S. and Anderson, G. (2009) 'The science and careers of CSI', in M. Byers and V.M. Johnson (eds) *The CSI Effect: television, crime and governance*, Lanham: Lexington Books.
Vlessing, E. (24 July 2008) 'Brits, Kiwis buy *Flashpoint*', *Playback*. Online. Available HTTP: <http://playbackonline.ca/2008/07/24/flashpoint-20080724/> (accessed 15 February 2011).
—— (27 October 2008) 'Canwest goes drama shopping', *Playback*. Online. Available HTTP: <http://playbackonline.ca/2008/10/27/canwest-20081027/> (accessed 20 February 2011).

—— (3 February 2010) 'CTV leaves CBS behind on "The Bridge"', *The Hollywood Reporter*. Online. Available HTTP: <http://www.hollywoodreporter.com/news/ctv-leaves-cbs-behind-bridge-20230> (accessed 22 June 2012).
Waldman, D. (2005) 'A case for corrective criticism: *A Civil Action*', in A. Sarat, L. Douglas, and M.M. Umphrey (eds) *Law on the Screen*, Stanford: Stanford University Press.
Watercutter, A. (20 September 2011). 'TV fact-checker: Ex-NYPD cop brings realism to *Unforgettable*', *Wired Magazine*. Online. Available HTTP: <http://www.wired.com/underwire/2011/09/tv-fact-checker-unforgettable/> (accessed 24 July 2012).
Williams, R. (1961) *The Long Revolution*, London: Chatto & Windus.
—— (1976) *Keywords: a vocabulary of culture and society*, New York: Oxford University Press.
Wilson, P. (6 December 2006) 'Don't put the Hammer down; Hamilton's had lots of nicknames, but this one's like the city – no pretence', *The Hamilton Spectator*: G2.
Wolf, D. and Burstein, J. (2003) *Law and Order: crime scenes*, New York: Sterling Publishing.
Woodmansee, M. (1998) 'The cultural work of copyright: Legislating authorship in Britain, 1837–42', in A. Sarat and T. Kearns (eds) *Law in the Domains of Culture*, Ann Arbor: University of Michigan Press.
Writers Guild of Canada. (2003) *We need more Canada on TV: crisis in Canadian drama*. Online. Available HTTP: <http://www.writersguildofcanada.com/files/Crisis%20in%20Drama.pdf> (accessed 21 February 2011).
Yar, M. (2009) 'Book review of Eamonn Carrabine's *Crime, culture and the media*', *Theoretical Criminology*, 13: 411–13.
Young, A. (1996) *Imagining Crime: textual outlaws and criminal conversations*, London: Sage.
—— (2008) 'Culture, critical criminology and the imagination of crime', in T. Anthony and C. Cunneen (eds) *The Critical Criminology Companion*, Sydney: Hawkins Press.

Index

Please note that page numbers relating to Notes will have the letter 'n' following the page number. References to Figures or Tables will be in italics.

ABC network, US, 54, 141
above-the-line personnel, 54, 55, 58n
academic criminology, 2, 11, 15, 56, 171
acceptable television programming, boundaries, 117
accident frauds, 157; *see also* fraud, insurance
actants, 36, 101
action sequences, 64
actor–network, defined, 4
actor–network theory (ANT), 3–4, 6, 7–8, 31, 101, 173, 175; academics within actor-networks, 37; actor–networks of production, 40, 43–5; actors in, 4, 36; ant metaphor for researcher, 39; assembling of actor–networks, 43, 47, 62, 99; and auteur theory, 36, 37; black boxes, successful final products as, 3, 44, 169; case studies, 4–7; definitions, 4; failed actor–networks, 44, 45; horizontal vs. vertical approaches, 43; making of television fictional crime stories, study of, 2; methodological limitations, 56–7; and production of culture perspectives, 39–56; size, scale and scope, 49; St. Brieuc Bay scallop controversy, 36; story-revision, 99, 100; translation in, 37–9; writers' room, 61, 91
actors, defined, 4, 36
acts, in episodes, 64, 93n, 170

Adalian, J., 54, 87
Adams, C.J., 108
adaptation, modes of, 168n
administrative criminology, 13
Adorno, T., 20, 33n, 40, 41, 170
advertising, 89; *see also* commercial breaks
aesthetics, criminological, 13, 14
Allen, V., 58n, 136
Alley, R.S., 47, 54
Alliance Atlantis (Canadian film and television production/distribution company), 9n
Altheide, D., 25
American Medical Association (AMA), 95n
Anand, N., 37, 42, 90
Anderson, G., 22
Andreeva, N., 146, *147*
anecdotal stories, 8, 61, 74
anthrax, 146
antisocial behaviour, effects research, 28–9
archetypes, 71
Arresting Images (Doyle), 25
art: cultural products as, 19–22; literature and film, 34n
artefacts, cultural, 50
articulation, 50
Ascherson, N., 52
Asimow, M., 17

assembling of actor–networks, 43, 47, 62, 99
Associates, The (Canadian lawyer drama series), 134
asterisk symbol, 120–2
ATF (Alcohol, Tobacco and Firearms), US Bureau, 86
atherosclerosis, lower limb, 89–90
Attalah, P., 51, 168n
Atwood, M., 134, 165n, 166n, 167n
audience, 19, 26–7; consumer, 98, 127, 128, 129n, 132n; fragmentation, 1, 53, 142, 166n; reception, 30, 34n
auteur theory/auteurist products, 20, 21, 36, 37
'Autotopsy' (*Cra$h & Burn* website section), 9–10n

Babe, R.E., 91
'bad apples'/police corruption plot in *The Bridge*, 6, 8, 73, 172; appearance and disappearance of 'bad apples,' 97, 103, 105, 112, 119, 125; vs. 'bad seeds,' 125; entering the 'kitchen' of television production, 104–5; meat eating pattern of police corruption, 108, 130n; and ripening concept, 102; Standards and Practices (S&P) department, 117, 118, 120, 127, 141, 173, 174; story documents, 97, 98, 101, 102–3; *see also Bridge, The* (police drama)
Baker, W.E., 44
Bakhtin, M., 131n
Baltimore, US, 153
Banet-Weiser, S., 63, 139
Barak, G., 23
Barken, A., 32, 115
Barnard, L., 149
Barr, M., 151
Barthes, R., 130n
Basch, P., 121
BBC Worldwide, 5
Beam, A., 53, 133, 135
beats/beat sheet, 63, 64, 95n, 105–9, 121
Beaty, B., 6, 9n, 51, 91, 149, 166n
Becker, H.S., 46
Bell, D.F., 10n
below-the-line workers, 54, 58n

Bennett, D., 33n
Berenson, A., 93n
Berger, P.L., 57n
Bergman, P., 17
Berkowitz, R., 136
Bernstein, A., 151
Bertelsmann, 58n
Biber, K., 14
bibles, television, 56, 59n
Bielby, D.D., 42, 44, 46
Bielby, W.T., 42, 44, 46
'big picture,' 4, 39, 41, 47, 99
binary logic of representation, 14, 22
Binning, C., 130n, 151
biography, 43, 71
Black, D., 17, 18
black boxes, successful final products as, 3, 44, 169
Blackman, S., 134
'boarding' of episodes, 64
Body Multiple, The (Mol), 89–90
bonus material, on DVD, 52, 99
Bordwell, D., 24, 93n, 112
BORIS (Big Organized Russian Insurance Scam), 156, 159, 164
Bourdieu, P., 23, 55
Box Office Mojo, 33n
BPEs (Broadcaster Performance Envelopes), 167n
'brass wall' metaphor (old boys' network), 107, 108, 109, 110, 114, 115, 125
breaking of a story, 74–88; writers' room, 8, 63–4
Bridge, The (police drama), 8, 53, 65–87, 150, 153; as American–Canadian co-production, 65, 93–4n, 104, 113, 135, 170–1; 'Anytime' setting, 70; 'Anywhere' setting, 65–6, 68, 135, 151; asterisk symbol, 120–2; beats/beat sheet, 63, 64, 95n, 105–9, 121; breaking of a story, 63, 74–88; character lists, 120, 122–4; 'cowboy' designation, 114–15; Errors and Omissions (E&O) insurance, 8, 65, 66–70, 91, 94n, 127, 174; Final Draft, 121; final revised shooting script, 97, 124–9; formation of episodes, 60–96; frames of reference/frame-by-frame

Index   199

analysis, 47–9, 99–100; full white production draft, 117–20, 122–3; 'Injured Cop,' breaking story of, 74–88; investigative procedure, 100–4, 106; linearity of investigation, writers' assumption of, 106; local knowledge, 75–88; money laundering, 106, 107; mystery structure of story, 79–80; network draft, 113–16, 117, 119, 120; network outline, 109–12, 130–1n; newspaper articles, 76; paper trail, following, 101, 128–9; pink production draft (final revised shooting script), 97, 124–9; police corruption plot *see* 'bad apples'/police corruption plot in *The Bridge*; producers, 120–4, 132n; restaurant settings *see* restaurant settings, in *The Bridge*; re-writing, 97, 99, 105, 120, 121, 124, 129; robbery and hostage-taking in, 106, 108, 113, 119, 131n; sale of to South Africa, 153, 177; showrunner role in, 65, 66, 69, 70–3, 75, 79, 89, 113–14, 127, 132n, 174–5; storytelling preference and artistic vision of showrunner, 70–3; technical consultants, 8, 73, 75–88, 151–2; time scheme changes, 112–13; Toronto setting, 65–6, 68; transformation of episodes, 97–132; universality of, 65, 66, 69, 70–1; writers' room, 56, 62–4, 73, 80; writing process, 5, 47–9; *see also Flashpoint* (police procedural)
broadcaster, 136, 164
Broadcaster Performance Envelopes (BPEs), 167n
broadcasting laws, 90–1
Brogden, M., 94n
Brown, M., 3
brute perception, 18
Buchanan, R., 18
budgets per episode, 167n
bullet points, 122
bureaucratic documents, 122
Burlington Skyway Bridge (Hamilton), 162, 168n
Burns, G., 37
Burstein, J., 161

Byers, M., 1, 30, 97
bypasses, theoretical and methodological, 7–8

cable television networks *see* premium cable networks
Cagney and Lacey (prime-time TV series), 50
Caldwell, J.T., 39, 42, 43, 47, 50, 52, 54, 55
Callon, M., 35, 36, 156
Cameron, T., 150–1
Canada, 6–7; central symbol for, 134; representational strategies, 150–64; television see Canadian television; Toronto *see* Toronto, Canada
Canadian Audio-Visual Certification Office (CAVCO), 167n
Canadian Broadcasting Corporation (CBC), 51, 145, 146, 165, 166n
Canadian Charter of Rights and Freedoms, 94n
Canadian dream, 162, 163, 164
'Canadian media-identity problematic,' 135
Canadian Multiculturalism Act (1985/1988), 160
Canadian Radio-Television Telecommunications Commission (CRTC), 142, 145, 158, 174
Canadian Screenwriter Magazine, 59n
Canadian television: accessing television productions, 52–6; American television compared, 6, 51; broadcasting landscape, 142–5; communications perspective, 51; content, 149–50, 158; crime dramas and relevance of place, 133–68; cultural capital, mobilizing, 54–6; Francophone identity, Quebecois television, 9n, 58n; funding of television drama, 51, 58n, 149–50; middleness, 166n; pilots, 165n; 'prosocial' content, 141, 142; specialty channels, 9, 142, 143, 145–50; television production studies, doing, 50–6; 'untried' productions, 53–4, 56, 128; *see also specific programmes*
Canadian Television Fund (CTF), 51, 149

Cantor, J.M., 37, 90–1, 142
Cantor, M.G., 37, 47, 90–1, 98, 127, 142
Canwest Global (Canadian broadcaster), 145, *147*, 148, 168n
Capital, 20
capital, circuit of, 49
capitalistic mode of production, 40–1
Carman's Dining Club, Toronto, 110
Carrabine, E., 11, 12, 30, 33n, 176
case studies, 4–7, 40; future research, 174–6; *see also specific studies*
CAVCO (Canadian Audio-Visual Certification Office), 167n
Cavender, G., 22
CBC (Canadian Broadcasting Corporation), 51, 145, 146, 165, 166n
CBS (American broadcaster), 1, 62, 65, 66, 70, 72, 73, 78, 87, 89, 104, 114, 115, 130n, 131n, 141; Program Practices, 117, 118, 119; *see also Bridge, The* (police drama)
certificates of insurance, 66
Chancer, L., 23
character lists, 120, 122–4
Chase, A., 15
Chatto, J., 110
Chicago, US, 136
Childhood (PBS documentary series), 55
Chomsky, N., 41
Chris, C., 143
chronotope, 113, 131n
cinematic portrayals of law, 18
circuit of culture, 49, 50
Clover, C., 18
cognitive-behavioural tradition, 28
Cohen, S., 12, 14
Cole, S., 2
Coleridge, S.T., 77
collaborative action, 4, 36–7, 46–9; drafting, 121–2
collective conscience, 33n
Collins, R., 6, 167n
Colombo, J., 130n
commercial breaks, 64, 89, 93n, 176
community policing, 94n
compensatory position, 165n
Compesi, R.J., 37, 46

competence, of television writer, 121, 131n
consciousness, 26; false, 40–1
Conseil d'Etat, making of law at, 36, 101–2
conservative view of the law, 26–7
conspiracy theory, 41
consumer audience, 98, 127, 128, 129n, 132n
content analyses, qualitative, 13, 19, 22, 26, 30, 32, 177
content restrictions, 131–2n
conventional criminology, 13
Coppola, F.F., 107
co-productions, 7, 46–7, 54, 86, 130n, 135, 164; *see also Bridge, The* (police drama); collaborative action
COPS (American reality television program), 27, 131n
copyright infringement, 66
copyright laws, 90
copyright permission, 70
Cornea, C., 92n
Corporation for Public Broadcasting (CPB), 58n
corrective criticism, 16, 17
Couldry, N., 39
counter-images, 141–2
Courtés, J., 101, 131n
courtroom experience, portrayal of, 18, 177–8
CPB (Corporation for Public Broadcasting), 58n
Cra$h & Burn (Canadian cable television drama, formerly *Lawyers, Guns and Money*), 9n, 137–9; Hamilton, Ontario setting, 136; pilot, 5, 6, 56, 67, 136, 137; plot, 133, 138, 161; showrunner, 67; writer's room, 63
crime: in Canadian television, 51; causes, 15; correcting representations of, 22–7; and culture, 12; fear of, 12, 13, 28–9; knowledge about, 171–2; mass-mediated, cultural representations, 12; operationalization, 29; and ordinary people, 12, 16, 22, 23, 31; semiotic approaches, 18, 19–22, 25; statistics, 22, 23; 'true crime' story, 86; violent, 14, 22, 32

Crime and Media: A Reader (Greer), 30
crime dramas: docudramas, 5, 58n, 67, 68, 86, 95n, 143; genre of, 1–2; relevance of place in, 133–68
crime news, 30
criminological aesthetics, 13, 14
criminologists, 2, 12, 130n, 140
criminology: academic, 2, 11, 15, 56, 171; conventional/administrative, 13; criminological aesthetics, 13, 14; cultural, 2, 12–14; Marxist-inspired, 38; newsmaking, 23; popular, 2–3, 11, 12, 15–18, 21, 24, 176–8; public, 23; sub-cultural, 13–14; theories, 2, 15
criticism, corrective, 16, 17
CRTC (Canadian Radio-Television Telecommunications Commission), 142, 145, 158, 174
CSI: Crime Scene Investigation (North American television drama), 9n, 22, 30, 135, 141, 143; academic scholarship, 58n; *CSI* effect, 2, 16, 58n, 170; *CSI: Miami* (spin-off series), 1; popularity, 1–2
CTV (Canadian television network), 62, 65, 70, 73, 87, 89, 104, 115
cultural artefacts, 50
cultural capital, 54–6
cultural criminology, 2, 12–14
Cultural Criminology (Ferrell and Sanders), 13
cultural discount, 152–3, 168n
'cultural dupes,' 33n
cultural products, 2, 19–27, 31; as art, 19–22; facticity of, 22–7; mass production, 20; message vs. the medium, 24–6; presumed ideological effect on a mass audience, 26–7; as symptomatic of a culture's ideological leaning, 24, 26
cultural studies, 11
cultural uplift, 139
culture: circuit of, 49, 50; and economy, 20; high, 22; mass culture *see* mass culture/mass media; popular *see* popular culture; of production, 42–3, 57n; production of culture perspectives,

and ANT, 39–56; *see also* cultural criminology; cultural products
culture industry, 8, 11–12, 24; 'big picture,' 4, 39, 41, 47, 99; vs. the culture industry, 33n; as deceptive, 41; and industrial production, 41–3; origin of term, 40; paradigmatic, 20, 33n; study of, 8, 40–5
Currie, E., 23

D'Acci, J., 50, 51
Davis, M., 152
Dawn, R., 135, 161, 168n
daylight, shooting in, 131n
Deadwood (HBO drama), 158, 168n
defamation, 67, 68, 94n, 124
Defiant Ones, The (crime film), 77
Defining Women (D'Acci), 50
deMint, J., 58n
Denmark, police in, 94n
Denvir, J., 17
Deutsch, S.K., 22
deviance, 14, 28; 'delight of,' 13
Dialectic of Enlightenment (Horkheimer and Adorno), 33n
dialectical thinking, 57n
Dickens, C., 17
Dioso-Villa, R., 2
directors, hiring of, 176
Discovery Channel, 143
'Discovery Dan,' 143, 166n
disinformation campaigns, 23
Disney, 58n
distortion, media, 38
Djankov, S., 40
docudramas, crime, 5, 58n, 67, 68, 86, 95n, 143
documentary, 24, 52, 67, 77
Doktori, H., 118
Donaldson, M.C., 68
Dornfeld, B., 55
Douglas, P., 19, 60, 63, 64, 73, 84, 99
Dowler, K., 29, 38
Doyle, A., 25, 27, 30, 33n, 74, 86, 154
Doyle, J., 165
Dragnet (US television production), 76–7, 135

Druick, Z., 51, 58n
du Gay, P., 49–50, 57n
Due South (Canadian–American co-production), 46–7, 136, 148
Duran, D., 159
Durkheim, E., 33n
DVDs, bonus material on, 52, 99
dynamic movement, 35, 45, 49–50

economy, and culture, 20
educational impact of mass media, 19
electronic format of story documents, 102, 130n
Elephant (film), 21
Elkins, J.R., 18, 19
Ellis, J., 33n, 54, 71, 79, 115, 142
Ellis, M., 151, 167–8n
Emergency Task Force (ETF), Toronto police, 73, 76, 82, 84, 88, 92, 115, 123, 151
England, as The Island, 134
English novels, 90
English-Canadian imagination, 133, 134, 165n
entertainment, 18, 19
episodic representations, 8, 61, 64, 93n, 99, 100
ER (US medical drama), 1
Ericson, R.V., 12, 18–19, 22, 23, 29, 32, 57n, 86, 94n, 127, 139, 140, 154
Errors and Omissions (E&O) insurance, 8, 65, 66–70, 91, 94n, 127, 174
essentialist position, 165n
ethnic minorities, representation of, 118
ethnography, 2, 13, 40, 47, 52, 56, 60
Ettema, J.S., 4
Everyman, construct of, 161
Ewick, P., 26
Exhibit A (forensic crime docudrama), 5, 58n, 143
expenditures, above- and below-the-line, 59n
experimental studies, 28
Eyerman, R., 42

F2: Forensic Factor, Cold Blood (re-titled *True CSI* in UK), 5

facticity/facts: accuracy of, in writing, 60; cultural products, 22–7; fact-checking, 67; matters of fact, 171; policing, 77; raw facts, 74; scientific facts, 61, 62
false consciousness, 40–1
fandom, 55, 56
Faulkner, R.R., 44
Favourite Website Award (FWA), 9–10n
FBI (Federal Bureau of Investigation), 86
FCC (Federal Communications Commission), 117, 127, 131n, 141, 142, 174
fear of crime, 12, 13; effects research, 28–9; and mass media, 19
Federal Bureau of Investigation (FBI), 86
Federal Communications Commission (FCC), 117, 127, 131n, 141, 142, 174
Feilzer, M., 23
femininity, 50, 83
Ferrell, J., 2, 3, 13, 21, 28
Feuer Domash, S., 27
fictional drama, 2; fiction filter, 74, 75, 88, 92, 173; and knowledge of crime, 172–4; laboratories of fiction-making, other, 176–7; translation into textual form, 38, 62
fieldwork, 5–6, 52
film: conventional vs. critical, 26; Hollywood, 15, 42, 58–9n; and law, 15, 17–18, 19; outside of Hollywood, 20; as visual medium, 16–17
film theory, 18
filter, fiction, 74, 75, 88, 92, 173
Final Draft, 121, 173
final products: concentration on, 36; fiction as, 61; final revised shooting script, in *The Bridge*, 97, 124–9; successful, as black boxes, 3, 44, 169
financial documentation, 56
Fine, G.A., 57n
Fiske, J., 19, 29
Fixmer, A., 7, 53
Flashpoint (police procedural), 53, 76, 79, 82–8, 115, 133, 135, 144, 150, 153, 165n; Strategic Response Unit (SRU), elite tactical police force, 82, 151; *see also Bridge, The* (police drama)
folly, in audiences, 19

food, semiotics of, 130n
forensic crime docudramas, 5, 58n, 86
forensic criticism, 17
forensic evidence, in television dramas, 2, 22
Forensic Factor (Canadian crime-related docudrama), 58n, 86, 143, 176–7
Foucault, M., 12
FOX network, US, 117, 141
fragmentation, audience, 1, 53, 142, 166n
frames of reference: frame-by-frame analysis, 99–100; shifting between frames in writing process, 47–9
Francophone identity, Quebecois television, 9n, 58n
Frank, S., 31, 95n
Frankfurt School, 33n
fraud, insurance, 56, 138, 156, 157, 159
freedom of expression, 94n
Freeman, M., 17
French administrative law *see* Conseil d'Etat, making of law at
French-language Canadian television productions, 9n
Freudian explanations of crime, 15
Friedman, L.M., 15, 22, 31
The Frontier symbol, 134, 135, 158–9
Frye, N., 133
full white production draft, in *The Bridge*, 117–20, 122–3
Fulton, R.G., 152
funding of television drama, 51, 54, 58n, 149–50, 167n
FX (US network), 145

'gags,' 77
Garland, D., 11, 26
gaze, of viewers, 33n
GE, 58n
Geertz, C., 71–2
general liability insurance, 66
generalizability of television production practices, 56, 69
generalized symmetry principle, 36
genre of crime dramas, 1–2
Gerbner, G., 28
Gherardi, S., 143–4

Gillers, S., 16, 31
Giraud, M., 97
Gitlin, T., 42, 46, 57n, 79, 92, 96n, 140, 166n
Gittins, S., 143
glance, of viewers, 33n
global media industries, 152–3
Godfather, The, 107, 130n
Golding, P., 40
Golick, J., 93n
Good Witch II, The (made-for-television movie), 149
Goodman, D.J., 19, 25–6
Goodrich, P., 62
Gottdiener, M., 42
Government of Canada, 144
Gray, H., 51, 89
Greenfield, S., 17, 36
Greer, C., 27, 30
Greimas, A.J., 101, 131n
Grimm (fantasy-crime drama), 76
Grindstaff, L., 51, 55
Gripsrud, J., 46, 128
Griswold, W., 90
Gross, Paul, 148

Haggerty, K.D., 56
Haggis, P., 136
Hall, S., 13–14, 32, 33n, 57n
Haltom, W., 27
Halton Hills (Town) v. Kerouac, 94n
Hamilton, Ontario, 9, 136, 137, 148–50, 168n; Hamilton Mountain, 162, 163; Hamilton Professional Firefighters Association, 148–9; particularities, 6, 153–64; *see also Cra$h & Burn* (Canadian cable television drama, formerly *Lawyers, Guns and Money*); Toronto, Canada
'Hammer, The,' 161–2
handcuffing, 77
Harari, J.V., 10n
Hartley, J., 28, 34n
Hastings, T., 146
Havens, T., 39, 42, 152
Hawaii 5.0 (US crime drama), 76, 78, 135
Hayward, K., 13

204 Index

HBO (cable television network)/HBO Films, 21, 33n, 136, 137–9, 150, 158, 166n; as The Frontier of television programming, 138–9, 158–9; *see also Wire, The* (HBO crime drama)
Hemmingway, E., 39, 43, 61, 127
Henderson, A.M., 55, 118
Herman, E.S., 41, 42
Hesmondhalgh, D., 24, 40
heterogeneity, 37, 41, 61, 75
high culture, 22
High Level Bridge, York Boulevard (Hamilton), 168n
Hill, K., 55, 134
Hirsch, P.M., 28
Hollywood films, 15, 42; above-the-line personnel and below-the-line workers, 58–9n
Hollywood Reporter, The (trade magazine), 59n
Hollywood: The movie colony, the movie makers (Rosten), 55
Honolulu Police Department (HPD), 78
Horan, D., 170
Horkheimer, M., 20, 33n, 40, 41, 170
Horton, T., 159
Hoskins, C., 152
Hughes, M., 28
human interest, 77
humanities-oriented analyses, vs. social science approach, 4, 27
human/non-human *a priori* separation, 36
human–technology hybrids, 39
Hutcheon, L., 135–6, 165–6n
Hutchings, P.J., 14
hypodermic needle theory, 29, 170

ideologies, 12; cultural, 24; ideological leaning of a culture, 24, 26; law-and-order, 14, 26, 27; Marxist, 27, 38; mass audience, presumed ideological effect of cultural products on, 26–7; messages, 24; socio-political, 1
imagination, 14; English-Canadian, 133, 134, 165n; social, 16
indecency and obscenity rules, 117, 131n
independent television companies, 58n

in-depth interviews, 5
Inderbitzin, M., 23
index cards, 63
indoctrination, legal, 18
induction, 69
industrial production, 40, 41–3
industrial reflexivity, 52
industrial smokestacks, Hamilton, 162
infomercial, 89
information, 62
Information Age, 74
infringement of copyright or trademark, 66
inscription devices, 38, 61
Inside the Writers' Room (Meyers), 93n
insurance, 154–61; certificates of, 66; Errors and Omissions (E&O) insurance, 8, 65, 66–70, 91, 94n, 127, 174; fraud, 56, 138, 156, 159; no-fault regime, 154; scams, 156, 157, 159, 164
intellectual property, 90, 95n
International Television Audience Award, 1
Internet, 74
Internet Movie Database, 94n
inter-rater reliability, 57
interressement, 156
intertextuality, 173
interviews, 2, 5, 40, 47
irreduction principle, 37
The Island, as English symbol, 134
Italian-American Civil Rights League, 130n

'Jaws of Life' (hydraulic rescue tool), 148, 149
Jenkins, H., 21, 29
Jewkes, Y., 12, 27, 33n
Johnson, C., 153
Johnson, R., 18, 30, 49
Johnson, V.M., 1, 30, 97
jurisdiction confusion, in co-productions, 68
jurors, viewers as, 18

Kafka, F., 17
Kalifa, D., 105
Kamir, O., 18, 19, 20

Karamano, A., 110
Katz, J., 13
Killingsworth, J., 166n
Kirby, D.A., 77, 95n
Knapp Commission Report on Police Corruption, 108
Knight, S., 150
Knorr-Cetina, K., 60
knowledge: communication of, 60, 61; construction of, 57n; of crime, 171–2; cultural and social capital, 55, 56; sources, 75, 95n
knowledge moves, 91, 92
Kompare, D., 1, 2, 9, 167n
Kotsopoulos, A., 51, 58n
Krashinsky, S., 165
Kurasawa, A., 20

LA Law, 16, 31
La Traverse, A.M., 143
laboratories: of fiction-making, 176–7; Latourian, 8, 61–2, 88, 133; limitations of studies, 133; scientific, 38, 61
Lam, A., 95n
Lasswell, H.D., 29
Latour, B., 2, 7, 10n, 23, 31, 32, 60, 62, 63, 73, 74, 75, 76, 92, 98, 104, 121, 133, 136, 137, 150; actor–network theory, 35–9, 43–7, 57n, 61, 101; on Pasteur, 37, 57n, 146; study of Conseil d'Etat, 36, 101–2
Latourian laboratory, writers' room as, 8, 61–2, 88, 133
law: broadcasting, 90–1; conservative view of, 26–7; and content of television representations, 90; and film, 15, 17–18, 19; liberal view of, 26; ordinary people's perceptions of, 12, 16, 22, 23, 31; people's, 16; representations of *see* law, representations of; role in revision process, 127–8
Law, J., 4, 5, 31, 35, 37, 56
law, representations of: correcting, 22–7; fictional, 16; inaccurate, 22, 23, 24, 30, 171; and literature, 17, 34n; semiotic approaches, 18, 19–22, 25; social problems as legal problems, 26; sociolegal, 16, 17, 18, 20, 21, 24

Law and Order, 93n, 138, 141, 143, 161
law films, 17, 18
Law Goes Pop (Sherwin), 16–17
law-and-order ideologies, 14, 26, 27
lawsuits, avoiding, 66–9, 70, 75, 124
lawyers, films portraying, 17
Lawyers, Guns and Money (Canada cable television drama, later known as *Cra$h & Burn*), 5, 9, 137–9, 138, 153, 158, 159; opening title sequence, *163*; technical consultants, 168n; *see also Cra$h & Burn* (Canadian cable television drama, formerly *Lawyers, Guns and Money*)
Lazarsfeld, P.F. et al (1968), 29
lead role, 57n
Lebo, H., 130n
Lee, F.L.F., 153
legal practice, 16–17
legal studies, popular, 15–18, 21, 24; law and film, 17–18
Lenz, T., 26, 27
Levine, E., 51, 55, 58n, 135
Levinson, S., 17
lex populi (people's law), 16
LGM see Lawyers, Guns and Money (Canada cable television drama, later known as *Cra$h & Burn*)
libel, trade, 66, 67, 127
liberal view of the law, 26
line producers, 167n
linear transmission model, 25–6, 29
literary classics, representation of law in, 17
literature, and law, 17, 33n
literature review, 12–14
Liu, K., 110
Livingstone, S., 28
Loader, I., 23
local knowledge, 75–88
Lost Girl, 167n
Lotz, A.D., 142
Lucas, S., 147
Luckmann, T., 57n
Lyons, J., 50, 51

Macaulay, S., 15, 31
Macdonald, I.W., 44

Machura, S., 17, 177–8
MacNeil, W.P., 16, 17, 20
macro-level political economy approaches, 40, 43
Mafia, Italian, 107, 109, 119, 130n
Mamet, D., 60
Man against Nature theme, in American novel, 90
Mann, D., 37, 99
Maras, S., 98, 99
Marenin, O., 94n
Marlow, I., 165
Marshall, L., 90
Marx, K., 40, 49
Marxist ideologies, 27, 38
masculinity, 50
Mason, P., 12
mass audience, 9; presumed ideological effect of cultural products on, 26–7
mass culture/mass media, 12, 14, 16, 18, 19, 22; meaning of 'mass,' 25; medium vs. the message, 24–5; propaganda model, 41; representations, 18
mass production, 20
material-semiotic analysis, 4, 31, 37, 57n
Matheson, S.A., 135, 143, 150, 168n
Mawby, R.I., 94n
Mayer, V., 42
McCann, M.J., 27
McChesney, R., 42
McGrath, D., 113, 148
McKee, R., 71
McLaughlin, E., 23
McLuhan, M., 25
McShane, M., 22
'mean world view,' 28–9
meaning, and textual production, 41
'meat and potatoes' policing, 108, 130n
media, the, 7, 11, 30–1
media distortion, 38
media effects, studying, 27–9, 30; antisocial behaviour and fear of crime, 28–9
media ownership patterns, 40
'medical mill,' 154
medium specificity, 25
Meehan, E., 37

Merton, R.K., 163–4, 168n
methodological limitations, 56–7
Meyers, L., 93n
Miami Vice (cop show), 50–1, 135
Microsoft Word, 121
'midlevel' perspective, 42
Miller, M.J., 51
Miller, W.I., 17
Ministry of Cultural Heritage, Canada, 149, 158
Mirus, R., 152
misinformation, communication through fictional television programs, 2, 172
Mnookin, J.L., 30
modernity, 60, 61
modes of adaptation, 168n
modes of production: capitalist, 40–1; industrial production, 40, 41–3; operationalization, 40
Mods and Rockers, UK, 14
Mol, A., 53, 89, 90
money laundering, 106, 107, 114
Montagu, K., 146
Montague (Township) v. Page, 94n
Mopas, M., 2
moral panics, 14
Moscovitch, P., 86
'Mounties' (Royal Canadian Mounted Police officers), 135, 136, 159
MuchMusic, 142
mugging, 14, 32
Muller-Doohm, S., 33n
multiculturalism, 159, 160
Mulvey, L., 33n
Muraskin, R., 27
murder, over-representation of by mass media, 22
Murdock, G., 40

narratives/narrative regimes, 18, 29, 63, 77, 101, 140; narrative resolution, 120
NBC network, US, 141
negative effects of television, emphasis on, 28
Netherlands, police in, 69
network draft, in *The Bridge*, 113–16, 117, 119, 120

network era, 142, 166n
network executives, 109
network feedback, 112, 113
network notes, 113
network outline, in *The Bridge*, 109–12, 130–1n
network television, 136
networks: commercial broadcasting, 93n; definition of 'network,' 4, 35; phone calls, 56; premium cable, 2, 9, 118, 142, 148; Standards and Practices (S&P), 117, 118, 120, 127, 141, 173, 174; television, 42; *see also* actor–network theory (ANT); post-network era
New York City/New York State, 138, 157, 158–61; Brighton Beach, 153
Newcomb, H., 47, 54, 55
Newman, M.Z., 63
news media, 12, 14, 23, 33n, 40; sociological production studies, 57n
news production, 61
NewsCorp, 58n
newsmaking criminology, 23
newspaper articles, 76
newspaper production, 140
niche markets, 9, 136, 142, 164
Nichols, B., 95n
Nicolini, D., 143–4
9/11 terrorist attacks, US, 1, 138
novels, British and American, 90
numerical representations, 60, 93n

O'Brien, M., 19
obscene material, 117, 131n
O'Connor, A., 33n
Office, The (situation comedy), 145
Ohmann, R., 96n
Onstad, K., 143, 150–1
Ontario Health Insurance Plan (OHIP), 154
oppositional terms, 14, 22
origins of television crime dramas, 8
Oswald, B., 53

paper trail, following, 101, 128–9
paradigmatic culture industry, 20, 33n
Parker, M., 146

Parker, W.H., 152
participant-observation, 47, 56
Pasteur, L., 37, 57n, 146
Patch, N., 135
Patriquin, M., 153
Peelo, M., 12
people's law, 16
Peterson, R.A., 37, 42, 90
pilots, 133; Canadian, 165n; *Cra$h & Burn*, 5, 6, 56, 67, 136, 137; defined, 10n; development, 136; 'freeway' built during development, 137; purpose, 146–7; scripted American, *147*; 'theatre of the proof,' 146
pink production draft (final revised shooting script), 97, 124–9
place: broadcasting landscape in Canada, 142–5; funding of television drama, 149–50; generic city, 150–3; Hamilton, Ontario City, 148–50, 153–64; insurance world, 154–61; pilots, 146–7; popular vs. quality productions in post-network era, 9, 136, 139–45, 166n, 170; relevance in Canadian crime dramas, 8–9, 133–68; representational strategies, 150–64; thematic and visual translations, 161–5; Toronto as 'world class' city, 9, 150–3
plagiarism, 67
Playback (trade magazine), 59n
Podias, K., 2
Podolny, J.M., 44
point-of-view identification, 27
Polan, D., 139, 142, 161
police cooperation, 8, 86
police corruption plot, in *The Bridge see* 'bad apples'/police corruption plot in *The Bridge*
police practices, 94n
police procedurals, 76, 79
Policing the Crisis (Hall), 14
political economy approaches, 40–1, 42, 43
Poovey, M., 61
popular culture, 7, 11, 58n, 117, 170; cultural product, studying, 21, 22, 26; popular criminology and popular legal studies, 15–16

popularity: as ambiguous concept, 1; criminology, 2–3, 11, 12, 15–18, 21, 24, 176–8; *CSI: Crime Scene Investigation* (North American television drama), 1–2; definitions, 21; and entertainment, 18, 19; law and film, 17–18; legal studies, 15–18, 21, 24; measurement, 9n; popular vs. quality productions in post-network era, 9, 136, 139–45, 166n, 170; texts, 23
positivism, 13, 28
Posner, R.A., 17
postmodernism, 19
post-network era, popular vs. quality productions in, 9, 136, 139–45, 166n, 170
premium cable networks, 2, 9, 118, 136, 142, 148
Presdee, M., 13
primary creative personnel vs. technical craftspeople, 59n
prime-time North American crime dramas, 2, 12, 25, 53, 58n
Prince Edward Viaduct, Toronto, 168n
privacy, invasion of, 67, 68
procedural storytelling, 76, 79, 135, 143, 166n; *see also Flashpoint* (police procedural)
process-centric perspective, 32, 178
producers, 120–4, 132n, 167n
'producer's gate,' 54
Producer's Medium, The (Newcomb), 55
product-centric perspective, 34n
production, 7, 30, 61, 133; actor–networks of, 40, 43–5; of culture perspectives *see* production of culture perspectives, and actor–network theory; in-house, 54; mass production, 20; modes of, 40–3; of newspapers, 140; of prime-time North American crime dramas, 2, 12, 25; six-facet model (Peterson and Anand), 42; sociological production studies, 36, 37, 42, 57n; and success, 21–2
production of culture perspective, and actor–network theory, 39–56; actor–networks of production, 40, 43–5; Canada, television production studies in, 50–6; collaborative action, 4, 36–7, 46–9; convergences, 45–50; and culture of production, 42–3, 57n; divergences, 39, 40–5; dynamic movement, 45, 49–50; modes of production, 40–3; textual production and meaning, 41; uncertainty, 45–6
programming risk, 9n
propaganda model of mass media, 41
property crime, under-representation of by mass media, 22
Propp, V., 125, 131n
'prosocial' content, 141, 142
psychoanalytic theories, 15, 18
public criminology, 23
public interest, 142

qualitative methodologies, 13, 47
quality vs. popular productions, 9, 136, 139–45
quantitative methodologies, 13
Quebecois television, 9n, 58n
quotidian texts, 42

Raboy, M., 91
Rafter, N., 2, 3, 12, 15, 16, 26, 166n
randonné, conceptualization of, 10n
Rapping, E., 1, 26–7, 97
Rashomon (crime film), 20
rational choice theory, 13
Ravage, J., 37
Rawlings, P., 15
realism, 77
reality television, 1, 74, 95n, 131n
reflexivity, industrial, 52
'rehabilitation clinic,' 154
Reiner, R., 12, 28, 29, 30, 33n
representational stability, 98
representational strategies, Canadian crime drama, 4, 6, 150–64; generic city, 150–3; Hamilton particularities, 153–64; Toronto as 'world class' city, 9, 150–3
representations: accuracy, 77; binary logic of representation, 14, 22; competing, of policing, 75–88; of crime *see* crime, representations of; episodic, 8, 61, 64,

93n, 99, 100; of ethnic minorities, 118; fictional, 14; of law *see* law, representations of; news, 14; North American system, 6; numerical, 60, 93n; pop culture, 7, 11; richness of meaning in, 41; translation of, 37–9, 161–5; *see also* representational strategies, Canadian crime drama

Rescue Me (US drama), 145

research, 11–32; on antisocial behaviour and fear of crime, 28–9; bypasses, theoretical and methodological, 7–8; correcting representations of crime and law, 22–7; criminology, 11, 12, 15–18; culture industry, 11–12; empirical, on cultural production, 7; ethnography, 2, 13, 40, 47, 52, 56, 60; experimental studies, 28; fieldwork, 5–6, 52; future, 174–8; interviews, 2, 5, 40, 47; key findings, 169–74; literature review, 12–14; media effects, 27–9; methodology/methodological limitations, 2, 5–6, 13, 56–7; ordinary people, 12, 16, 22, 23, 31; participant-observation, 47, 56; popular criminology and popular legal studies, 15–18; qualitative methodologies, 13, 47; quantitative methodologies, 13; research table, resetting, 29–32; semiotic approaches, 19–22; study of crime, media and culture, 18–29

restaurant settings, in *The Bridge*: breakfast diner notion, 105, 112–24; entering the 'kitchen' of television production, 104–5; Italian 'steakhouse,' 105–9, 113, 119, 130n; Mediterranean restaurant, 109–12, 113, 119

revenge genre, 17

revision process (*The Bridge*), 8, 102; final revised shooting script, 97, 124–9; messiness of, 99, 100; role of law in, 127–8; summary, *126*

re-writing (*The Bridge*), 97, 99, 105, 120, 121, 124, 129

Rice, L., 117, 118

rich description, 40

Riles, A., 122

Ring, M., 42

'ripening file,' in French administrative law, 101–2, 122

risk-averse storytelling approach, 2

Robson, P., 17, 24

Rookie Blue (police drama), 53, 54, 133, 135, 150, 165n, 168n

Rosenberg, C.B., 31

Rosenthal, A., 94n

Rosten, L., 55

Sacco, V.F., 29

Sandeen, C.A., 37, 46

Sanders, C., 13

Sarat, A., 16, 17, 19, 20–1, 29

Scafidi, S., 90

Schiller, H.I., 40

Schneider, M., 130n

Schramm, W., 28

Schudson, M., 41, 57n

Science and Technology Studies (STS), 35, 39

scientific laboratories, 38, 61

screen performers, television actors as, 4

screenwriting practices, 6

screenwriting software, 173

script clearance report, 124

script coordinator, 129–30n

Script Magazine, 59n

script-writing process, 61

Seaman, W.R., 128

Seglins, D., 76

self-regulation, 141

self-theorizing, 43

semiotic approaches, 18, 25, 130n; material-semiotic analysis, 4, 31, 37, 57n; representations of crime and law, 19–22

sensationalism, 23

serials, 63, 73

Serres, M., 10n, 57n

72 Hours: True Crime (Canadian crime-related docudrama), 58n

Sex and The City, 138

Shakespeare, W., 17

Shattuc, J.M., 51, 128

Sherwin, R.K., 16–17

Shield, The, 118

Showcase (Canadian specialty channel), 9, 136, 144, 145–50
Showrunner Award, 92n
showrunner role, 8, 92–3n, 99; in *The Bridge*, 65, 66, 69, 70–3, 75, 79, 89, 99–100, 104–5, 113–14, 127, 132n, 174–5; in *Cra$h & Burn/Lawyers, Guns and Money*, 137, 159–60, 164, 176
Silbey, J., 24
Silbey, S.S., 16, 26
Simon, D., 21, 139, 140–1, 153
site-specificity, 35
Six Feet Under, 139
six-facet production model (Peterson and Anand), 42
slander, 67
Slings & Arrows (Canadian mini-series), 148
Smith, D.E., 128
Smith, V., 146
Smoodin, E., 29
Smythe, D.W., 40
Snow, R., 25
social capital, 55, 56
Social Construction of Reality, The (Berger and Luckmann), 57n
social imagination, 16
social reality, 23
social science approach, vs. humanities-oriented analyses, 4, 27
sociolegal representations of law, 16, 17, 18, 20, 21, 24
sociological production studies, 36, 37, 42, 57n
socio-political discourses, capture in dramatic form, 1
Sodano, T., 55, 128
Somalis, 159
Sony Entertainment Television, 177
Soothill, K., 12
Soprano, T., 166n
Sopranos, The (television drama), 138, 139, 145, 166n
Sparks, R., 11, 23, 130n, 150
specialty channels: Canada, 9, 142, 143, 145–50; United States, 58n
spectatorship, 14
St. Brieuc Bay scallop controversy, use of ANT in, 36

Staiger, J., 28, 30
Stallybrass, P., White, A., 163
Stam, R., 20
Standards and Practices (S&P), network executives, 117, 118, 120, 127, 141, 173, 174
Stark, S., 76
Statue of Liberty, New York, 138
Stein, N., Burke, D., 156
Steinert, H., 20, 33n
Stelter, B., 87
Stepakoff, J., 58n, 64, 92n
Stevens, D.J., 2, 22
story documents, 98, 101, 102–3, 173; activation of, 128; file cabinet, 129–30n; as mediators, 126; outlines, 109–12, 130–1n
story-plot distinction, 93n
storytelling: biographically-oriented trade, 43, 71; *The Bridge*, 64; culture of, 61; Hollywood, 99; preference and artistic vision, 70–3; procedural, 79, 135, 143, 166n; revision process *see* revision process; risk-averse approach, 2; in writers' room, 137; *see also* writers' room
Strange, C., 36
Strategic Response Unit (SRU), elite tactical police force (in *Flashpoint*), 82, 151
Strathern, M., 122
Straw, W., 165n
Street, J., 108
STS (Science and Technology Studies), 35, 39
Stursberg, R., 165
sub-cultural criminology, 13–14
subversive potential of popular texts, 22–3
Sullivan, R., 6, 9n, 51, 91, 149, 166n
Surette, R., 12, 22
suspension of disbelief, 77
Sweet Hereafter, The (film), 20–1
symbolic capital, 55

talk shows, 51
Tate, M.A., 58n, 136

technical consultants, 8, 31, 73, 151–2, 168n; anecdotes of, 75–88; excerpt of exchange with writers, 80–2; professional attire, divesting of, 80
Tedesco, R., 143
Telefilm Canada, 51, 149
television: actors, 4, 37; American broadcasting networks, 46, 53, 54; bonus material, on DVD, 52, 99; in Canada *see* Canadian television; evolution of texts, 36; forensic evidence in dramas, 2, 22; as hybrid institution, 37; independent television companies, 58n; making of fictional crime stories, 2; negative effects, emphasis on, 28; networks, 42; origins of dramas, 8; reality, 1, 74, 95n, 131n; talk shows, 51; as visual medium, 16–17; witness, position as, 71; *see also specific programs*
television actors, 4, 37
television bibles, 56, 59n
Tell Me You Love Me (HBO drama), 168n
text-centred approaches, 18
texts: popularity, 22–3; quotidian, 42; subversive potential of popular texts, 22–3; television, evolution of, 36; televisual, 98; text-centred approaches, 18
The Movie Network (TMN), 148
The Sports Network (TSN), 142
'theatre of the proof,' 146
Theoretical Criminology (journal), 13
third position, 57n
Thomas, R.R., 78
Thompson, J.B., 20
Thompson, K., 24, 93n, 99
Thompson, R.J., 37
Tim Hortons franchise restaurants, Canada, 159
time scheme changes, 112–13
TimeWarner, 58n
Tinic, S., 51, 66, 68, 134, 135, 167n
To Serve and Protect (reality TV show), 131n
top-down approaches, 43
Toronto, Canada, 7, 53–4, 56, 58n, 135; accident ring run, by Samalis, 159; *The Bridge* set in, 65–6, 68; vs. Chicago, 136; Emergency Task Force (police), 73, 76,
82, 84, 88, 92, 115, 123, 151; as 'Hollywood North,' 53; police service, 86; Police Union, 68, 72; Prince Edward Viaduct, 168n; as 'world class' city, 9, 150–3; *see also* Canada; Canadian television; Hamilton, Ontario
'track changes' function, in Microsoft Word, 121
trade libel, 66, 67, 127
trade magazines, 59n
trademark infringement, 66
transgression, criminal, 13
translations, 4, 7, 136, 173; in actor–network theory, 37–9; equivalent vs. making equivalent, 137; reverse, 153; thematic and visual, 161–5
transmission, linear model, 25–6, 29
travel guide metaphor, 7
truth, semblance of, 77
Turow, J., 95n
24 (US drama), 93n
Twin Towers, 138
Tzanelli, R., 19

Uggen, C., 23
Ulbrich, S., 177–8
uncertainty, 45–6
Unforgiven (film), 17
Unit, The (US military drama), 60
United States (US)/American television: American broadcasting networks, 46, 53, 54, 57n; *The Bridge*, requirement for success in, 66; Canadian vs. American television, 6, 51; conglomerate companies making TV shows, 58n; financing of television programs, 51, 54; The Frontier, as symbol of, 134, 135, 158; generalizability of television production practices, 56; New York City/New York State, 138; North American entertainment, 2, 12, 25, 53, 56; prime-time crime dramas, 2, 12, 25, 53, 58n; specialty channels, 58n; television productions, 174–5; writer's rooms, 6
universality, 3, 6–7, 75, 76, 135; *The Bridge*, 65, 66, 69, 70–1

'untried' television productions, 53–4, 56, 128; *see also Bridge, The* (police drama)
US Bureau of Alcohol, Tobacco and Firearms (ATF), 86

Vaidhyanathan, S., 90
Valier, C., 14
Valverde, M., 12, 19, 91, 113, 131n, 154
Van Sant, G., 21
VanDerWerff, T., 135
VanLaerhoven, S., 22
Variety (trade magazine), 59n
vengeance, 17
verisimilitude, 31, 77
Veronica Mars (television drama), 21
veterans, 58n
Viacom, 58n
violent crime, 14, 22, 32
visual media, film and television as, 16–17
Vlessing, E., 70, 146, *147*, 148, 153

W (Women Network) network, Canada, 143
Walby, S., 12
Waldman, D., 30
walking expedition metaphor, 10n
'well-tried' shows, 175–6
West Wing, 134
Whedon, J., 93n
whiteboards, in writers' room, 62–3, 64
Whizbang Productions, 5, 148–9, 154
Williams, F., 22
Williams, R., 24, 32, 33n
Wilson, W.J., 33n, 161–2
window broadcasts, 166n

Winter Olympics, 2010, 70
Wire, The (HBO crime drama), 21, 33n, 118, 140–1, 153
witness, television as, 71
Wolf, D., 161
Woodmansee, M., 90
Woolgar, S., 2, 62, 63, 76; actor–network theory, 61
work sectors, 43
'world class' city concept, 9, 150–3, 167n
Writers Guild of America strike, 2007 and 2008, 87
Writers Guild of Canada, 144; Showrunner Award, 92n
writers' outline, 109–12, 130–1n
writers' room: actor–network theory, 91; American, 6; breaking of a story in, 8, 63–4; *The Bridge*, 56, 62–4, 73, 80; bulletin boards, 63; *Cra$h & Burn*, 63; entering, 8, 60–4, 171–2; *Flashpoint*, 87; and the Internet, 74; as Latourian laboratory, 8, 61–2, 88, 133; script-writing process, 61; storytelling in, 137; thinking workshop of, 100; whiteboards, 62–3, 64; writing workshop, 100; *see also Bridge, The* (police drama)

Yar, M., 29
Young, A., 12–13, 14, 21
Young, J., 13

ZOS: Zone of Separation (television drama), 148

For Product Safety Concerns and Information please contact our EU
representative GPSR@taylorandfrancis.com
Taylor & Francis Verlag GmbH, Kaufingerstraße 24, 80331 München, Germany

www.ingramcontent.com/pod-product-compliance
Lightning Source LLC
Chambersburg PA
CBHW051643230426
43669CB00013B/2414